Volatile Knowing

Volatile Knowing

*Parents, Teachers, and the Censored
Story of Accountability in America's
Public Schools*

KAIA TOLLEFSON

FOREWORD BY MAXINE GREENE

LEXINGTON BOOKS

A division of
ROWMAN & LITTLEFIELD PUBLISHERS, INC.
Lanham • Boulder • New York • Toronto • Plymouth, UK

LEXINGTON BOOKS

A division of Rowman & Littlefield Publishers, Inc.
A wholly owned subsidary of The Rowman & Littlefield Publishing Group, Inc.
4501 Forbes Boulevard, Suite 200
Lanham, MD 20706

Estover Road
Plymouth PL6 7PY
United Kingdom

British Library Cataloguing in Publication Information Available

Library of Congress Cataloging-in-Publication Data

Tollefson, Kaia.
  Volatile knowing : parents, teachers, and the censored story of accountability in
America's public schools / Kaia Tollefson.
     p. cm.
  Includes bibliographical references and index.
1. Educational accountability—United States. 2. Public schools—United States. I.
Title.
  LB2806.22.T65 2008
  379.1'580973—dc22   2007042858

ISBN: 978-0-7391-1559-6 (cloth : alk. paper)
ISBN: 978-0-7391-1560-2 (pbk. : alk. paper)
ISBN: 978-0-7391-4571-5 (electronic)

Printed in the United States of America

Dedication

In memory of my mother, Joyce Elaine Tollefson, a woman of strength.

*In the 18 years that I knew her
she taught me that it takes courage to live your own life,
that boundaries are movable,
and that singing and laughing are two good ways to keep your balance
in the world.*

Contents

Foreword

This eloquent, indignant, and scholarly book pulls down the screens obscuring the damage being done by the practices of accountability being imposed on public schools. As this author sees it, these practices intentionally stand in the way of teachers' and parents' sense of agency. They normalize those eager to innovate, to respond to the needs and interests of diverse students. Linked to them of course, as Kaia Tollefson argues sharply, is the domination by high-stakes testing and a distortion of the schools' presumably democratic purposes. The distortion, as she sees it, is effected by those who view the schools as serving the interests of business and industry, training the workers and technicians required by the system. Dr. Tollefson views the schools, therefore, as subservient to a market ideology in which public school students are thought of as "human resources" rather than as individuals entitled to equal opportunities to learn, become, and participate in a free society; they are subject to industrial demands rather than empowered to choose themselves in a not always hospitable world.

None of this is new, of course, to critical readers of educational literature. The thumbprints of Noam Chomsky, Karl Marx, Henry Giroux and other familiars are evident, particularly at the start; but none of the movements they represent overtake Dr. Tollefson's postmodern rejection of totalities in her often crystalline prose. She makes at least two novel contributions to the literature; and these allow her to open unexpected perspectives for her readers. The first is making audible the dialogues and discussions carried on by mixed groups of parents and teachers who particularize and ground accounts of what is being done to the schools today. They speak from experience in actual classrooms and in the homes and neighborhoods of the students, making accessible what is happening, defining what ought to be. The presentations of what they think and say derive from a particularly careful and authentic use of qualitative research, permitting the reader to tune into points of view ordinarily submerged.

The other novel contribution to the literature is the introduction of Michel Foucault's treatment of power. Dr. Tollefson chooses quite brilliantly to look through the perspectives of his "disciplines of power" as they work within the public school on teachers (the memos, the scheduling, the signing in before meetings, the interferences with curriculum). She finds Foucault's "panopticon" a proper metaphor for the structures of power that control so many teachers without their being aware of it. Describing how control is achieved by the public school panopticon, Professor Tollefson writes about its pyramid shape, the cells arranged on hierarchical levels, with the lowest containing multiple cells, the highest containing one. There is individualizing throughout; and each cell contains one individual prevented from communicating with any other by a brick wall. The parents and teachers located on the bottom levels inevitably inhabit what Freire called a "culture of silence," kept in order and in place by the disciplines of power.

Dr. Tollefson calls for a deliberate empowerment that will enable people to recognize and deal with those disciplines. Her hope lies in the generation of energy that may occur when people speak together and make connections with one another. This happens infrequently where teachers and parents and administrators are concerned in the domains of education. This author is quite aware of the open questions; and that very awareness may well move her readers to define and eventually act upon possibilities of change. The idea of countering power and the disciplines of power through dialogue and authentic exposure may empower those who occupy the lowest levels of the panopticon to rub the blinders off their eyes and come together for new beginnings.

This is a book that unnerves and awakens. Its readers may well see what they have seldom seen, hear what they have never heard.

Maxine Greene
Teachers College, Columbia University
July 2007

Acknowledgements

My deepest thanks go to all of the parents and teachers who participated in this project with me. I wish that I could thank each one by name here, but in the interests of confidentiality I offer instead my continuing and heartfelt gratitude. I am deeply appreciative of their generosity of time, enthusiasm, and laughter over the months that we worked together. Their individual and collective passions for the wellbeing of all children and for the ideals of the public good embodied in our nation's system of education are a continuing source of inspiration to me. Their willingness to share their thoughts with each other, to cross the unofficial but deeply inscribed divide that has historically existed between parents and teachers in our public schools, allowed me to explore my questions about the current accountability movement in education in a real and powerful way.

Where these research participants helped me to understand the terms and the effects of the accountability movement in the everyday experience of being teachers and parents in the public schools, others supported my ability to frame those experiences in a larger context. To Dr. Maxine Greene, in particular, whose work has significantly shaped my understanding of why education must be dedicated to the cultivation of imagination and the pursuit of possibilities, I owe much. For her generosity in offering the foreword to this book, for her philosophy that places the least advantaged child at the very center of why our public schools exist, and for her ability to write the most lyrical sentences that are yet powerful enough to move the world, I am grateful. I also thank Dr. Betsy Noll for her encouragement, wisdom, and ability to push my thinking in unfailingly critical and productive ways. More importantly, I appreciate her contributions to my work that stemmed from her professional disposition, which I have described in other contexts as "ethical to the bone." With her depth of knowledge and professional/ethical grounding in the conduct of qualitative research, she has been my moral compass a number of times when the role of researcher was too heavy to handle alone. My thanks, too, to Dr. Edward DeSantis, Dr. Kathryn Herr, Dr. Liz Keefe, and Dr. Peter Phillips for their support, thoughtful critique, and helpful contributions to my work.

A number of friends and family members provided their support and critical commentary for this project over the years, and their generosity of time, support, and care is something I will not forget. For this, in particular, I thank Kristi Sackett, Jane Erlandson, Carol Brandt, Deborah Krug, and Judy Reagan. Finally, my thanks to the one who taught me to dare the freefall. It has made all the difference.

CHAPTER 1

Accountability in the Schools:
What the People Don't Know

> By shifting the locus of authority to outside bodies, it undermines the capacity of schools to instruct by example in the qualities of mind that schools in a democracy should be fostering in kids: responsibility for one's own ideas, tolerance for the ideas of others, and a capacity to negotiate differences.
>
> Deborah Meier[1]

> Unless the mass retains sufficient control over those entrusted with the powers of their government, these will be perverted to their own oppression, and to the perpetuation of wealth and power in the individuals and their families selected for the trust.
>
> Thomas Jefferson[2]

Local control of the schools has historically been a deeply valued American tradition. Today, however, educators, parents, and other community members have been replaced by corporate and political leaders who have assumed control over defining the ends and means for accountability in education[3]—but not for ensuring that all children have adequate food, shelter, health and dental care, school facilities, and educational resources.[4] With such basic readiness-to-learn elements as these out of reach for the nation's poorest children,[5] it is clear that educational accountability as it is currently conceptualized in the United States is not founded in the goal of promoting equal opportunities in education. Neither is it founded in the goal of ensuring that all children have access to a balanced curriculum in which art, music, and the social sciences enjoy the same essential status as the "practical" subjects of reading, writing, math, and the "hard" sciences. In short, accountability in the current era in education is not about ensuring that our schools are focused on addressing the intellectual, social, and emotional needs of students; it is about optimizing children's potential as the nation's future workforce.

1

The idea that the public schools exist for the primary purpose of serving the nation's economic interests (versus ensuring education as the means by which the people can "retain sufficient control over those entrusted with the powers of government," for example) is so widely accepted that the following illustration of it in an excerpt from a recent *New York Times* editorial may be viewed as unremarkable:

> The United States can still prosper in a world where its labor costs are higher than the competition's, but it cannot do that if the cheaper workers abroad are also better educated. Business leaders who have firsthand experience with this problem warn that this country could become a third-rate economic power unless it radically remakes its schools. But the education community is in deep denial.[6]

Within the context of this "common sense" argument for school reform, students' primary educational purpose is to develop to their fullest potential as human resources rather than as human beings. This rationale for school reform and for the goal of accountability in education is about advancing "national" interests that coincide neatly with political agendas and corporate concerns. An interpretation of the national interest that coincides with a humanistic agenda and democratic concerns would naturally result in a vastly different understanding of the primary function of the schools. Such an interpretation would view the number of serious problems that certainly do exist in the public school system from the perspective of the nation's least advantaged child rather than from that of its most powerful citizens. It would take into account what has been known for decades about the circumstances under which human beings are genuinely motivated to want to try hard, to do their best, and to achieve—academically and otherwise.[7] Such an interpretation of what is in the national interest would require a public school system that is uncompromisingly devoted to providing challenging educational opportunities for all children, in which the underlying focus is always to understand more about how human beings are motivated to accomplish goals that they see as meaningful and worthy. It would be devoted to helping children to develop the knowledge and skills they need to grow into their future roles—not only as workers but as stewards of their economy, their government, and their environment.

In today's sociopolitical context in which the public good is subordinated to private interests, however, the government "of the people, by the people, and for the people" that Lincoln described is an unrealized ideal. This reality is nowhere more perfectly illustrated than in the politically orchestrated accountability movement in education. At the time of this writing, this accountability movement is represented in federal education law familiarly known as "No Child Left Behind" (NCLB). While significant revisions to this law are likely to occur through current reauthorization proceedings, it is less likely that the reality it presumes will shift any time soon. In this construction of reality, local administrators, teachers, and students are held accountable to goals backed by corporate interests and established in law by the federal government.[8] This gross inversion of democratic intent threatens not only the future of public education, but also the ideals of freedom and democracy that only an informed and attentive public can hope to realize.

Citizens today are encouraged to believe that federal control of accountability in education is in the nation's best interests, and that the tradition of local control is merely a quaint holdover from earlier, simpler times. Times change, but if Thomas Jefferson was correct, the danger of entrusting the public good to elected officials does not. In 1819, he wrote to John Adams, "No government can continue good, but under the control of the people." Thirty years earlier the same theme appeared in his letter to Edward Carrington, a fellow Virginian in the Continental Congress: "If once the people become inattentive to the public affairs, you and I, and Congress and Assemblies, Judges and Governors, shall all become wolves. It seems to be the law of our general nature, in spite of individual exceptions."[9] In the present context of a public education system in which children are presented among the "raw materials" and "tools at hand" that are available for serving "America's" economic interests,[10] it would appear that the wolves have already breached the schoolhouse door, and that local advocacy is no less important to guarding the ideals of democracy than it was two hundred years ago.

Proponents of top-down accountability mandates are clearly not aligned with the idea that governmental control must rest in the hands of the people. The inversion of democratic intent exemplified in today's accountability movement in education is championed by conservatives who call for national standards but not for a system of funding education that would aggressively address the "savage inequalities" that define reality in so many of our nation's deeply segregated schools.[11] They rightfully demand that the education system must be accountable for closing the achievement gap, but they are not similarly invested in the idea that our health care system must be equally accountable for closing the health care gap.[12] These conservative champions of educational equity and accountability see it as reasonable that all children should be able to achieve the same high academic standards—regardless of whether those children are healthy or unhealthy, fed or unfed, housed or homeless. They trumpet the failure of American students to compete academically in an international arena and they depict the education community as being in "deep denial" over international comparisons of achievement, but they are mysteriously silent about the fact that there is a greater discrepancy in access to good schools and health care for wealthy and poor children in this country than in most other industrialized nations of the world.[13] They loudly proclaim the importance of America's ability to be a global competitor academically, but they offer not even a whisper about the fact that the United States is reportedly "the only country in the developed world, except for South Africa, that does not provide health care for all of its citizens," that our infant mortality rate ranks twenty-sixth out of twenty-nine member nations of the Organization for Economic Cooperation and Development, or that we come in dead last in terms of "the degree to which financial contributions to health systems are distributed fairly across the population."[14]

These "accountability" proponents are numerous and vocal but not without opposition. Scholarly critiques and other challenges to the accountability movement in education exist (e.g., district- and state-level lawsuits against the federal government, and teacher-, parent- and student-led protests against standardized tests). However, these tend to focus on critiquing the *means* of federally established accountability measures—currently embodied, as previously mentioned, in the under-funded mandates of NCLB[15] and performance goals aimed at ensuring that every public school makes "adequate yearly progress." The more fundamental project lies in considering the question of its ends: What are the public schools accountable *for*, and where does the authority for answering that question lie?

Sustained public attention to such a question is unlikely, however, for the same reason that explains widespread acceptance for the past six years of federal legislation ironically known as "No Child Left Behind" in a social context that is partially described by a one-in-five poverty ratio for American children.[16] That irony is easily explained by the simple fact that the people don't know. The mainstream media is not in the habit of offering critical perspectives on the fundamental question of ends versus means in the realm of public school accountability.[17]

It makes sense that both the public's general acquiescence to the accountability movement and the lesser-known criticisms of it tend to be focused on its more superficial, visible aspects. It makes sense because it is the superficial and the visible that typically take priority in the for-profit corporate media. Deeper issues go largely unexamined,[18] which is certainly a troubling reality for a people whose freedom is intimately linked with the existence of a free and critical press. For example, the "academic atrophy in social studies, history, geography, civics, languages, and the arts" reported in Gerald Bracey's fourteenth annual report on the condition of public education in America[19] is not presented in the media as a direct consequence to the manner in which educational accountability is conceived, defined, and implemented in our schools. Academic atrophy in these areas is simply a given, a reality accepted by parents and teachers alike as the way things are—not because they collectively want the arts and social sciences out of the curriculum, but because the public has been trained to understand that these subjects are expendable, unnecessary because they do not serve "America's" economic interests.

If teachers, parents, and other community members were to debate such questions as what is and is not expendable in the schools and what is and is not in the nation's best interests educationally, they would require access to information on a number of topics from a variety of perspectives (e.g., differing ideas about such things as the purpose of education, the role of public schools in a free society, the variety of ways in which success in education can be defined and measured, and the "savage inequalities" that exist in children's experiences of school in America). This diversity of perspective, however, has been spectacularly rare in mainstream media coverage of issues in education.[20] Instead, the uniform language of market ideology—that is, of standardization, competition, and accountability—dominates educational discourse not only in the media, but in the halls of government and schools as well.[21] The existence of market ideology in the governance of public schools has achieved a kind of "natural" aura, revealing a colossal, collective assumption of rightness for private interests to dominate social thought about the role of public education in America. In *The Struggle for Control of Public Education,* Michael Engel describes this phenomenon, which he calls the "virtually unchallenged dominance" of market ideology. He describes it and warns of the threat that it poses to democratic education—ostensibly an essential purpose of the schools in a nation that lays claim to the language of democracy:

> current-day discussions about the future of education are conducted almost entirely in the language of the free market: individual achievement, competition, choice, economic growth, and national security—with only occasional lip service being given to egalitarian and democratic goals. . . . market ideology's virtually unchallenged dominance threatens the very existence of public education as a social institution, because its logic ultimately eliminates any justification for collective and democratic control of the schools. Market ideology and democratic values in education are mutually exclusive.[22]

While the existence of market ideology as an influence on the mission of public schools is certainly not surprising (such is to be expected in the context of capitalism), what is problematic for the future of a free society is the diminishing opportunity for citizens to explore alternative ideologies as the basis for determining the appropriate ends and means of education and accountability in their schools. It can certainly be argued that students who are motivated and well-served by an education system that functions in the competitive reward-and-punish mode of the market deserve continued access to that kind of training in their schools. (Some research suggests that 20 to 25 percent of American children are genuinely motivated by extrinsic controls.[23]) But students who need schoolwork to be intrinsically motivating if they are to genuinely invest themselves in it deserve another definition for educational accountability. A one-size-fits-all ideology for determining the ends and means of education and accountability in the public schools does not bode well for the ideals of freedom and democracy. Without popular media coverage of these issues or easy access to a public forum for discussing and debating them, it is unlikely that educators, parents, and other community members, including local political and business leaders, will realize what is at stake before it is too late.

The problem goes deeper still, however, beyond that of informational access. Even if a critical perspective on accountability mandates were routinely available in the mainstream media, it is questionable whether that information would find its way into conversations between teachers and parents. Simply put,

parents and teachers don't generally talk with each other about substantive issues in education. Philosophical, political, and policy-level discussions between
them are overwhelmingly more the exception than the rule. Parents have historically and routinely been relegated to the sidelines when it comes to discussing
politics and policies in the schools; education research establishing this point is
consistent and strong.[24]

The *de facto* rule in schools, as pervasive as it is indefensible, is that parents
and teachers are not "supposed" to venture into conversation beyond the immediate interests of the child who brought them together. The goal of parent involvement in the schools is commonly understood to be focused on enhancing
the success of an individual child, classroom, or school. It is not intended to encourage parents to advocate for the rights of all children to have access to excellent educational facilities and resources, for example, or to facilitate home-
school-community discussions about "the public good" or the relationship between education and freedom. "Parent involvement" is far more narrowly conceived.

I am convinced that in order for the future of public education and the ideals
of freedom and democracy to hold, the next step that teachers, administrators,
and academics must take is to figure out how to genuinely engage parents and
other community members in discussions and debates about essential questions
in education—questions having to do with such foundational themes as purpose,
access, and accountability. This book offers insight into one approach for accomplishing that. It is intended to add a new perspective on the accountability
discourse in education: that of everyday citizens—a particular group of parents
and teachers together—who studied and discussed information about the accountability movement that is available in academic texts but typically not in the
mainstream media. In part, this book is the story of six teachers and six parents,
diverse in terms of race, socioeconomic status, and school affiliation (some from
"exemplary" schools and some from "failing" schools) who met every two
weeks for six months to study a variety of texts on accountability and to discuss
the varying effects of accountability mandates in their neighborhood schools.
(These twelve were participants in the research project upon which this book is
based. Methodology for this qualitative case study is described in Appendix A.)

The discovery of new possibilities and the potential for positive change—
that is, the "volatile knowing" that parents and teachers can create with each
other—is the promise of democracy. Nonetheless, opportunities for teachers and
parents to talk with each other about school politics and policies are unusual.
Bucking this deeply engrained reality through participation in this research project was a transformative experience for the majority of parents and teachers in
the study, as well as for me. My hope is that others will benefit from the sharing
of that experience. One way for the potential benefit of this kind of teacher-
parent exchange to be viewed is in the context of a relatively new and growing
area of study in education: the establishment of learning communities for educators. In learning communities (e.g., Critical Friends Groups, Teaching Circles,

Professional Learning Communities), educators have ongoing opportunities to critically examine their own professional practices together, to consult with each other on dilemmas they encounter in their work, and to engage in discussions about critical issues in education. To my knowledge, there has been little attention in this body of literature to the idea of including parents in the creation of learning communities in the schools. This text can offer a window into the potential power that exists in doing so.

Countless parents and educators who have long been frustrated by their status as somehow "less than" when it comes to articulating educational dreams and desires for their children and schools need opportunities to open that conversation up, to challenge the exclusion of parents and teachers alike in defining the concept of accountability in our schools, and to broaden our understanding of who belongs in a learning community.

"Aristocrats fear the people," wrote Jefferson, "and wish to transfer all power to the higher classes of society."[25] There exist aristocrats in America, wolves in our schools who would define for us the ends and means of accountability in education. They fear the idea of the people coming together. They call this the problem of excessive democracy.[26]

I call it hope.

Notes

1. Deborah Meier, *Will Standards Save Public Education?* (Boston: Beacon Press, 2000), 4–5.

2. University of Virginia Library, "Electronic Text Center for the Thomas Jefferson Digital Archive," <http://etext.virginia.edu/jefferson/> (6 Sept. 2005).

3. Landon E. Beyer, "Educational Reform: The Political Roots of *A Nation at Risk*," *Curriculum Inquiry* 15, no. 1 (1985): 37–56; David C. Berliner and Bruce J. Biddle, *The Manufactured Crisis: Myths, Fraud, and the Attack on America's Public Schools* (Cambridge, Mass.: Perseus Books, 1995); Donaldo P. Macedo, "Literacy for Stupidification: The Pedagogy of Big Lies" in *Breaking Free: The Transformative Power of Critical Pedagogy*, edited by Donaldo P. Macedo (Cambridge, Mass.: Harvard Educational Review, 1996); Michael Engel, *The Struggle for Control of Public Education: Market Ideology vs. Democratic Values* (Philadelphia: Temple University Press, 2000); Henry Giroux, "Pedagogy of the Depressed: Beyond the New Politics of Cynicism." *College Literature* 28, no. 3 (Fall 2001); Linda Miller-Kahn and Mary L. Smith, "School Choice Policies in the Political Spectacle," *Education Policy Analysis Archives* 9, no. 50 (2001); Peter Phillips and Project Censored, *Censored 2003: The Top 25 Censored Stories* (New York: Seven Stories Press, 2002); and Deborah Meier and George Wood, eds., *Many Children Left Behind: How the No Child Left Behind Act Is Damaging Our Children and Our Schools* (Boston: Beacon Press, 2004).

4. Dale Johnson and Bonnie Johnson, *High Stakes: Children, Testing, and Failure in American Schools* (Lanham, Md.: Rowman & Littlefield Publishers, 2002); Jonathan Kozol, *Savage Inequalities: Children in America's Schools* (New York: Harper Perennial, 1991); Berliner and Biddle, *The Manufactured Crisis*; and The Children's Defense

Fund, "The State of Children in America's Union: A 2002 Action Guide to *Leave No Child Behind,*" <http://www.childrensdefense.org> (13 Nov 2002).

5. Children's Defense Fund, "The State of Children in America's Union." 20 percent of American children are born into poverty.

6. "Back to School, Thinking Globally," *New York Times*, September 6, 2005, Editorial Section. <http://www.nytimes.com/pages/pageone/> (6 Sept 2005).

7. Alfie Kohn, *Punished by Rewards* (New York: Houghton Mifflin Company, 1993); Kennon M. Sheldon and Bruce J. Biddle, "Standards, Accountability, and School Reform: Perils and Pitfalls," *Teachers College Record* 100, no. 1 (1998): 164–181; and Spence Rogers, "Increasing Student Motivation to Learn." Presentation at the National Schools Conference Institute's *Effective Schools Conference*, Phoenix, 1998.

8. The current incarnation of federal education law is "No Child Left Behind." *United States Department of Education* <http://www.nclb.gov/> (18 Jan 2003); "Fair Test, the National Center for Fair and Open Testing." <http://www.fairtest.org>; Johnson and Johnson, *High Stakes;* Susan Ohanian, *What Happened to Recess and Why Are Our Children Struggling in Kindergarten?* (New York: McGraw-Hill, 2002); and Meier and Wood, *Many Children Left Behind.* Even when this particular law is revised and reauthorized, however, it is unlikely that the trend to centralize decision-making and to impose top-down education policies will soon be reversed.

9. University of Virginia Library, "Electronic Text Center for the Thomas Jefferson Digital Archive."

10. National Commission on Excellence in Education (NCEE), "A Nation at Risk: The Imperative for Educational Reform." (U.S. Department of Education, 1983) <http://www.ed.gov/pubs/NatAtRisk/> (16 Feb 2001). This document is widely considered the launching point of the present-day accountability movement in education.

11. Kozol, *Savage Inequalities.* Jonathan Kozol, *Shame of the Nation* (New York: Crown Publishers, 2005).

12. Conservative political and corporate leaders' concerns for the well-being of America's least advantaged children are highly visible when it comes to how those children are doing in schools and whether they have access to highly qualified teachers. When it comes to whether those same children have access to excellent health care and highly qualified doctors and dentists, however, that concern is considerably harder to detect. For example, at the time of this writing a presidential veto has been promised in response to a movement in Congress to expand the State Children's Health Insurance Program. Nine million of the nation's seventy-four million children are currently uninsured, which is peculiarly unproblematic for corporate and political leaders so vocally devoted to the well being of the nation's least privileged students. Children's right to have immediate and routine access to highly qualified professionals does not apply in every context, as it turns out for these champions of selective equity. As George W. Bush put it, "I mean, people have access to health care in America. After all, just go to an emergency room" (Krugman 2007).

13. Children's Defense Fund, "The State of Children in America's Union"; University of Maine, "The United States Health Care System: Best in the World, or Just the Most Expensive?" <dll.umaine.edu/ble/U.S.%20HCweb.pdf> (6 Sept 2005); Berliner and Biddle, *The Manufactured Crisis.*

14. University of Maine, "The U.S. Health Care System," 3–6.

15. This 670-page reauthorization of the Elementary and Secondary Education Act (ESEA) of 1965 was itself due to be reauthorized in 2007. Legislative analysis offered by the International Reading Association in July 2007 is representative of current thought

about that process; more importantly, it underscores the point that accountability is presently conceived as a matter of course to be appropriately defined in political rather than educational arenas: "Currently we believe that both the House and Senate are working to change how the accountability system is conducted to allow for use of growth models, but specifics haven't been finalized. Among the questions are how to hold school accountable yet be realistic in working with ELL and handicapped populations. . . . While many observers are saying NCLB will not be reauthorized this year, the process is still moving forward" <http://www.latadvisory.blogspot.com/> (26 July 2007).

16. Children's Defense Fund, "The State of Children in America's Union," 15.

17. Berliner and Biddle, *The Manufactured Crisis*; Alfie Kohn, *The Schools Our Children Deserve: Moving Beyond Traditional Classrooms and 'Tougher Standards'* (New York: Houghton Mifflin Company, 1999); Engel, *The Struggle for Control of Public Education*; Giroux, "Pedagogy of the Depressed"; Miller-Kahn and Smith, "School Choice Policies."

18. For example, "in 2005, the year that saw the Katrina disaster and the culmination of [Michael] Jackson's rather less consequential trial, the networks deemed the pop star's legal problems twice as newsworthy as the economic plight of tens of millions of poor citizens, running 44 stories on Michael Jackson to 22 for poverty" (deMause and Rendall 2007).

19. Gerald Bracey. "The 14th Bracey Report on the Condition of Public Education." *Phi Delta Kappan* (October 2004): 166.

20. Berliner and Biddle, *The Manufactured Crisis*; Kohn, *The Schools Our Children Deserve*; Engel, *The Struggle for Control of Public Education*; Giroux, "Pedagogy of the Depressed"; Miller-Kahn and Smith, "School Choice Policies."

21. Kohn, *The Schools Our Children Deserve*; Peter Sacks, *Standardized Minds: The High Price of America's Testing Culture and What We Can Do to Change It* (Cambridge, Mass.: Perseus Publishing, 1999); Jim Donlevy, "The Dilemma of High-Stakes Testing: What Are Schools For?" *International Journal of Instructional Media* 27, no. 4 (2000): 331–338; James. V. Hoffman, "The De-Democratization of Schools and Literacy in America," *Reading Teacher* 53, no. 8 (2000): 616–624; Michael Apple, *Education the "Right" Way* (New York: RoutledgeFalmer, 2001); "No Child Left Behind"; Percy Ednalino, "Teacher Won't Administer CSAP Tests" (*Denver Post,* January 27, 2001); and Johnson and Johnson, *High Stakes.*

22. Engel, *The Struggle for Control of Public Education*, 3, 6.

23. Rogers, "Increasing Student Motivation to Learn."

24. Kimberly Waggoner and Alison Griffith, "Parent Involvement in Education," *Journal for a Just & Caring Education* 4, no. 1 (January 1998); Michelle Fine, "[Ap]parent Involvement: Reflections on Parents, Power, and Urban Public Schools," *Teachers College Record* 94, no. 4 (Summer 1993); Kathryn Nakagawa, "Unthreading the Ties that Bind: Questioning the Discourse of Parent Involvement," *Educational Policy* 14, no. 4 (September 2000); Carol Vincent, "Parent Empowerment? Collective Action and Inaction in Education," *Oxford Review of Education* 22, no. 4 (December 1996); Daphna Birenbaum-Carmeli, "Parents Who Get What They Want: On the Empowerment of the Powerful," *Sociological Review* 47, no. 1 (February1999); Miller-Kahn and Smith, "School Choice Policies"; and Claire E. Smrekar and Lora Cohen-Vogel, "The Voices of Parents: Rethinking the Intersection of Family and School," *Peabody Journal of Education* 76, no. 2 (2001): 75–100.

25. University of Virginia Library, "Electronic Text Center for the Thomas Jefferson Digital Archive."

26. Howard Zinn described the emergence of this phrase in the parlance of modern-day politics: "As the United States prepared in 1976 to celebrate the bicentennial of the Declaration of Independence, a group of intellectuals and political leaders from Japan, the United States, and Western Europe, organized into 'The Trilateral Commission,' issued a report. It was entitled 'The Governability of Democracies.' Samuel Huntington, a political science professor at Harvard University and long-time consultant to the White House on the war in Vietnam, wrote the part of the report that dealt with the United States. He called it 'The Democratic Distemper' and identified the problem he was about to discuss: 'The 1960's witnessed a dramatic upsurge of democratic fervor in America.' In the sixties, Huntington wrote, there was a huge growth of citizen participation 'in the forms of marches, demonstrations, protest movements, and 'cause' organizations.' There were also 'markedly higher levels of self-consciousness on the part of blacks, Indians, Chicanos, white ethnic groups, students and women, all of whom became mobilized and organized in new ways. . . .' There was a 'marked expansion of white-collar unionism,' and all this added up to 'a reassertion of equality as a goal in social, economic and political life.' . . . What worried Huntington was the loss in governmental authority. . . . His conclusion was that there had developed 'an excess of democracy,' and he suggested 'desirable limits to the extension of political democracy.'" Howard Zinn, *A People's History of the United States: 1492–Present* (New York: Harper Collins, 1995), 546–548.

CHAPTER 2

Challenging the Virtually Unchallenged:
A Personal Experience

My perspective on the problem of "aristocrats" defining the ends and means of public school accountability is primarily that of a teacher. For twenty-five years, I have worked in a variety of teaching and administrative positions. I have taught elementary, middle school, and college students; I have been a teachers' association president, a curriculum and staff development coordinator, and an elementary school principal. My work now is in teacher education.[1]

The importance of the problem I am exploring here crystallized for me when I returned to the classroom to teach fifth grade a few years ago. I took a temporary leave from my graduate studies and from working with student teachers to do this; prior to then, it had been eight years since I had taught children full time. I had not lived the intensification of the accountability movement over the previous decade as a public school teacher, and I believed that I needed to experience it in order to understand the real-world context that I was helping new teachers to enter. I took a fifth grade position because I had never before taught elementary-aged students; I wanted to make myself as new to the profession as possible in order to understand the experience of a beginning teacher as best I could. I spent the year as an experienced novice and was humbled to realize—although I had previously considered myself a hard worker as a middle school teacher and then as an administrator—that I had never fully appreciated what it takes to try to do a good job of teaching at the "elementary" level.

In returning to the classroom I experienced again the daily joys and sorrows of teaching: the exhilaration of hearing a quiet Native American girl who struggles academically pose a profound question to her classmates during a Socratic discussion ("How come things that are supposed to be good are always light and blonde-haired, and things that are bad are dark?"); the ache in my heart for the tough little boy who whispered to me during a school assembly, "Don't tell anybody, especially my mom, but I wish I could join the drill team." The sweetness of the same boy who, on deciding whether or not he wanted to participate in a class sleepover at the school, wrote a note asking whether any lights would be left on at night. ("Don't tell anybody, but I'm afrade of the drk.") The painful confiding of the girl who agonized over her mother's drug use, distraught with repeated imaginings of her death. ("Oh, please don't tell my dad that I told. He'll kill me if he finds out.") The boy who proudly described his father's accomplishments in this country, ending with a whisper, "And he's not even a legal citizen here."

Daily joys and sorrows, and always the balancing act of knowing when "telling" is in a child's best interests. Such is the constant fare of emotional highs and lows in classroom teaching that I remembered and that I was expecting to experience again. What I was not emotionally prepared for was the constant weight of presence that I felt over my shoulder. This was the presence of a hierarchical school structure, ultimately directed, it seemed, not by students, parents, teachers, principals, the superintendent, or the school board—but by "them": policy makers at state and federal levels who claimed the right to dictate the terms of success and failure for me, my students, and my school.

This demoralizing presence made itself known from my first day as a new employee. During an inservice session with about twenty other newly hired teachers in the district, we learned from an enthusiastic textbook representative that the district's recently adopted math program was designed so well that "a monkey could teach it." Judging by the looks on the faces of several first-year teachers, this was perceived by many as a very good thing. After waiting to no avail for the assistant superintendent in the room to take issue with the comment, a friend and I finally did. Our administrator remained silent throughout the conversation that resulted from our asking, "What is it that we bring to this program as professionals, beyond what monkeys might be able to do with it?" Clearly, there is great need for quality instructional materials that can provide a supportive framework for teachers, and I understood the new teachers' apparent relief at having been told that such a resource would be available to them. However, I could not understand this administrator's silence in the face of the message, particularly to such an impressionable audience, that teaching is a rote activity. In hindsight, that silence makes sense if teaching is defined in accordance with the market values of efficiency and productivity rather than in the more democratically oriented terms of critical thought and depth of understanding.

Throughout the year, in observation and in conversation with my administrators, I saw them as managers rather than leaders, unable or unwilling to work with members of our education community toward our own definitions for words like education, teaching, learning, and success. I made a point of speaking with my principal about this on a number of occasions, but came away each time feeling an odd mixture of anger and understanding. She was new to her job that year, too, and seemed overwhelmed—as well as somewhat frantic in her desire to deliver good test scores in March. District-office administrators were only visible to me throughout the year as members of the surveillance teams who visited classrooms during their school site visits, checking for teachers' compliance with mandated measures designed to ensure the district's goal of "excellence in education." This I interpreted to mean "excellence in test scores," as the district-office visits stopped in March, the month of test administration.

With my own philosophy about teaching and learning subordinated by the system to the market demands of accountability, efficiency, and quantitative measures of achievement, I struggled that year to hold onto a sense of personal and professional integrity. One of Webster's definitions for integrity is the "state of being complete or undivided." I did not achieve this state. I wrestled with my conscience almost daily as I chose to disobey mandates from my superiors that conflicted with what I saw as my ethical responsibilities as a teacher. The largest moment in my resistance to what I perceived as unethical demands came in March. It may have surprised me almost as much as anyone.

Believing that it is possible for standardized tests to serve some useful purposes, but that in today's pressurized climate of accountability they are destructive of the kinds of things I value (e.g., curricular depth, thoughtfulness, and the importance of being able to take risks as a teacher and as a learner), I decided not to participate in administering them. I felt justified in this decision because of the consistency I had found in the literature regarding the negative effects of an over-reliance on standardized test scores for evaluating educational achievement.[2] Linda McNeil and Angela Valenzuela provide a concise summary of these effects. While their research was specific to the "harmful impact" of the Texas Assessment of Academic Skills (TAAS, currently known as TAKS, the Texas Assessment of Knowledge and Skills), its adverse effects are echoed throughout this body of research. "Beneath the accountability rhetoric," they wrote, the following realities about TAAS-based teaching and testing are consistently found[3]:

- It violates what is known about how children learn.
- It reduces the quality and quantity of curriculum.
- It distorts educational expenditures, diverting scarce instructional dollars away from such high quality curricular resources as laboratory supplies and books toward test-prep materials and activities of limited instructional value.
- It provokes instruction that is aimed at the lowest level of skills and information, and it crowds out other forms of learning, particularly for poor and minority students.
- It is divorced from children's experience and culture.
- It is imposing exit measures that are particularly inappropriate for LEP (Limited English-Proficient) students.
- It is widening the gap between the education of children in Texas' poorest (historically low-performing) schools and that available to more privileged children.

Because of my familiarity with this kind of information, I believed that my participation in the administration of our school's standardized tests would be tantamount to colluding with a system that was designed to ensure that there would be children, families, educators, and whole communities to occupy the places of winners and losers in the public schools. I requested—and was denied—a two-week leave without pay for the duration of the testing window.

My principal told me that she would "be fired in five minutes" if she were to grant that leave request. I had written a lengthy memo to her explaining why I felt obliged to resist; in it I cited research about the effects of emphasizing standardized test results, and I attached what I thought were pertinent excerpts from the National Education Association's Code of Ethics. She was very supportive in theory, telling me more than once that she agreed with what I had written. In actuality, however, the response that she repeated on more than one occasion subverted my professional concerns to her personal ones. "I just need you to give those tests," she said. "I have to be concerned about my own position, too. I know I'd be fired in five minutes if I gave you leave without pay during the testing window. I have two boys in college, and I need to make this salary. I just need you to give those tests."

Her words made me feel simultaneously worried for her wellbeing and angry at being manipulated by an emotional appeal. This was Carol Gilligan's "ethic of care"[4] put to use as a strategy for containing resistance. Another use of this same strategy, after it became clear that I was not going to change my mind, was her agonized query, "But what about your *children,* Kaia? What about your *kids?*" In my journal that night (2/26/02), I wrote:

> Her saying, 'But what about your *children*' just infuriated me. I kept thinking on the way home, when is anyone but a teacher asked that question? Why are teachers held more responsible for what's 'good for children' than principals, superintendents, businessmen, and politicians? When are any of them asked this question with the same levels of passion and condemnation?

My principal didn't apparently appreciate the irony of her question or consider the possibility that it may represent the most important challenge of our time.

One of the most difficult aspects of this whole experience for me, a difficulty that continues to this day, has to do with my conflicting thoughts over how to characterize this administrator in my own mind—much less on paper. This was a woman who had given every indication of being glad to have me in her school. We had a positive and mutually respectful relationship. She invited me to serve on her leadership council, allowed me to run my classroom as I wished, and supported activities and projects that I wanted to pursue but that weren't typical practices at the school (e.g., a class sleepover, student-led parent conferences, the formation of a writing assessment team made up of parents). Even when my resistance to administering the tests challenged her authority, we maintained a mostly positive and highly civil rapport. My appreciation for her in this regard remains high, making any simplistic representation of her personal response to a professional problem inappropriate. It is appropriate, I believe, to view her words and actions through a broader lens—one that is large enough to bring the ideological framing of her position into focus. With market ideology ensconced as the driving force behind school governance, her room to maneuver was limited. With insistent demands for accountability and standardization pressing inexorably down from above and a bit of teacher resistance poking up from below, the view from the middle may have offered her few options.

While my principal's approach was to make the issue personal, appealing to what Gilligan has called the feminine ethic of care, my superintendent, predictably, made it a legal one when I took my request for a leave without pay to her. "I spoke with the [school] district's attorney, and she said we can't just go against the state's mandates. I just don't have any flexibility on this," she said. During the course of a 90-minute conversation with her (in follow-up to the memo I had sent, similar to the version I had given my principal), certain themes were repeated. The superintendent made four references to their attorney, three to my reputation as a "good teacher," and three to what she saw as the dismal outlook for my future employability if I persisted in refusing to administer standardized tests. Such statements made it plain that my teaching ability was of less value than my obedience.

Throughout our conversation it was clear that my educational priorities, some of which were personally shared by the superintendent, were ultimately of little importance. Instead, administrative allegiance appeared to lean heavily in the direction of political and corporate priorities. This was evidenced by a number of revealing statements, such as the following: "There was talk for awhile of doing away with the NRTs [Norm-Referenced Tests], but the business community wouldn't hear of it"; "We work in a state-driven system"; "There is nothing wrong at all with educating parents in a very balanced manner about these tests, but we have to be careful not to inflame the state board"; and "If I were a new teacher now, I don't know that I could make it. I know that the pressure is huge."

This was a woman who struck me as sincere. She seemed genuinely invested in the interests of children. "If we'd been serving the needs of all kids to begin with, we wouldn't be here," she rightly observed early in our conversation. This concern for "all kids," however, had not motivated her administration to ensure that the members of our relatively affluent community were fully informed of the consequences of attaching extreme importance to standardized test scores, particularly in the poorer schools and regions of the state. The following excerpt is from my journal entry that night (3/05/02) when I recorded the content of this conversation based on the notes I had taken:

> Then she said that she understood the role of the dissenter in a democracy, that dissent had played a valuable role in our country's history. 'But,' she said, 'there's another part of democracy. It means following laws. We're a law-abiding society. Being in a democracy means that you work from within to try and change the system, and that if you don't get your way, you go along with what's decided.' I said I thought that sounded fine, except that the parents I spoke with didn't know anything about these issues surrounding testing.

In the absence of information, democracy of any type is an illusion. In the words of James Madison,

> A popular Government without popular information or the means of acquiring it, is but a Prologue to a Farce or a Tragedy or perhaps both. Knowledge will forever govern ignorance, and a people who mean to be their own Governors must arm themselves with the power knowledge gives.[5]

Although Madison's words are perfectly aligned with my argument, it must be said that the ideology that motivated his sentiment is not the same as the one motivating me. He, of course, was advocating for informational access on behalf of "the 'more capable set of men' who recognize that it is the responsibility of the government 'to protect the minority of the opulent against the majority.'"[6]

The ideology motivating my actions was actually described well, if not always enacted, by my superintendent. It has been called "strong," "living," "participatory," and "popular" democracy.[7] This model requires far more of the citizen than liberal democracy, which posits voting as the defining act of citizenship. I follow the lead of others who have rejected such passive understandings of democracy,[8] a problem Karl Hess described in observing that "People who simply drop scraps of paper in a box or pull a lever are not acting like citizens; they are acting like consumers, picking between prepackaged political items."[9]

The kind of democracy to which my superintendent had referred is stronger, more active. In *The Quickening of America,* Frances Lappe and Paul DuBois wrote that an active conception of democracy requires that "we learn to solve problems with others—that we learn to listen, to negotiate, and to evaluate. To think and speak effectively. To go beyond simple protest in order to wield power."[10] What my superintendent appeared willing to overlook is that this kind of popular democracy presumes the people's access to balanced and accurate information. Few of the teachers and none of the parents with whom I spoke that year indicated that they had previous knowledge of critical literature on the accountability movement. In the absence of that information, this administrator's appeal to democracy rang hollow, although I did not doubt her sincerity. I did see it as another strategy for containing resistance, particularly in view of her associating democracy with obedience. Her repeated references to the district's lawyer and her intimation that I would be operating outside of the lawful boundaries of democracy if I did not administer standardized tests seemed primarily designed to make a problem go away.

As a one-time school administrator myself, I understand that my refusal to participate in administering the tests was insubordinate and that my administrators would have been within their rights to terminate my contract on the spot. What becomes less defensible from an administrative standpoint, however, is the refusal to make room for conscientious objection by way of granting the leave without pay that I had requested—particularly in view of the fact that such a leave had been granted the previous year to a woman who was a teacher in the same district, allowing her a week away from her classroom so that she could participate in a musical group touring Mexico. With this form of administrative support offered for personal considerations but not political ones, the choice that I saw was whether I should behave in a way that would be perceived as insubordinate by others or as unethical by myself.

At my school, I was not alone in my opposition to the way the tests were being used to drive the agenda for teaching and learning. Two primary-grade teachers, in particular, were publicly supportive of the stance I had taken. Other teachers at the school complained at length and in private about the grave ills they saw resulting from the district's seemingly exclusive focus on high test scores; many scoffed at the "efficient" strategies that we were taught to use in order to achieve them. I heard the comment, "I wish I could afford to resist it, too," more than once. This was sad, to me, for a number of understandable reasons. It suggested that the speakers were fearful of the consequences if they were to speak their truths; it indicated either an unwillingness or an inability to claim collective power; and it revealed a sense of resignation. (This situation is certainly exacerbated by such things as teacher isolation, rigid scheduling, and other entrenched and constraining realities that I will explore in Chapter 7.)

The short version of the rest of this story is that I found parents and students alike to be very supportive of my continued refusal to administer the tests, when I explained my reasoning in meetings with both groups. Two families wrote a letter to the principal, asking that their children be excused from taking the tests; many parents and a few teachers told me of their surprise in finding out that families have this right in their state,[11] and of their anger at not having known of it before. In the end, the school counselor administered the tests in my classroom while I worked on a project for the fifth-grade staff. I was not fired. Instead, I was told that I was wanted back for the following school year, but only if I would agree to participate in future standardized test administrations. (Oddly, the principal told me that this was the superintendent's stipulation; the superintendent told me that it was the principal's.) I entertained the idea of complying with this condition in order to have the opportunity to work from within the district, helping others in the community to learn about the accountability movement and research findings on its effects, especially on impoverished and demoralized students and schools. Having learned already, however, that the district obviously had higher standards for obedience from its employees than it did for teaching ability or critical thought, I wasn't eager to return. I chose instead to resign from what had initially been a three-year mental commitment.

With nearly two decades in education behind me, it was very difficult throughout that year to claim the right to define myself as a teacher and to hold onto my own professional values. As hard as this was for me, I ached for my colleagues who were in their first years of teaching. A few who had been my students at the university and were now in their first, second, and third years of service in area schools, confided that their experience as teachers was a far cry from what they had learned about student-centered practices in their foundations and methods courses. They spoke often in anger and sometimes with tears about feeling betrayed, vulnerable, and constantly anxious about what their students' standardized test scores would say about them. One said matter-of-factly that she "didn't feel like a teacher." Her school, located in the "war zone" of a neighboring community, mandated the "teacher-proofed" language program *Success for All*. District administrators would visit her classroom at least twice a month, she said, to make sure that she was on the right lesson and had the right posters on the wall. "I read from a script, every day!" she raged indignantly when we met for coffee one Saturday afternoon. "I mean, why did I even go to college? My kids deserve better than this!"

These young teachers' stories made me angry. Without the invitation to spend their novice years experimenting in safety, making mistakes and learning from them with the help of experienced mentors, they were urged instead to focus their efforts on becoming efficient data-collectors and to care only about quantifiable results. I went home particularly frustrated one night after a staff meeting at my school, during which a first-year teacher had said that he worried about whether he was "meeting the needs of all of the student segments" in his room. This young teacher was learning to integrate the dehumanizing language of the market; he had adopted the vocabulary that transformed the individual children in his care into collective "segments."

The early instigators of today's accountability movement, the members of the National Commission on Excellence in Education who wrote *A Nation at Risk*,[12] were not at all shy about dehumanizing children. In this 1983 report on the state of education in America is a section called "The Tools at Hand" in which the "raw materials needed to reform our educational system"[13] are listed. First on that list of tools are "the natural abilities of the young that cry out to be developed and the undiminished concern of parents for the well-being of their children." In the midst of an accountability movement spawned in this context, in which children head a list of the "raw materials . . . waiting to be mobilized through effective leadership," it makes sense that my young friend would refer to the children in his care as "student segments." There is a problem with this "sensible" conclusion, however, that Karl Marx named 160 years ago. In *The Wages of Labour*, he wrote, "If human life is to be regarded as a commodity, we are forced to admit slavery."[14]

With the "virtually unchallenged dominance"[15] of market ideology in America's schools firmly established, children are aptly designated as laborers in a compulsory system designed to serve the needs of the state.

Notes

1. When I tell my students a short version of the story in this chapter, I emphasize my belief that it is the job of new teachers to learn how to teach well, not to challenge their administrators or be insubordinate in the face of accountability mandates they may not agree with. I also emphasize another belief, that this story turned out the way it did because I was twenty years into my career at the time, and my fifth graders' parents (who

knew I was working on a PhD in education) saw me as experienced and capable. Although I was new to the school the year that these events took place, I am careful to clarify with education students the fact that the social and cultural capital I carried into my classroom that year was very different from that of the typical new teacher. This is why I emphasize the idea that a new teacher's job is to learn how to teach well. Not only do I believe that a new teacher's career would be a short one if s/he began it by overtly resisting accountability mandates; I also think that only a teacher who is trusted by parents in a school and who knows how to invite them to substantive discussion about issues in education is in a position to facilitate the crucial work of redefining accountability in the schools.

2. Kennon M. Sheldon and Bruce J. Biddle, "Standards, Accountability, and School Reform: Perils and Pitfalls," *Teachers College Record* 100, no. 1 (1998): 164–181; Jim Donlevy, "The Dilemma of High-Stakes Testing: What Are Schools For?" *International Journal of Instructional Media* 27, no. 4 (2000): 331–338; Alfie Kohn, "Standardized Testing and Its Victims," *Education Week* 20, no. 4 (2000): 60, 46–47; Linda McNeil and Angela Valenzuela, "The Harmful Impact of the TAAS System of Testing in Texas: Beneath the Accountability Rhetoric," Harvard University: The Civil Rights Project, 2000; Alfie Kohn, "The Case Against 'Tougher Standards,'" http://www.alfiekohn.org (2001); and Stan Karp, "Let Them Eat Tests," *Rethinking Schools* 16, no. 4 (2002): 3–4.

3. McNeil and Valenzuela, "The Harmful Impact of the TAAS System of Testing in Texas," Introduction, ¶10.

4. Carol Gilligan, *In a Different Voice* (Cambridge, Mass.: Harvard Univ. Press, 1983).

5. In Robert McChesney and John Nichols, *Our Media Not Theirs* (New York: Seven Stories Press, 2002), 24.

6. Noam Chomsky, "Renewing Tom Paine's Challenge," in *Our Media Not Theirs* by Robert McChesney and John Nichols (New York: Seven Stories Press, 2002), 16.

7. Michael Engel, *The Struggle for Control of Public Education: Market Ideology vs. Democratic Values* (Philadelphia: Temple University Press, 2000), 46–48.

8. Maxine Greene, *The Dialectic of Freedom* (New York: Teachers College Press, 1988); Jean Bethke Elshtain, *Democracy on Trial* (New York: Basic Books, 1995); John Dewey, "The Democratic Conception in Education" (1916), in *Educating the Democratic Mind*, by Walter C. Parker (Albany: State University of New York Press, 1996); and Engel, *the Struggle for Control of Public Education*.

9. Hess, 1979 in Walter C. Parker, ed., *Educating the Democratic Mind* (Albany, New York: State University of New York Press, 1996), 9.

10. Lappe & DuBois, 1994, in Engel, *The Struggle for Control of Public Education*, 47.

11. A parent or guardian's right to exempt a child from participation in state- and federally-mandated tests varies from state to state.

12. Peter Sacks, *Standardized Minds: The High Price of America's Testing Culture and What We Can Do to Change It* (Cambridge, Mass: Perseus Publishing, 1999).

13. National Commission on Excellence in Education (NCEE), "A Nation at Risk: The Imperative for Educational Reform," (U.S. Department of Education, 1983), "The Tools at Hand" section.

14. Karl Marx, *Early Writings* (New York: Penguin Books, 1844/1992), 293.

15. Engel, *The Struggle for Control of Public Education*, 6.

CHAPTER 3

Making Sense of the Accountability Movement: Organized (and Profitable) Malevolence Against the Public Schools

How to describe a nation that views its children as raw materials? How to explain a school system in which attention is fixed on coercing students' achievement of standardized skills and knowledge on a uniform timeline—rather than on stimulating their curiosities, developing their critical thinking abilities, and ensuring their love for learning? A certain set of priorities is clearly evident in the pervasive pattern of dehumanizing children in America's schools. It does not follow that these are "America's" priorities, although effort is certainly invested in convincing the American public that it is natural for the nation, not the child, to enjoy the ownership rights of education. Whose priorities *are* served, then, by the subversion of children's interests to politically defined and imposed accountability mandates? An exploration of this question requires another look at the privileging of market values over democratic ideals in the governance of the nation's public schools.

Exploring an Oxymoron: Unchallenged Ideology in American Schools

Making sense of the current accountability movement in education means making sense of the virtually unchallenged dominance of market ideology in the schools. Toward this end it is productive to ask: how have market values come to dominate our educational discourse so thoroughly? How is it possible that in this pluralistic society, where difference is assumed and sometimes celebrated, such singularity of thinking could possibly prevail on a topic as complex as the ends and means of education and accountability in a free society? I join others[1] in answering that this has been achieved through a manipulation of the American public into a fearful, defensive posture, accomplished by means of what

Michael Apple calls "open season on education"[2] and by what David Berliner and Bruce Biddle refer to as a "campaign of criticism"—a massive disinformation campaign of "organized malevolence"[3] against the public school system. Berliner and Biddle named this phenomenon "the Manufactured Crisis," noting that in recent years

> ideologically driven criticism of the schools has grown more strident, and negative findings known to be questionable or wrong are now being cited in that criticism—findings that are often drawn from unidentified or secondary sources, and are used as ritualized support for lambasting education.[4]

One enabling feature of such "organized malevolence" is the American people's lack of access to balanced media coverage about the state of education in the country's schools, and about the serious problems that they do, indeed, face.[5] In studying the data that were and were not used in the engineering of an overwhelmingly negative public perception of the nation's schools, Berliner and Biddle ultimately arrived at two conclusions which flatly contradict incessant media messages of a failing school system: (1) "on the whole, the American school system is in far better shape than the critics would have us believe," and (2) "where American schools fail, those failures are largely caused by problems that are imposed on those schools."[6] Gerald Bracey's analyses of achievement data in his annual reports on the condition of public education, published each year in *Phi Delta Kappan,* consistently reinforce Berliner and Biddle's conclusions. Such findings may fall strangely upon ears conditioned for ritualized lambasting of education.

Lawrence Stedman, highly critical of Berliner and Biddle's analysis of achievement data and adamant that "there is a real achievement crisis," nonetheless agrees "that right-wing forces have been attacking the public schools and exploiting the evidence."[7] Additional points of concurrence include Stedman's assertions that "U.S. performance in the international arena is not as dismal as school critics have asserted,"[8] that "in the 1980s, school critics often exaggerated the size and extent of the test score decline," and "in spite of enormous changes in society and school populations, U.S. achievement has been remarkably stable for many decades."[9] While the level of this achievement is troublesome enough for Stedman to argue convincingly that the crisis in education is real, the underreported stability of achievement rates for the past several decades—despite a variety of "enormous changes in society and school populations"—suggests that critics have been more interested in highlighting school failure rather than the nation's failure to ensure adequate food, shelter, health care, school facilities, and educational resources for all of its children.

This points to a problem that threatens the future of public education—and, indeed, of the very idea of the "public good" in America. This problem lies in the reality that overly negative perceptions of the nation's school system—a system that has historically existed, in part, for the purpose of ensuring that citizens are capable of protecting Constitutional definitions of personal and public welfare—have been engineered by those whom Peter Phillips calls the "corporate and governmental elites"[10] who stand to gain from distorting the truth. (Three specific kinds of private gain will be described later in this chapter.)

To further complicate the problem of state and federal leaders in business, government, and the media failing to provide a variety of perspectives on the state of education in America is the previously mentioned failure of many teachers, administrators, parents, students, and other community members to share their own perspectives on education with each other. Without genuine opportunities or invitations to do so, members of these different groups do not typically discuss with each other such things as the wide variety of purposes for education or the damaging effects of extrinsic "motivational" strategies on students and teachers. In my experience, the majority of those who are involved in the processes of teaching and learning in the schools do not see it as their *place* to participate in such debates, accepting, instead, state and federal decrees mandating educational policies that they had no part in creating. I have come to believe that this handing over of personal and professional power is a logical response by an uninformed public that has no access to a popular medium for readily exploring other realities in education. Surely, Berliner and Biddle's assertion of a "manufactured crisis" and the existence of savage inequalities in education, documented by Jonathan Kozol in 1991 and by others since then,[11] would qualify as two of those other realities deserving of a public forum.

The problem with all of this is that private interests have effectively precluded genuine public participation in determining the appropriate ends and means of education and accountability in the nation's schools. This curbing of citizens' access to their own participatory responsibilities has been undertaken by right-wing forces bent on ascribing failure to the entire institution of public education—rather than on focusing appropriate attention and resources on addressing possible underlying causes of "failure" in particular school contexts (e.g., racism and segregation, poverty, the conflation of high standards with standardization, low expectations, internalized oppression, hopelessness, the damaging effects of extrinsic controls on intrinsic motivation to teach and to learn).[12] The work of supplanting a public discussion on education among citizens with the private voices of elite corporate and political interests is aided by the absence of "media democracy" in America—that is, the absence of a diversified major media system devoted to the First Amendment ideal of an informed public.[13] Rather than working to ensure balanced and accurate reporting on the state of the nation's public schools, major media coverage of educational issues is instead comprised largely of the "myths, half-truths, and sometimes outright lies"[14] which have been deployed in the attack on public schools.

Media complicity in establishing the "manufactured crisis" is not surprising, given the reality that government deregulation of media ownership[15] has paved the way for as few as ten "giant firms" to dominate the global media system.[16] In such a political climate, it stands to reason that corporate interests have superceded Constitutional ideals in the schools as well as in the public airwaves. In this context, Michael Engel's claim that public education is now thoroughly driven by market ideology rather than by democratic values is justified. In the current education arena, he wrote,

> certain themes [have] seemed to receive unqualified acceptance from everyone involved with the school system: cooperation with the business community, the prime importance of computer technology, corporate models of school governance, an emphasis on collaboration among various 'stakeholders' in the system, the economic rationality of school choice, and rigid state standards and assessments in the name of reform.[17]

Without balanced media coverage, few citizens may question the appropriateness of such "common sense" parameters governing the debate about school reform. Without a popular medium for exploring and debating alternative views about the appropriate ends and means of education, it is unlikely that public education will be popularly valued for any number of reasons beyond economic rationality. With mass media resources securely controlled by corporate interests, Americans are vulnerable to whatever profitable "reality" is constructed for them. In this context, focused media attention is simply not given to certain kinds of issues, such as the extent to which "local taxpayers are being robbed of corporate tax revenues at a time when school costs are rising to meet additional needs."[18] Indeed, as Paul Harris noted,

> In the 1950s the proportion of federal income from company taxes was 33 percent, by 2003 it was just 7.4 percent. Some 82 of America's largest companies paid no tax at all in at least one of the first three years of the administration of President George W. Bush.[19]

So skillfully have corporate and governmental elites managed to control and define the country's gaze toward education that popular demands for *their* accountability to the public rarely occur. This is advantageous to the politically powerful, of course, since it is the schools of the poor—those serving children whose families lack the social capital to demand accountability from their leaders—that are consistently "failing."[20] Such a condition can be rectified only if the public demands an opportunity to redefine and refocus the accountability discourse. Lacking knowledge, however, few Americans are aware that they have not had this opportunity, that they weren't invited to participate when the market-driven terms of the debate were effectively established with the Reagan-era publication of *A Nation at Risk: The Imperative for Educational Reform.*[21] Lacking knowledge, the resulting lack of public solidarity and the people's inability to resist are assured.

Consider Rosa Parks, not a poor, black woman too tired at the end of the day to move another step, but an activist with a thirty-year commitment to civil rights, steeped in the solidarity of the NAACP, and educated in the discourse of civil disobedience.[22] Mrs. Parks' stance in "excessive democracy"[23] was firmly rooted in knowledge. How can the kind of agency and resistance that she undertook be enacted—or even be enabled to occupy space in the minds of teachers, students, parents, and other citizens—without benefit of the kind of information, education, and solidarity that she and other heroes of the 1960s had won? The importance of this line of thinking is illustrated by Noam Chomsky's description of a crucial strategy employed by "the world of private power"[24] in reversing the "problem" of excessive democracy:

> Much of the right-wing fervor behind the drive to destroy Social Security and public schools, and to block efficient and popular programs of public health care, reflects the understanding that such programs rely on values that must be extirpated: the natural and deep-seated values of sympathy and solidarity, the conviction that one should care about what happens to the child or disabled widow on the other side of town. These pernicious ideas must be driven from the mind. People must be atomized and separated if they are to be ruled by the responsible men, for their own good.[25]

If Chomsky is correct, that it has been the project of "the responsible men" to extirpate "the natural and deep-seated values of sympathy and solidarity"— that is, to pull them up by the roots, to destroy them completely—then popular belief in the "manufactured crisis" and widespread support of "savage inequalities" in education is a logical measure of their success. The crucial point here, of course, is that this success cannot yet be legitimately claimed. People without access to information have not had opportunity to explore either the existence of or the potential for sympathy and solidarity with each other relative to educational issues.

Maxine Greene cited a 1989 "Talk of the Town" column from *The New Yorker* that effectively explains the importance of having access to information, of having the kind of detailed knowledge that the American public has been denied in the corporate-led drive for a marketized system of public schooling:

> Ambiguous and unpredictable, details undermine ideology. They are connective. They hook your interest in a way that ideas never can. If you let in the details of some aspect of life, you almost have to allow that aspect to be what it really is rather than what you want or need it to be.[26]

One example of a text that provides this kind of crucial, detailed knowledge—but which lacks mainstream visibility—is *High Stakes*, by Dale Johnson and Bonnie Johnson. These two resigned their tenured professorships at a midwestern university that "prides itself on the huge numbers of teachers it turns out,"[27] disillusioned with what they experienced as "obliviousness to the real needs of teachers and children" in its college of education. After spending one year in their new positions at a state university in northern Louisiana, they returned to the classroom to ground themselves in the current realities of the public schools. Their new university went out of its way to support this venture, going so far as to arrange unpaid one-year leaves of absence.

The book that the Johnsons wrote was not planned at the outset of their year in a poverty-stricken school in northern Louisiana, but they ended up writing the story of their experience because they realized, as the year went on, that it was a story that desperately needed to be told. The connective details they share provide an intimate look at the effects of an accountability system that targets children, teachers, and schools rather than politicians, corporate leaders, and society. With the details of their day-to-day lives at "Redbud Elementary," they allow their readers to experience the terrible injustices they routinely witnessed. For example, while the school's 600+ children and their teachers did not have access to "hot water, a library, current textbooks, reference materials, playground balls and equipment, a place for sick children to lie down, art supplies, or vermin-free classrooms,"[28] they were held responsible for the same achievement standards as the affluent children down the road who did enjoy high-quality conditions for teaching and learning. Dale Johnson, who taught fourth grade that year, wrote:

> I am filled with anger at the state bureaucrats and politicians who designed and mandated this uncompromising accountability system. Our Redbud pupils have so many strikes against them. They are often sick. They have rotting teeth and cry because of severe toothaches. Many come from dysfunctional homes. They are ill-clad and wear ill-fitting shoes. Several do not get enough food or enough rest. They live with acute poverty in substandard homes, often surrounded by drug dealers and users and drunks. The harsh accountability system imposed by the state kicks them further.[29]

I believe that this type of detailed knowledge—the kind of information that is not honored in the corporate media's "news" and its ritualized lambasting of education—is a necessary precondition for rekindling what Chomsky called the "deep-seated values of sympathy and solidarity." In a related vein, Maxine Greene wrote:

> One of the reasons I have come to concentrate on imagination as a means through which we can assemble a coherent world is that imagination is what, above all, makes empathy possible. . . . Of all our cognitive capacities, imagination is the one that permits us to give credence to alternative realities. It allows us to break with the taken for granted, to set aside familiar distinctions and definitions.[30]

There is a relationship between Chomsky's notion of "sympathy and solidarity" and Greene's ideas about "imagination," "empathy," and the work of assembling a "coherent world." Chomsky voices the "conviction that one should care about what happens to the child or disabled widow on the other side of town," and Greene contends that this conviction is acquired through knowing some of the details of that child's or disabled widow's reality. In the next chapter I will describe a research project that grew from these ideas. It brought parents and teachers together for the purpose of studying and discussing a critical perspective of the accountability movement that is typically unavailable in the mainstream media. Through this study, it was my project to see what, if anything, would happen in the realms of sympathy and solidarity when teachers and parents explored elements of "the manufactured crisis" and the "savage inequalities" in education together. I wanted to hear the conversations that would occur when some of the details were known. I wanted to learn how a small group of teachers and parents would respond to the kind of news about schools that "the press seems not to notice."[31]

Private Gain from Public Loss: A Typology of Profits

Academics who are critical of the intensification of the accountability movement in recent years have written extensively, highlighting the problem of ceding the public schools to the private interests of market ideology.[32] Other writers have detailed the zeal with which public officials are willing to hold teachers, students, and schools accountable for academic achievement—even though the latter groups, particularly in poor communities, are typically divorced from the process of determining what those achievements should be and how success should be defined.[33] These critics have also noted the decided lack of enthusiasm that policy makers tend to exhibit for holding themselves accountable for what the late Senator Paul Wellstone called a national disgrace: America's failure to ensure that all children enjoy equal opportunities to learn in healthy and welcoming environments.

Critical voices are effectively muted, however, when freedom of the press is reduced to the dominant reality of for-profit media.[34] Ethnographies and critical essays revealing the flaws of market ideology and the corporate takeover of America's schools typically appear in scholarly books and academic journals, not in forums readily accessible to the general public. Popular forums, privately owned, do not generate profit by disclosing the facts of the savage inequalities that exist between schools, nor by critiquing the privatization of education. They do, however, generate profit by reinforcing the message that schools, teachers, students, and families are failing. These profits come in a variety of forms. In education literature critical of the accountability movement and of the rise of market ideology in the governance of public schools, there is evidence of at least three kinds of private profit—political, financial, and familial—that may accrue to those who are in a position to manipulate perception of the public schools. A description of each follows.

Type 1: Political Profit—Diversionary Benefits

Political profiteering at the expense of the public schools comes from the diversionary benefit to be had by powerful politicians who are complicit in dismantling popular faith in public education. This is what Berliner and Biddle conclude with their observation that "both [Reagan and Bush] administrations had reasons for diverting America's attention from federal failures to deal with

domestic problems, and one way to do this was to blame those problems on educators and the schools."[35] The classic example of such political misdirection of
public attention is embodied in what Peter Sacks calls "a marvel of alarmist
propaganda,"[36] that is, the Reagan administration's infamous report on the state
of education in America.

A Nation at Risk: An Exemplar of Diversionary Rhetoric

I began teaching in 1983, four months after The National Commission on
Excellence in Education (NCEE) released its "Open Letter to the American
People" entitled *A Nation at Risk: The Imperative for Educational Reform.* My
entire career has been carried out in the context of this era in education,
launched by the report's now-notorious introduction:

> If an unfriendly foreign power had attempted to impose on America the medio-
> cre educational performance that exists today, we might well have viewed it as
> an act of war. . . . We have, in effect, been committing an act of unthinking,
> unilateral educational disarmament.[37]

This strident call for reform is based almost entirely upon a rationale that
argues for the nation's need to regain superior international status as a global
competitor:

> Our Nation is at risk. Our once unchallenged preeminence in commerce, indus-
> try, science, and technological innovation is being overtaken by competitors
> throughout the world. . . . What was unimaginable a generation ago has begun
> to occur—others are matching and surpassing our educational attainments. . . .
> America's position in the world may once have been reasonably secure with
> only a few exceptionally well-trained men and women. It is no longer.[38]

This rationale for educational improvement is not founded upon a public
commitment to advancing the promises of America to all citizens. The premise,
rather, is that the nation's public school system must be reformed with the goal
of ensuring that citizens can be more effectively utilized in the pursuit of
"America's" economic goals. The fact that the gap between the rich and poor in
this country is at its largest recorded point in over thirty years[39] dispels the notion that school reform for the past two decades has been in pursuit of economic
goals for the American people. Nevertheless, this purpose for school reform has
not lost ground since 1983. Indeed, writers on the subject generally agree that
the current era of reform, characterized as it is by industry's influence on the
policies and practices affecting public schools, was launched twenty years ago
with the immediately popular proposals of the NCEE. As Michael Engel wrote:

> The commission's prestige and the urgency of its rhetoric led to wide publicity
> for its findings, despite their rather weak empirical support. Its specific propos-
> als were strengthening high school graduation requirements in what it called

the Five New Basics (English, mathematics, science, social studies, and computer science), more rigorous and measurable standards, a longer school day, improved teacher education, and increased financial support for schools—although not necessarily from the federal government.[40]

Despite a steady barrage of criticism leveled at the Commission for its poor methodology, shallow conclusions, and incendiary tone,[41] the powerfully backed report remains the solidly anchored flagship of the corporate takeover of American education. While the release and the contents of the report were avidly covered by the media, subsequent and substantial criticisms of it were not. Media coverage drew considerable scholarly attention, in fact, for its lack of integrity. Peter Hlebowitsch, for example, observed that "major news magazines like *Time, Newsweek* and *U.S. News and World Report* covered the essential details of the report in a fashion that was tantamount to advocacy."[42]

Not only have scholarly critics of *A Nation at Risk* failed to make headlines over the years. Important post-publication comments by Commission members themselves also failed to make banner news—comments which, had they been publicized, would logically have called the report's authority into question and scuttled widespread public faith in its findings and recommendations. For example, when the NCEE was criticized for ignoring National Assessment of Education Progress data that indicated higher achievement levels in math and verbal skills by junior high and elementary students, Commission member William O. Baker is quoted as having said, remarkably, that "We disregarded what we didn't believe."[43] (Baker was one of two corporate representatives on a government-sponsored commission on education that included not one teacher—public or private, K-12 or college.)

While "the document became the top news story on the nation's top three television networks" within a few hours of its release,[44] then, the same enthusiasm for providing media coverage did not extend to ensuring that the public became aware of its flaws (such as the methodological negligence described by Baker). Furthermore, project director Milton Goldberg reportedly stated that the document's purpose was intentionally propagandistic. Four years after its publication, Doran Christensen explained:

> *A Nation at Risk* was not, as admitted by the commission's director (Goldberg, 1984), intended to illuminate the problems of the schools, but rather to 'rouse' the public through stark and emotional rhetoric. . . The major purpose of the report was to attract media attention.[45]

In 1999 Peter Sacks wrote, "As one of the most widely distributed and aggressively marketed policy statements to emerge from the Reagan administration, the landmark report would become a veritable New Testament for the modern-day accountability movement."[46] The terms for school reform, established in 1983 and founded in propaganda, have not been popularly challenged or changed since then.

Writing only two years after its publication, Landon Beyer commented that "The narrow perspective on educational and social issues represented by the report . . . may serve to hide the political interests it in fact embodies."[47] Further, he characterized *A Nation at Risk* as

> a politicized attempt to cover the social and economic reasons for [Americans'] loss of purpose and vision. Throughout the report . . . schools are the source of a variety of economic, military, and spiritual ills. Yet the possibility that schools may *reflect* a range of social problems that continue to plague American society is not examined.[48]

According to Beyer, "One of the most important questions we need to ask is who benefits from the way America's institutions are organized and run, and what alternatives are there to these patterns."[49] Who, then, benefits from what Henry Giroux describes as "the emergence of a view of education in which schools are defined as a private rather than a public good"?[50] Who profits when shoddy research and weak empirical evidence are used as the basis for casting schools as the definitive source, rather than as a possible reflection of "a variety of economic, military, and spiritual ills" facing the nation?

No Child Left Behind: An Exemplar of Diversionary Rhetoric for the New Millennium

One way to identify who the winners and losers are in any society is to follow the advice offered by the Children's Defense Fund in their assessment of "The Bush Administration's Track Record in Leaving No Child Behind":

> Follow the money and you find what we truly care about and stand for as a nation. Budgets represent moral and social choices, not just economic ones. They are a test of what we value as a people. . . . 'The biggest percentage of our budget should go to our children's education. Education is my top priority,' President Bush said in February 2001. His 2002 budget then proposed 40 times more money for tax cuts than for education. . . . The Bush administration's budget choices before and after September 11th leave millions of children behind. . . While thousands of children, parents, and grandparents stand in unemployment and soup kitchen and homeless shelter lines waiting for food and a stable place to live all across America, lobbyists for powerful corporations like Enron and rich individuals and special interests line up inside Congress and the White House to get hundreds of billions of dollars in new tax breaks and government handouts.[51]

Children living in poverty is one of those domestic problems from which some of the country's most powerful leaders would arguably prefer to divert America's attention. That it is one of the nation's most significant social problems is incontrovertible, though the details may not be widely known. For example, according to the Children's Defense Fund, the United States ranks 12th among industrialized countries in the percentage of children living in poverty, 16th in living standards for the poor, and 17th in efforts to lift children out of poverty—but 1st in Gross Domestic Product, defense expenditures, health technology, and the number of millionaires and billionaires. Perhaps unsurprisingly, in this context, the United States is one of only two of the 154 members of the United Nations that has not ratified the U.N. Convention on the Rights of the Child. The other is Somalia, which has no legally constituted government.[52] Such information is politically overshadowed by the zealous rhetoric of the Right in which schools are admonished to "leave no child behind."[53] In the mid-1980s, Beyer used the example of children in poverty to support his claim that the conservative attack on the schools was a "politicized attempt" to obscure social and economic failures:

> Again, consider the current situation faced by poor and minority children in the United States. The irony should not escape us that a substantial portion of these children's predicament is the direct result of policies put forward by the administration that authored *A Nation at Risk*. . . . Since 1979, 3.1 million children (or 3,000 per day, 125 per hour) have fallen into poverty.[54]

Is the average American more familiar with the message that the public school system is failing or with the fact that today, according to the Children's Defense Fund, one in five of our nation's children live in poverty?

> America's fifth child would fare better as a citizen of another nation. . . . If America's poverty prevention safety net for children was as effective as it is in France, two out of three poor children would escape poverty. If she lived in 23 other industrialized nations, she would be guaranteed health insurance, an income safety net, and the chance for a parent to stay at home with pay after childbirth.[55]

It would be surprising if citizens were more aware of such details than they are about an education system that has supposedly placed our nation at risk. The facts that "poverty rates are *far* worse in our country than in other Western democracies" and that "family incomes and financial support for schools are *much* more poorly distributed in our country than in other industrialized nations"[56] do not seem to generate the same kind of attention as the results of international comparisons of student achievement. While schools are held primarily accountable for society's rightful goal of leaving no child behind, political leaders typically fail to promote their own accountability to the "12 million children [who] are poor, and millions [who] are hungry, at risk of hunger, living in worst case housing, or homeless."[57] Only in the wake of Hurricane Katrina's devastation of the Gulf Coast region in September of 2005 did chronic, generational American poverty debut, briefly, on television screens around the world. It took catastrophe to make visible what our nation's leaders, typically, do not.

Political misdirection of public attention with the "leave no child behind" rhetoric is further unveiled in a comparative look at the winners and losers in the economic plan that took shape at about the same time as the NCLB legislation. According to the Citizens for Tax Justice,[58] people whose average income was $1,117,000 (the top 1 percent) received 37.6 percent of the total tax cut in the Bush plan that was signed into law in June 2001. Charging schools with society's moral obligation to leave no child behind seems especially preposterous in view of the reality that while this law was being shaped (as the 2001 reauthorization of the Elementary and Secondary Education Act of 1965), a $1.3 trillion tax cut—designed to benefit primarily those whose children are unlikely to ever want for food, shelter, or access to excellent health care and educational opportunities—was being enacted. This tragic absurdity was illustrated at the time in the Children's Defense Fund's 2002 publication, *The State of Children in America's Union*:

> For the money we will spend on the $1.3 trillion Bush tax cut plan passed by Congress and signed by the President in June 2001, America could: Provide every uninsured child health coverage; *and* provide Head Start, preschool, and quality child care for every eligible child who needs it; *and* help rebuild crumbling schools and reduce classroom sizes in the early years when children need a solid basic skills foundation; *and* help 10 million needy individuals, mostly in families with children, get food stamps; *and* provide housing vouchers to the 3.6 million children living in families with the "worst case" housing needs (paying more than half their income on rent or living in severely substandard housing); *and* help provide services to protect millions of abused and neglected children.[59]

From the inflammatory *Nation at Risk* to the co-option of *Leave No Child Behind* (the trademarked mission statement of the Children's Defense Fund), it is evident that in the past quarter-century children's health, safety, and educational wellbeing have not figured prominently in the political determination of who should profit from school reform.

Profit accrues to those with the power to define. According to Michael Apple, "One of the most important objects of the rightist agenda is changing our common-sense, altering the meanings of the most basic categories, the key words we employ to understand the social and educational world and our place in it."[60] In a political context in which military spending and tax relief for the wealthy soar while desperately needed social services are cut,[61] a common-sense definition of "accountability" would not lay primary responsibility for educational achievement on the shoulders of teachers (an unempowered and, not coincidentally, predominantly female workforce, typically from working class backgrounds, earning an average salary of about $45,000 a year[62]), when the neediest students they teach do not have the food, housing, and medical care they need to survive, much less to learn. When teachers' working conditions reveal the reality that the poorest schools they serve do not have even the most basic resources for their students,[63] and "accountability" is exclusively defined in relation to achievement standards (versus federal and state standards ensuring equitable opportunities to learn, for example), then the spectacular political success of having changed common sense must be admitted. In this, it is arguably clear that political profit in the form of a diversionary benefit is to be had by those who control the terms of the accountability discourse.

Type 2: Financial Profit—Investment Returns

A second kind of profit is purely financial, benefiting the emerging host of education entrepreneurs who offer a range of products and services in pursuit of their share of the two trillion dollar global expenditure on education each year.[64] Increasingly, financial profits from public education are reaped by the corporate elite. From the perspective of the entrepreneurs who invest in school markets, claims Apple, "the $700 billion education sector in the United States is ripe for transformation. It is seen as the 'next health care'—that is, as a sphere that can be mined for huge profits."[65]

The staggering reach of the move to privatize schools was illustrated in Maude Barlow's February 2001 story in *The Ecologist*, "The Last Frontier." It was chosen as that year's second most important censored story in the United States by Sonoma State University's *Project Censored*. Barlow described a little-known development in the global economy that "is the most far-reaching negotiation ever undertaken on the trade in services and will affect the lives of every human being on the planet."[66]

> A global trade agreement now being negotiated will seek to privatize nearly every government-provided public service and allow transnational corporations to run them for profit. The General Agreement on Trade in Services (GATS) is a proposed free-trade agreement that will attempt to liberalize/dismantle barriers that protect government-provided social services. . . . Health care, education, and water services are the most potentially lucrative. . . . The World Trade Organization has hired a private company called the Global Division for Transnational Education to document policies that 'discriminate against foreign education providers.' The results of this study will be used to pressure countries with public education systems to relinquish them to the global privatized marketplace.[67]

In a follow-up commentary, Barlow noted, "Yet very few people know that it is taking place. . . The mainstream press has all but ignored this story."[68] Clearly, there is merit in Apple's observation that "Over the past two to three decades, the right has mounted a concerted attack on what many of us took as natural. The entire public sphere has been brought into question."[69] The enormity of the challenge to individual liberty and to the future of the very concept of public welfare is sobering, indeed, particularly in the context of Michael Engel's assertion that "In a totalitarian system . . . it is the exclusive responsibility of the political elite to determine educational goals and values, as well as the process for achieving them, and it is the duty of the citizens to accept the entire package without question."[70] My recent experience as a fifth grade teacher taught me that Engel's description of a totalitarian state in education applied to my situation (and, it is important to note, I was teaching in a relatively affluent and progressive school compared to what I knew to be true for many of the student teachers I had once supervised, who were now in their first years in the profession). Although I had brought nearly two decades of experience in education into my position in that school district, I learned that it was not my place, as far as my superiors were concerned, "to determine educational goals and values." It was my job, rather, "to accept the entire package without question." In a totalitarian setting, without balanced media treatment of issues in education, how will the people in any community learn enough to know that the public good is up for private auction?

Beyond the GATS story, other examples of private financial gain from public school coffers abound. Christopher Whittle is perhaps the classic example of the new breed of education entrepreneur. Chief executive and founder of the Edison Project, "the first school-management company traded on a stock exchange,"[71] he is also the creator of Channel One,[72] the "controversial in-school news and advertisement program sent to what it calls a 'captive audience' of 8 million students a day for close to $200,000 per 30-second ad."[73] Whittle, responding to financial woes subsequent to a recent crash in the value of Edison shares,

> recently told a meeting of school principals that he'd thought up an ingenious solution: Take advantage of the free supply of child labor, and force each student to work an hour a day, presumably without pay, in the school offices. 'We could have less adult staff,' Mr. Whittle reportedly said at a summit for employees and principals in Colorado Springs. 'I think it's an important concept for education and economics.' In a school with 600 students, he said, this unpaid work would be the equivalent of '75 adults' on salary. Although Mr. Whittle said he could have the child-labor plan in place by 2004, school board officials were quick to say they would have nothing to do with the proposal.[74]

In Mr. Whittle's world, it would appear that Barbara Miner's conclusion is correct—that "the real emphasis is on investment returns rather than student welfare and educational development."[75] As for the students who attended the 150 schools operated by Edison in 2002—often what Doug Saunders described as the "worst-off high schools in some of the most abject slums in the country"[76]—rather than finding the nation rallying in response to a pattern of school failure by addressing what the late Senator Paul Wellstone called the "crushing lack of opportunity" that was their reality,[77] they found instead that their right to a high quality education had been put on the market with the goal of making the exorbitantly privileged even wealthier.

A final example of the corporate windfall occasioned by "school reform" is illustrated by McGraw-Hill. An incident from my recent public school experience indicates how well positioned this publishing company is for mining profits. One of their representatives, sent to "train" teachers in the use of the new

McGraw-Hill language arts adoption, all but winked when she remarked on how clever "we" (i.e., the district) had been in choosing that adoption: McGraw-Hill was also the publisher of the standardized tests our students would take in the spring. "Perfect alignment" was the phrase she used to describe this homogenizing influence on education.

As one of the top firms dominating a $700 million a year testing industry,[78] McGraw-Hill has been perfectly positioned to profit even further from what Stan Karp called "the euphemistically named 'No Child Left Behind Act.'"[79] Federally mandated testing was the cornerstone of this piece of legislation for the new millennium, which mandated:

- annual tests in reading and math from grades 3-8 and at least once in grades 10-12;
- additional annual tests in science beginning in 2007, given once between grades 3-5, 6-9, and 10-12;
- use of these tests to determine whether schools are making 'adequate yearly progress' towards 100 percent proficiency for all students within 12 years.[80]

Little wonder that the publishing world's "Big Three" in standardized testing (McGraw-Hill, Houghton-Mifflin, and Harcourt General) were "identified as 'Bush stocks' by Wall Street analysts."[81] F. Peter Jovanovich from Pearson Education, while addressing a room full of Wall Street analysts just after the 2000 presidential election, "displayed a quote from President-elect Bush calling for state testing and school-by-school report cards, and announced, 'This almost reads like our business plan.'"[82] Seven years later, Congressman Mike Honda commented with refreshing candor on the connection between public education policy and corporate health, saying, "The testing companies, they're the ones that are probably making, having the benefit of our educational policies."[83] Whatever words may have followed the Congressman's first impulse to use the word "making" in this context, the implication is clear: the money in holding teachers and children accountable to "national" interests is good.

Type 3: Familial Profits—Amoral Familism

A third type of profiteering at the expense of public interests in education rides in on the coattails of political and corporate manipulations of public perceptions. This is the private profit enjoyed by families of privilege who lead what Linda Miller-Kahn and Mary Lee Smith call "the credential race . . . a zero-sum game [in which] one person only gains relative to another's loss."[84] In describing this kind of profit I will borrow Edward Banfield's concept of "amoral familism," a term he used to explain the inability of the families in a poor Italian village in 1958 (post-World War II) to "act together for their common good or, indeed, for any end transcending the immediate, material interest of the nuclear family."[85] In the context of the "credential race," I use the label of amoral familism to signify what Daphna Birenbaum-Carmeli described as powerful parents' "legitimised . . . prioritisation [sic] of their own children's interests, while oppressing less powerful parents, teachers and principals."[86]

Miller-Kahn and Smith illustrate the concept of amoral familism as it relates to private gain resulting from the manipulation of public perception of the schools. In their paper on "School Choice Policies in the Political Spectacle," they describe the events that took place in a school district in Boulder, Colorado throughout the 1990s. During this time "interest groups took advantage of federal, state, and district policies meant to promote school choice and molded them into a system of schools that met individualistic interests rather than the common good."[87] Miller-Kahn and Smith used Murray Edelman's theory of political spectacle[88] to explain how influential families used their privileged positions to attain benefits from the school district that did not extend to less powerful and less privileged families. These "local elites"—which Amy Stuart Wells and Irene Serna defined as "those with a combination of economic, political, and cultural capital that is highly valued within their particular school community"[89]—used flawed data and elements of political spectacle theory to convince the public that Boulder schools were failing, despite significant evidence to the contrary.

This could not have been accomplished without media support. The authors noted the essential role of a complicit media in the process of ensuring that the political spectacle engineered by the influential would take root in reality in the Boulder community:

> First, a political agenda is usually launched by an actor who bases his or her message of crisis by reporting statistics more dramatic than technically accurate. . . . Second, newspapers construct and reinforce a sense of crisis in policy matters. . . . Third, media reduce complex situations to simple sound bites and visual symbols. . . . Fourth, media take strong perspectives on policy issues and craft news articles and select or solicit opinion pieces that reinforce those perspectives. . . . Fifth, the perspective that local newspapers take is often consistent with corporate interests nationally rather than local concerns.[90]

The agents of amoral familism in Boulder organized and named their group Parents and Schools. They "adopted the rhetoric of national achievement crisis, even against the evidence of the local test scores," in keeping with Edelman's point (reiterated by Miller-Kahn and Smith) that "policy makers and political actors often invoke crises—whether real or not—to justify actions on behalf of private rather than public values."[91] Members of Parents and Schools then advocated successfully for policy changes that they believed would benefit their own children. "Whether the consequence of their proposed policy changes disadvantaged anyone else's children was not their concern."[92] Ultimately, the benefit of school choice that the local elites secured resulted in "16 choice schools attended by 20 percent of the district students . . . [which] 'deserves the name *skimming* because some schools are drawing a disproportionate number of students from the high scoring pool."[93]

An unsurprising effect of the work of Parents and Schools is that "Boulder schools have become substantially more stratified by ethnicity since the district adopted school choice policies."[94] Also unsurprising is Miller-Kahn's and Smith's observation that the school board, in making difficult decisions about school consolidation as enrollment patterns shifted, often took "the more expedient route, targeting the families with the least cultural capital, those who would likely put up the least resistance."[95] The effect of amoral familism as it applies to manipulations of the public school system for personal advantage, illustrated in Boulder, is to further empower the already powerful.

Looking to the public schools with private profit in mind—whether from a political, financial, or familial perspective—is clearly consistent with the atomizing goal of Chomsky's "responsible men," that is, the extirpation of "the natural and deep-seated values of sympathy and solidarity, the conviction that one should care about what happens to the child or disabled widow on the other side of town."[96] It is tempting to stop here, with blame for public school profiteering laid squarely at the feet of the "responsible men"—and women—who have engaged in the political, financial, and familial maneuverings thus far described. While those private interests surely bear a large degree of responsibility for the attack on public sympathy and solidarity, it must also be recognized that this responsibility extends further, into many of our own homes, where a much subtler and more pervasive form of amoral familism exists. The term applies also to the many loving and well-meaning families who, in Stephen Ball's words, "find themselves thrust into an education market-place"[97]:

> Being unable to affect the social situation of progressively less equal shares, but having the opportunity only to try and secure an advantageous share for those whose interests they hold in trust, they are under pressure to adopt a conservative and prudential social stance, thus contributing to cumulative social changes they have not directly chosen, and may very well not endorse.[98]

In other words, many well-intentioned people (who have no desire to secure benefits for their own children at others' expense) find themselves feeling powerless in the face of the monolith of market ideology to do anything but make sure that they have done their best by their own. In a political and social context in which market forces loom larger than humanitarian concerns and in which "the natural and deep-seated values of sympathy and solidarity" are under attack, the socially conscious, middle-class parent may see no alternative but to advocate on behalf of her or his own child. Without benefit of the kind of information, education, and solidarity that Rosa Parks and her colleagues had won during the Civil Rights years of "excessive democracy," how can that well-intentioned citizen hope to achieve and sustain widespread public concern for all children? How can she promote sympathy and solidarity on behalf of the impoverished boy who has failed Louisiana's high-stakes fourth grade test and who cries, "My papa gonna be mad at me. He will beat me" or for the girl who says, simply, "I'm going to kill myself"?[99] In a culture, or a living room, of amoral familism, the reality of vomiting, fearful, depressed, and suicidal children—who, typically, desperately want to attain the high achievement standards that the nation's leaders have set for them—are not of public concern. In the shadow of privatization, sympathy and solidarity lose out to political apathy,

> a form of political alienation that [Tom DeLuca] describes as 'the indefinite suspension of the ability to achieve and sustain political intentions due to the tightly spun web of depoliticizing ideology, language, social psychology, and technological and economic hegemony, which together form a mutually constituting and reinforcing system that for all practical purposes is closed'.[100]

In the context of today's "closed system" of educational discourse—or the "tightly spun web" of standardization, competition, and accountability—Apple observed, "Of the many voices now talking about education, only the most powerful tend to be heard."[101] The voices of the poor are not powerful enough to be heard, and the voices of the affluent, to borrow a metaphor from Audre Lourde, will certainly not be used to dismantle their own houses. What will it take, then, in the absence of a press committed to the ideal of an informed public, for average citizens to raise their voices on behalf of America's least privileged families—or on behalf of the children, parents, and teachers who have been named among "the essential raw materials"[102] that the nation has at its disposal for achieving global dominance? This is the question that motivated the research project described in upcoming chapters. That qualitative case study was designed to discover what happens when parents and teachers have the opportunity to become informed and to raise their voices together.

Notes

1. Landon E. Beyer, "Educational Reform: The Political Roots of *A Nation at Risk*," *Curriculum Inquiry* 15, no. 1 (1985): 37–56; David C. Berliner and Bruce J. Biddle, *The Manufactured Crisis: Myths, Fraud, and the Attack on America's Public Schools* (Cambridge, Mass.: Perseus Books, 1995); James. V. Hoffman, "The De-Democratization of Schools and Literacy in America," *Reading Teacher* 53, no. 8 (2000): 616–624; Alfie Kohn, "Standardized Testing and Its Victims," *Education Week* 20, no. 4 (2000): 60, 46–47; Michael Apple, *Education the "Right" Way* (New York: RoutledgeFalmer, 2001); and Linda Miller-Kahn and Mary L. Smith, "School Choice Policies in the Political Spectacle," *Education Policy Analysis Archives* 9, no. 50 (2001).

2. Apple, *Education the "Right" Way*, 1.

3. Berliner and Biddle, *The Manufactured Crisis*, xi, 4.

4. Berliner and Biddle, *The Manufactured Crisis*, 158.

5. Jonathan Kozol, *Savage Inequalities: Children in America's Schools* (New York: Harper Perennial, 1991); Berliner and Biddle, *The Manufactured Crisis*; Michael Engel, *The Struggle for Control of Public Education: Market Ideology vs. Democratic Values* (Philadelphia: Temple University Press, 2000); Dale Johnson and Bonnie Johnson, *High*

Stakes: Children, Testing, and Failure in American Schools (Lanham, Md.: Rowman & Littlefield Publishers, 2002).

6. Berliner and Biddle, *The Manufactured Crisis*, 12.

7. Lawrence Stedman, "Respecting the Evidence: The Achievement Crisis Is Real," *Education Policy Analysis Archives* 4, no. 7 (April 4, 1996), Overview section, ¶2. Emphasis in original.

8. Stedman, "Respecting the Evidence," International Assessments section, ¶1.

9. Stedman, "Respecting the Evidence," Conclusion, ¶1.

10. Peter Phillips, personal communication, November 11, 2002.

11. e.g., Johnson and Johnson, *High Stakes;* Linda McNeil and Angela Valenzuela, "The Harmful Impact of the TAAS System of Testing in Texas: Beneath the Accountability Rhetoric," Harvard University: The Civil Rights Project, 2000; Kohn, "Standardized Testing and Its Victims."

12. Kozol, *Savage Inequalities;* Kozol, *Shame of the Nation*; Berliner and Biddle, *The Manufactured Crisis*; Apple, *Educating the "Right" Way*; Johnson and Johnson, *High Stakes*; Mitchell Landsberg and Howard Blume, "Schools Chief Seeks End to Learning Gap," *Los Angeles Times*, August 19, 2007 <http://www.latimes.com/news/local/la-me-race19aug19,1,6409789.story?coll=la-headlines-california&ctrack=1&cset=true> (22 Sept 2007); Alfie Kohn, *Punished by Rewards* (New York: Houghton Mifflin Company, 1993).

13. Don Hazen and Julie Winokur, *We the Media: A Citizen's Guide to Fighting for Media Democracy* (New York: The New Press, 1997); "FAIR: Media Giants Cast Aside Regulatory 'Chains,'" *Fairness and Accuracy in Reporting* (March 2002), <http://www.fair.org/index.php?page=1659> (15 Aug 2002); Robert McChesney and John Nichols, *Our Media Not Theirs* (New York: Seven Stories Press, 2002).

14. Berliner & Biddle, *The Manufactured Crisis,* 4.

15. During the "deregulation drive of the Reagan era," networks were allowed to increase the number of stations they could own, from seven to twelve. (Jim Naureckas, "Media Monopoly: Long History, Short Memories." *Fairness & Accuracy in Reporting,* 2002. <www.fair.org/extra/9511/monop.html> 15 Aug 2002, ¶10). Then head of the Federal Communications Commission, Republican Michael Powell supported further inroads into the regulations governing media ownership: "he has said that we don't need a lot of regulations because antitrust laws are sufficient to prevent dangerous media monopolies." (Neil Hickey, "Behind the Mergers: Q & A," *Columbia Journalism Review* May/June 2002. <http://www.cjr.org/year/02/3/hickey.asp> 15 Aug 2002, ¶17.) Neil Hickey, editor at large of the *Columbia Journalism Review,* believes that this view jeopardizes the ideal of bipartisan media oversight—particularly in view of the fact that "the Bush administration [has] reorganized antitrust procedures to give the Justice Department sole oversight of mass media mergers, ending the system whereby the Federal Trade Commission also has jurisdiction in these deals" (Hickey, "Behind the Mergers, ¶18–19).

16. Peter Phillips and Project Censored, *Censored 2003: The Top 25 Censored Stories* (New York: Seven Stories Press, 2002); Robert McChesney and John Nichols, *Our Media Not Theirs* (New York: Seven Stories Press, 2002); Robert McChesney, "The Global Media Giants: The Nine Firms that Dominate the World," *Fairness & Accuracy in Reporting* (November/December 1997), <http://www.fair.org/index.php?page=1406>. A decade ago, Robert McChesney identified the nine "giant firms" dominating what he called the global media system: Time Warner, Disney, Bertelsmann, Viacom, Rupert Murdoch's News Corporation, TCI, General Electric, Sony, and Seagram. "A specter now haunts the world," he wrote, "a global commercial media system dominated by a small number of super-powerful, mostly U.S.-based transnational media corporations. It

is a system that works to advance the cause of the global market and promote commercial values, while denigrating journalism and culture not conducive to the immediate bottom line or long-run corporate interests" (McChesney, "The Global Media Giants," ¶1).

17. Engel, *The Struggle for Control of Public Education*, ix.

18. Robert Reich, Secretary of Labor in the Clinton Administration, "estimated that the overall corporate share of local property tax revenue declined 'from 45% in 1957 to 16%' in 1990. As Reich suggests, 'the inescapable conclusion is that American business isn't really worried about the future of the American work force." Moreover, the cities which have suffered most from this loss are industrial communities where people are often very poor and have little ability to fund the schools their children so badly need." (Berliner & Biddle, *The Manufactured Crisis*, 85.)

19. Paul Harris, "Is the US Heading for 'Developng Nations' Inequality Levels?" (*The Observer UK*, July 30, 2007), ¶7. <http://www.alternet.org/story/57727/> (30 July 2007).

20. Apple, *Educating the "Right" Way*; Kozol, *Savage Inequalities*; Johnson and Johnson, *High Stakes*; Berliner and Biddle, *The Manufactured Crisis*; Gary Anderson, personal communication, October 24, 2002.

21. This 1983 publication by the National Committee on Excellence in Education was the launching point of the current accountability movement in education. It will be described in more detail in this chapter, under the heading of "A Nation at Risk: An Exemplar of Diversionary Rhetoric."

22. Jannell McGrew, "Rosa Parks: A Woman Who Changed a Nation," *Montgomery Advertiser*, 1998. <www.montgomeryadvertiser.com/1news/specialreports/rosa/> (9 Nov 2002).

23. Howard Zinn, *A People's History of the United States: 1492–Present* (New York: Harper Collins, 1995).

24. Noam Chomsky, "Renewing Tom Paine's Challenge" in *Our Media Not Theirs* by Robert McChesney and John Nichols (New York: Seven Stories Press, 2002), 18.

25. Chomsky, "Renewing Tom Paine's Challenge," 18–19.

26. In Maxine Greene, *Releasing the Imagination: Essays on Education, the Arts, and Social Change* (San Francisco: Jossey-Bass Publishers, 1995), 95.

27. Johnson and Johnson, *High Stakes*, 5.

28. Elizabeth Keefe and Kaia Tollefson, review of *High Stakes: Children, Testing, and Failure in American Schools. Journal of Anthropological Research* 59, no. 1 (2003): 136.

29. Johnson and Johnson, *High Stakes*, 176.

30. Greene, *Releasing the Imagination*, 3.

31. Berliner and Biddle, *The Manufactured Crisis*, 59.

32. Greene, *Releasing the Imagination*; Alfie Kohn, *What to Look for in a Classroom and Other Essays* (San Francisco: Jossey-Bass Publishers, 1998); Peter Sacks, *Standardized Minds: The High Price of America's Testing Culture and What We Can Do to Change It* (Cambridge, Mass: Perseus Publishing, 1999); Engel, *The Struggle for Control of Public Education*; Henry Giroux, "Pedagogy of the Depressed: Beyond the New Politics of Cynicism," *College Literature* 28, no. 3 (Fall 2001).

33. Beyer, "Educational Reform"; Doran Christensen, "The Politics of Educational Reform: What Vested Interests Are at Stake?" Paper presented at the American Educational Studies Association, Chicago, 1987; Kozol, *Savage Inequalities*; Everett L. Walden, "Public Education: Sin Eater for *A Nation at Risk*," *Clearing House* 65, no. 4 (Mar/Apr 1992): 215–216; Berliner and Biddle, *The Manufactured Crisis*; Hoffman, "The De-Democratization of Schools and Literacy in America"; Alfie Kohn, "The Case

Against 'Tougher Standards'" (2001), <http://www.alfiekohn.org>; Johnson and Johnson, *High Stakes.*

34. Peter Phillips & Project Censored, *Censored 2003*; McChesney and Nichols, *Our Media Not Theirs*; "Fair: Media Giants Cast Aside Regulatory 'Chains'"; Hazen and Winokur, *We the Media*; Hickey, "Behind the Mergers"; Naureckas, "Media Monopoly."

35. Berliner and Biddle, *The Manufactured Crisis,* 148.

36. Sacks, *Standardized Minds*, 9.

37. National Commission on Excellence in Education (NCEE), "A Nation at Risk: The Imperative for Educational Reform" (U.S. Department of Education, 1983), Introduction, ¶3. <http://www.ed.gov/pubs/NatAtRisk/> (16 Feb 2001).

38. NCEE, "A Nation at Risk," Introduction, ¶2.

39. Children's Defense Fund, "The State of Children in America's Union: A 2002 Action Guide to *Leave No Child Behind*" (2002), v. <http://www.childrensdefense.org> <http://www.civilrights.org/issues/census/details.cfm?id=8367> (13 Nov 2002).

40. Engel, *The Struggle for Control of Public Education*, 27; Harris, "Is the US Heading for 'Developing Nations' Inequality Levels?"

41. James E. Albrecht, "A Nation at Risk: Another View," *Phi Delta Kappan* 76, no. 10 (June 1984): 684–685; William E. Gardner, "A Nation at Risk: Some Critical Comments," *Journal of Teacher Education* 35, no. 1 (1984): 13–15; A. Harry Passow, "Tackling the Reform Reports of the 1980s," *Phi Delta Kappan* 65, no. 10 (June 1984): 674–683; Beyer, "Educational Reform"; Christensen, "The Politics of Educational Reform"; Peter S. Hlebowitsch, "Playing Power Politics: How *A Nation at Risk* Achieved Its National Stature," *Journal of Research and Development in Education* 23, no. 2 (1990): 82–88; Fred C. Lunenberg, "The Current Educational Reform Movement: History, Progress to Date, and the Future," *Education & Urban Society* 25, no. 1 (1992): 3–18; Walden, "Public Education"; Berliner and Biddle, *The Manufactured Crisis*; Sacks, *Standardized Minds*; Engel, *The Struggle for Control of Public Education;* Hoffman, "The De-Democratization of Schools and Literacy in America."

42. Hlebowitsch, "Playing Power Politics," 85.

43. Edward B. Fiske, "Problem for Education: Commission Looks to Rise in Federal Role, While Reagan Looks to a Diminished Role," (*The New York Times*, 1983, B15), Critical Words from Boyer section, ¶2.

44. Hlebowitsch, "Playing Power Politics," 84.

45. Goldberg, 1984 in Christensen, "The Politics of Educational Reform," 9.

46. Sacks, *Standardized Minds*, 75.

47. Beyer, "Educational Reform," 43.

48. Beyer, "Educational Reform," 46, emphasis in original.

49. Beyer, "Educational Reform," 45.

50. Henry Giroux, "Pedagogy of the Depressed: Beyond the New Politics of Cynicism," *College Literature* 28, no. 3 (Fall 2001), Disavowing Pedagogy as a Political Practice section, ¶3.

51. Children's Defense Fund, "The State of Children in America's Union," v–vii.

52. Children's Defense Fund, "The State of Children in America's Union," 15.

53. "During his presidential campaign, President Bush adopted the Children's Defense Fund's (CDF) *trademarked* mission to Leave No Child Behind® as *his* motto." (Children's Defense Fund, "The State of Children in America's Union," iv, emphases added.)

54. Beyer, "Educational Reform," 47–48.

55. Children's Defense Fund, "The State of Children in America's Union," 6.

56. Berliner and Biddle, *The Manufactured Crisis*, 10, 5, emphases in original.

57. Children's Defense Fund, "The State of Children in America's Union," v.

58. in Children's Defense Fund, The State of Children in America's Union.

59. Children's Defense Fund, "The State of Children in America's Union, vi, emphases in original.

60. Apple, *Educating the "Right" Way*, 9.

61. "The Bush administration is now asking for a $48 billion increase in military spending, the largest hike since Ronald Reagan's first year in office. . . . That money, coupled with Bush's $1.3 trillion tax cut, is going to be taken away from social programs that are already underfunded. . . . It's going to come from mental health programs, education, health care, prescription drugs for the elderly, and public housing. . . . These cuts are going to affect millions of people." (Howard Zinn, *Terrorism and War*, New York: Seven Stories Press, 2002, 43.) That is to say, "by design and by default this country has chosen to turn disease, disputes, and war into profitable career fields. At the same time, it has made most unattractive the activity of educating our young. The question is not whether resources should be dedicated to the maintenance of health, domestic tranquility and international peace. Rather, the question is whether any society can afford to make their opposites profitable and to do so at the expense of education." (Kerr, 1983, in Berliner & Biddle, *The Manufactured Crisis*, 103.)

62. American Federation of Teachers at <http://www.aft.org>.

63. Johnson and Johnson, *High Stakes.*

64. Barlow, 2001, in Phillips & Project Censored, *Project Censored 2003.*

65. Apple, *Educating the "Right" Way*, 7.

66. Barlow, 2001, in Phillips & Project Censored, *Project Censored 2003*, 40.

67. Barlow, 2001, in Phillips & Project Censored, *Project Censored 2003*, 39–40.

68. Apple, *Educating the "Right" Way*, 40–41.

69. Apple, *Educating the "Right" Way*, 8.

70. Engel, *The Struggle for Control of Public Education*, 135.

71. Doug Saunders, "For-Profit U.S. Schools Sell Off Their Textbooks" (*Toronto Globe*, October 30, 2002), ¶3. <www.commondreams.org/headlines02/1030-02.htm> (4 Nov 2002).

72. Channel One was bought by K–III Communications Corporation for $300 million in August 1994. (Hazen & Winokur, *We the Media.*)

73. Hazen and Winokur, *We the Media,* 66. While the idea of trading televisions and satellite dishes to schools in return for the "captive audience" of 8 million children that Whittle delivered to advertisers may be morally repugnant to many, it apparently was not to Lamar Alexander, Secretary of Education to the first President Bush. In 1992, "John S. Friedman wrote about the suspicious alliance between corporate interests and White House education policies. . . . After his nomination as Secretary of Education, Alexander asked Whittle [and other business leaders] for their advice. In a series of meetings, three of which Whittle attended, the proposals that became America 2000 were mapped out, along with a voucher system [that would support private schools], according to one participant. . . . Alexander himself was on the Whittle advisory board that guided Channel One and worked for Whittle after leaving the [Tennessee] governorship in 1987. His compensation was $125,000 in consulting fees plus the opportunity to buy four shares of Whittle stock, for which he wrote a $10,000 check, according to the *Wall Street Journal.* . . . At the end of 1988, Whittle bought back the stock for $330,000, giving the Alexanders a healthy profit" (Berliner & Biddle, *The Manufactured Crisis*, 150–151).

74. Saunders, "For-Profit U.S. Schools Sell Off Their Textbooks," ¶8–10.

75. Miner, 2002, in Phillips & Project Censored, *Project Censored 2003,* 56.

76. Saunders, "For-Profit U.S. Schools Sell Off Their Textbooks," ¶2.

77. Paul Wellstone, "High Stakes Tests: A Harsh Agenda for America's Children" (Address at Teachers College, Columbia University, 2000), ¶22 <http://wellstone.senate. gov/columbia.htm> (22 Feb 2001).

78. Stan Karp, "Let Them Eat Tests," *Rethinking Schools* 16, no. 4 (2002): 3–4.

79. Stan Karp, "Let Them Eat Tests," 3.

80. Stan Karp, "Let Them Eat Tests," 3.

81. Stephen Metcalf, "Reading Between the Lines.," *(The Nation*, 2002), ¶10. <http://www.thenation.com/doc.mhtml?i=20020128&s=metcalf> (16 Jan 2003).

82. Metcalf, "Reading Between the Lines," ¶8; Gerald Bracey, "The Seven Deadly Absurdities of No Child Left Behind." <http://susanohanian.org/show_nclb_atroci- ties.html?id=1636> (17 Sept 2005).

83. Mike Honda, "Sec. Spellings Admits Lack of Educational Credentials" (Labor, Health, and Human Services Appropriations Subcommittee Hearing, March 12, 2007) <http://www.youtube.com/watch?v=5zSJexw0Gvs&mode=related&search=> (3 Aug 2007).

84. Miller-Kahn and Smith, "School Choice Policies in the Political Spectacle," Choice and Political Spectacle section, ¶4.

85. Banfield, in Walter C. Parker, ed., *Educating the Democratic Mind* (Albany, New York: State University of New York Press, 1996), 8–9.

86. Daphna Birenbaum-Carmeli, "Parents Who Get What They Want: On the Empowerment of the Powerful," *Sociological Review* 47, no. 1 (February1999), Introduc- tion, ¶5.

87. Miller-Kahn and Smith, "School Choice Policies in the Political Spectacle," Ab- stract.

88. "Political spectacle theory holds that contemporary politics resembles theater, with directors, stages, casts of actors, narrative plots, and (most importantly) a curtain that separates the action onstage—what the audience has access to—from the back- stage—where the real "allocation of values" takes place. . . . Edelman defines seven ele- ments of the theory: symbolic language; casting political actors as leaders, allies, and enemies; dramaturgy (staging, plotting and costuming); the illusion of rationality; the illusion of democratic participation; disconnection between means and ends; distinguish- ing action on stage versus action backstage." (Miller-Kahn and Smith, "School Choice Policies in the Political Spectacle, Introduction ¶11–12.)

89. 1996, in Miller-Kahn and Smith, "School Choice Policies in the Political Spectac- le," The Rise of the Local Elite section, ¶1.

90. Miller-Kahn and Smith, "School Choice Policies," Media Creating Spectacle sec- tion, ¶4.

91. Miller-Kahn and Smith, "School Choice Policies," Choice and Political Spectacle section, ¶2

92. Miller-Kahn and Smith, "School Choice Policies," Choice and Political Spectacle section, ¶2

93. Howe and Eisenhart, 2000, in Miller-Kahn & Smith, "School Choice Policies," Choice Effects in Boulder and Beyond section, ¶8.

94. Miller-Kahn and Smith, "School Choice Policies," Choice Effects in Boulder and Beyond, ¶ 8, 9.

95. Miller-Kahn and Smith, "School Choice Policies," Democracy: Deliberative and Faux section, ¶18.

96. Chomsky, "Renewing Tom Paine's Challenge," 18–19.

97. Stephen J. Ball, "Education Markets, Choice, and Social Class: The Market as a Class Strategy in the UK and the USA," *British Journal of Sociology of Education* 14, no. 1 (March 1993), The Ideology of the Market section, ¶2.

98. Jonathan, 1990, in Ball, "Education, Markets, Choice, and Social Class," The Ideology of the Market section, ¶2–3.

99. Johnson and Johnson, *High Stakes*, 177.

100. Engel, *The Struggle for Control of Public Education*, 47.

101. Apple, *Educating the "Right" Way*, 2.

102. NCEE, "A Nation at Risk," The Tools at Hand section.

CHAPTER 4

Redefining Accountability in Our Schools: Inviting Parents to the Learning Community

The Problem with "Parent Involvement"

It has become a truism to say that parents' involvement in their children's education is not only beneficial, but an essential prerequisite for student success. The political construction of "parental involvement" at local, state, and federal levels, however, has been framed in such a way as to reinforce the historic "unequal structuring of power and knowledge" between families and schools,[1] to separate the interests of parents and educators, often resulting in alienated and/or adversarial home-school relationships,[2] to further privilege families that already have large amounts of economic, social, and cultural capital,[3] and to promote the idea that "parent involvement" is an individual, rather than a collective responsibility.[4] Contrary to promoting the values of sympathy and solidarity, writes Carol Vincent,

> existing understandings ensure that individual parental involvement is the main route through which parents access the education system. In this way, they serve to limit and constrain parental agency.[5]

The social problems of amoral familism and political apathy are reinforced by a construction of parent involvement in which "parents are being organized as advocates for their children, other times as teacher bashers, often as bureaucracy busters, more recently, as culture-carriers, increasingly, as consumers,"[6] in the words of Michelle Fine. However they are cast, the common assumption is that parents' involvement in the schools should be primarily directed toward the goal of improving their own children's academic achievement.[7] This belief, facilitated and reinforced through education policies at community, state, and federal levels, is so prevalent as to have attained the status of common sense. Claire Smrekar and Lora Cohen-Vogel put it this way:

Widespread support for parent involvement is reflected by its inclusion in nearly every policy proposal aimed at improving the performance of our nation's schools. Repeated calls for 'parent empowerment' identify the improvement of family-school relationships as a key weapon in the struggle to slow the downward slide in academic indicators.[8]

In this construction, other reasons for parents' participation in the schools— for the purpose of ensuring that all children in every community have equal access to excellent teachers, resources, and facilities, for example, or to promote home-school-community conversations about the role of education in a democracy and the kinds of schoolwork that do and do not cultivate democratic dispositions and skills—are simply not in keeping with the common-sense parameters that have been established for parental involvement.

The problem with common sense, of course, is that the benefits associated with it can be exceedingly particular—not very common, after all. For example, while market ideology may be positioned as the logical and necessary driving force in education today, it is clear that this is a very profitable bit of common sense, from a particular and privileged perspective. The common sense approach to parent involvement in the schools also privileges a particular perspective: one that emphasizes an instrumental view of participation[9] in which parents become the means to an end that they did not author. Those who would embrace moral rather than amoral familism and egalitarian rather than market values as appropriate motivations for school reform are not empowered to make a difference when the parameters of parent involvement are defined for them, in a way that promotes parents' instrumentality as "common sense." Joel Spring makes the distinction between instrumental and agentic[10] views of participation clear:

current efforts at restructuring schools have more to do with trying to achieve improved management than with a real sharing of power. . . . During the Reagan-Bush years, conservatives advocated choice, site-based management, and parental involvement to counter the perceived mismanagement by the educational bureaucracy and as a means of more effectively transmitting the knowledge determined by state and federal governments. In other words, current calls for restructuring have little to do with democracy and a great deal to do with management. Parents' councils and site-based management groups cannot exercise any real power if the content of instruction is being determined by increasingly centralized government organizations.[11]

Parent involvement is an aspect of what Carol Vincent critically views as the empowerment discourse of the late 1980s and 1990s. The term empowerment itself, she says, operates as a "condensation symbol." Vincent explains that a condensation symbol (according to the concept's originator, Murray Edelman), is an element of political rhetoric which "operate[s] by 'condensing' specific emotions into a particular word or phrase, so that its usage provokes those emotions" even while "the exact meanings of the [term] are not clearly defined."[12]

Like "empowerment," the phrase "parent involvement" operates as a condensation symbol as well.[13] It is used regularly by teachers, parents, administrators, and policy makers despite the fact that parents and educators do not share the same understandings of what it means.[14] In Waggoner and Griffith's interviews of teachers, principals, and school volunteers, for example, they found that educators spoke of parent involvement in very traditional ways, with the school walls serving as the boundary lines for that involvement, typically framing it in terms of the school's needs. Volunteers, in contrast, described parent involvement in ways that illustrated "the broad range of work activities often unacknowledged by the normative notions of parent involvement in education."[15] They discussed the many ways that they were involved in their children's education within and beyond the boundaries of school walls, emphasizing family needs as well as those of the school.

Vincent argues that the rhetoric of parent involvement is, like other condensation symbols, invoked for the purpose of effecting "a warm glow of equality and joint endeavour."[16] The reality of parent involvement in education supports that argument, according to a number of other researchers on the topic who have found little in the way of equality or genuine collaboration between parents and educators.[17] Waggoner and Griffith dispel the myth of equality, noting that educators commonly use words like "assigned" during interviews when they were asked to describe the tasks parent volunteers were asked to do in the schools. Such language is an indicator of the imbalance of power that often typifies family-school relationships. This imbalance and the mythic existence of equality in this context are further illuminated by Nakagawa's observation:

> The language used to discuss parents in relation to schools controls how parents get involved and creates representations of the ideal parent. The ideal parent is used as a comparison for the actual parent; from the school's perspective, such a comparison often finds the actual parent wanting. Furthermore, in many instances, parent involvement is part of a strategy to improve education for children of color and lower income students. Thus, the construction of the ideal parent is directed toward ethnic minority parents and lower income parents.[18]

With the construction of the "ideal parent" in place, many educators are ideologically positioned to assume that low instances of parent involvement as they define it reflects a lack of interest in their children's development—a privileged judgment that is without foundation.[19]

Miller-Kahn and Smith dispense with the rhetoric of "equality and joint endeavour" by documenting the difference between under- and over-privileged parents in terms of the political influence that they wield in schools. (This was the story of the Parents and Schools group in Boulder, Colorado described in Chapter 3.) These two join many others[20] who have written of the vastly different positions that parents of means and parents in poverty occupy as consumers in the school marketplace. Under market ideology, public education itself has become a meritocracy in which, as Vincent says, the "government's championing of parental choice results in a situation in which the 'correct' response to instances of parental dissatisfaction with the school is 'exit.'"[21] Clearly, politically-motivated appeals for parental involvement do not deliver on the promise of "equality and joint endeavour" that they may imply.

The problem with parent involvement, in summary, is that—as "a key weapon in the struggle to slow the downward slide in academic indicators"[22]—it has been politically established as a condensation symbol, representing the normal, common-sense view of an appropriate family-school relationship. Effectively concealed is the culture of amoral familism and home-school antagonism that this construction encourages. In this context, an argument that Michelle Fine made a decade ago is relevant today:

> My point is simply that we need to see the teacher-parent adversarial relation as largely constructed by and serving the very bureaucracies (local, state, and federal) that are underfunding and overcontrolling public education. . . . It is only through organizing parents and educators, as a democratic coalition, that both privatization and controlling bureaucracy can be confronted.[23]

It was toward this end that the following research project was aimed.

Parents, Teachers, and the Censored Story of Accountability in the Public Schools

This study, conducted in 2003-2004, was grounded in my argument that: (1) the majority of educators, parents, and other community members have not had access to a diversity of perspectives on the state of the nation's public schools; (2) they have been disempowered as citizens through slanted coverage of education issues in the media; and therefore, that (3) they are badly under- and misinformed about much of the research on a variety of critical issues in education (e.g., the "manufactured crisis"; inequitable funding of schools and the "savage inequalities" in education; the ideological/historical roots of today's accountability movement; the intensification of the accountability movement and its effects on teaching and learning; the de-professionalization of teachers; the political construction of "parent involvement" in terms of functionalism and instrumentality; and the damaging effects of "extrinsic motivators"—i.e., coercions—on students' and teachers' intrinsic desire to teach and learn well).

Nearly all of the references available to me in constructing this argument were from academic articles and texts that had comprised my professional reading for nearly a decade. An obvious question, from a democratic perspective, became an insistent one in my own mind as I continued to read about the effects of standardization and imposed accountability mandates on students, teachers, schools, and communities. How do teachers, parents, and other citizens who do not have access to balanced media coverage of issues in education, nor to the luxury of access to academic texts or time for reading them, learn to find and discuss critical questions about education and accountability in the nation's public schools? Without benefit of either diversity or depth of information from "their" media system,[24] how can teachers, parents, and other citizens begin to see alternative possibilities for defining critically important words, like *education, teaching, learning, success,* and *accountability*?

With such thoughts in the foreground, my intention in this study was to learn how a purposefully selected group of participants, including both teachers and parents, would respond to a particular body of literature in education—texts that present a critical perspective on the accountability movement. Six teachers and six parents, diverse in terms of race, socioeconomic status, and school affiliation (some from "exemplary" schools and some from "failing" schools) met for two and a half hours every two weeks for a period of six months to study a number of texts together and to discuss the varying effects of accountability mandates in their neighborhood schools. (See Appendix A for a detailed description of methodology.)

In framing the study, I chose texts that would allow the group to explore a number of topics under the accountability umbrella, such as: (1) the use of standardized tests as the dominant means of defining and measuring student achievement; (2) the perpetuation of an unequal opportunity structure in education; (3) the de-professionalization of teachers; and (4) the political structuring of "parent involvement" in such a way as to promote individualism, competition, and consumerism while discouraging access to genuine power and the potential for collective action. The group read, in order, *High Stakes: Children, Testing, and Failure in American Schools* by Dale Johnson and Bonnie Johnson (2002), *What Happened to Recess and Why Are Our Children Struggling in Kindergarten* by Susan Ohanian (2002); *Will Standards Save Public Education?* by Deborah Meier (2000); *The Manufactured Crisis: Myths, Fraud, and the Attack on America's Public Schools* by David Berliner and Bruce Biddle (1995); and *The Schools Our Children Deserve: Moving Beyond Traditional Classrooms and "Tougher Standards"* by Alfie Kohn (1999). We also read *A Nation at Risk* by the National Commission on Excellence in Education (1983); an excerpt from C. Douglas Lummis's *Radical Democracy* (1996); and another excerpt from Michael Engel's *The Struggle for Control of Public Education: Market Ideology vs. Democratic Values* (2000). I facilitated text-based discussions on each of these readings.

The question that I set out to explore through this series of parent-teacher discussions and through a pre- and post-interview with each participant was simply: How do teachers and parents make sense of the accountability movement? Two sub-questions helped guide the study. The first had to do with the fact that my design was intentionally constructed to give parents and teachers the opportunity to talk together about critical issues in education. In this I followed Fine's (1993) lead in believing that the separation of teachers' and parents' interests effectively serves the interests of "the very bureaucracies . . . that are underfunding and overcontrolling public education."[25] In constructing the study in such a way as to invite parents and teachers to this conversation, it was incumbent upon me to recognize the imbalanced relation of power that has historically existed between these two groups.[26] Therefore, I built the recognition of this reality into my research design by making teacher-parent relationships an explicit subtext of the study. The first guiding question, then, was: How do participants' identities as parents and teachers influence group discussions and participants' experiences of those discussions? Another sub-question resulted from an assumption that I took into this study, which was that some kind of change would occur as a result of participation. A second guiding question was: Would action (either individually or collectively) result?

I approached this set of questions from the research paradigm of constructivism, what Egon Guba and Yvonna Lincoln had previously called "naturalistic inquiry."[27] Their explanation of the aim of constructivist inquiry effectively described the purpose for this study:

> The aim of inquiry is *understanding* and *reconstruction* of the constructions that people (including the inquirer) initially hold, aiming toward consensus but still open to new interpretations as information and sophistication improve. The criterion for progress is that over time, everyone formulates more informed and sophisticated constructions and becomes more aware of the content and meaning of competing constructions. Advocacy and activism are . . . key concepts in this view.[28]

With participants, my goal was to work toward group understandings of the critical issues in education that I named above, and then to document the effect of additional information on the reconstruction of those understandings. What I ultimately learned was as simple and as powerful as the idea of bringing teachers and parents together to talk about the politics of education. After what seemed like a lifetime of collecting, transcribing, and analyzing data, what I learned could fit on the back of a matchbook cover: *The energy that is generated when people gather purposefully to talk with each other—to find and to create connections through focused discussion of important texts and ideas—is transformative. This power of focused conversation (i.e., "volatile knowing") is potentially revolutionary.*

When I set out to explore my questions with the teachers and parents who agreed to be a part of this study group, I didn't anticipate finding such hope in the process. That optimism, however, resides in the long view. It is where the study ended, not where it began. I will return to the hopefulness of my matchbook-cover finding, but the road toward it begins in another place for the people who were a part of this project.

The Participants: Tensions, Frustrations, and Hope

Frustration is a palpable thing when teachers and parents get together to talk about education. At least, this was the case with the particular parents and teachers in our study group. To put that observation in context, however, it must be understood that I am not suggesting that the members of this group were representative of the categories of public school parents and teachers. I believe that this group was in fact unusual because of the high levels of education, community activism, and socio-political awareness and critique that its members brought to the table. One explanation for this is that my research questions and study design tended to attract participants who were attentive already to the topic of accountability in the schools and/or confident in their ability to participate in what was essentially an academic text-based discussion group. (The problem of exclusivity is real, and was a limitation of this study. The parents and teachers of this group provided a valuable beginning point in the work of bridging the home-school divide and broadening the definition of parent involvement, but clearly, much work lies ahead on the project of including historically marginalized voices in the conversation.)

This unusual group profile nearly caused me to lose a parent participant early on. During our first group meeting participants introduced themselves to each other and explained why they had decided to be a part of the study. While the impact of that initial meeting left me feeling emotionally charged and excited about the prospect of our next session together, a parent participant named Tessa had experienced an entirely different reality of it. She came to me after everyone else had left and said, "I'm not sure if I can stay with the group. I don't feel like I fit in here. Everybody else is all involved and doing so much, and I'm just a mom." Tessa did ultimately continue as a participant in the study. But it strikes me that the frustrations of a person who feels alienated in her role of being "just a mom" are probably typical of what many parents are experiencing in their relationships with schools and educators. For that reason I want to introduce Tessa first, of the twelve participants in the group. Hers is a voice that is seldom exercised in a public forum, which makes hearing and honoring it all the more important.

Parent Participant: Tessa[29]

Tessa is thirty-one years old; she is Asian and her son's father is Hispanic. Her only child is now in middle school, but he had once been a student in my fifth grade class. Tessa and her son had taken part in the parent and student meetings that I held when I explained my decision not to participate in administering the standardized tests. Although Tessa is a quiet person who rarely speaks in public, she wrote a letter to the school principal that year, stating that she did not want her son to be tested. I particularly valued her participation in our study group because her presence represented the more typical parent: she does not belong to the PTA, she is not an activist in her community. She is a single mom who is working hard to take care of her family, doing the best she can with the resources and the time and the information that she has. Frustrated sighs punctuated Tessa's remarks to the group during our first meeting as she explained why she decided to be a part of this research project:

> The reason why I'm here is just to learn more from a teacher's perspective. Because the little I get as far as teacher conferences . . .* But they don't even do a teacher conference any more. It's more of a student and mom conference. You don't really get to learn much from the teachers any more. And the group of teachers that my son has right now, they have this little clique amongst themselves that I've noticed, and it just doesn't suit me at all. So I was like, 'Okay, son, just survive this year. You know, it's almost over.' Hopefully next year he'll have teachers who actually want to talk to the parents and stuff like that.
>
> And I don't do PTA, because as far as I'm concerned it just reminds me of high school where you have your little rich ones here and your little 'I'm going to do this' there, and if you don't fit into one of the groups you're just out in the cold.

A quiet resentment at feeling excluded, being left "out in the cold" by teachers and other parents at her school, seemed to be compounded by Tessa's struggle to find and use her voice in strong and productive ways. This struggle was evident during our group discussions. Her participation in these conversations was consistently more internally than externally active, a reality that she seemed eager to change. In fact, one of the small ways in which my matchbook-cover finding is evidenced is in the progress that Tessa made over time toward her goal of becoming a more verbally active participant in this study. In the beginning, she wanted to quit because she felt like she didn't belong in the group. A few sessions later, in response to another participant's concern of, "I don't know if we leave space for you," Tessa replied with an apology. "Yeah, I'm sorry. I'm just a really quiet person." By our sixth meeting, she was able to describe her response to a discussion strategy we had used the week before by saying,

> Last week, reading the paragraphs one by one and then just discussing it all worked really well. Because it didn't have us go in circles, talking about the same thing over and over. And then everybody started having more thoughts, more ideas. And there were a lot of big words and stuff, but I felt fine saying, 'Okay, I don't understand this and I don't know what that is.' And at the same time, I felt a little bit more that I could talk a little bit more. Last time I probably talked the most so far.

---

* Ellipses, when quoting participants, always indicate a pause or an unfinished sentence rather than omitted words.

In the same meeting, Tessa told the story of a recent incident in her life that participation in this study group had caused:

> I went and had my tires changed. So I was sitting down, trying to do some reading out of our second book, and one of the customers that came in and sat next to me happened to be a teacher in one of the elementary schools. And she saw my book and we started talking! And she was just telling me how frustrated she was with the testing, and all kinds of stuff. And I was like, 'Well, didn't you know it's not mandatory?' And she was all, like, 'Really?' And then she started thinking and we talked some more. Her fear was that she was afraid to lose her job. And I was all, like, 'No! If it makes you feel that bad just talk to someone else in the school! And see if someone else will stand with you or something.' By the time she left she was ready to go and start trouble over there. [Kate: So we're going to create our own movement through the tire shops! (Group laughter.) Okay, parents, go to the tire shop! We'll just hang out in the tire shops and pass out pamphlets to everybody.]

People who don't know Tessa—people who can't hold in their minds either the image of the shy smile and self-deprecating shrug that tend to accompany her contributions to a discussion or the flare of resentment that sparks in her eyes at the thought of being left out in the cold by teachers and other parents— might not be able to appreciate the surprised pride in Tessa's voice when she exclaimed, "She saw my book and we started talking!" Small steps toward finding a public voice is one way of walking the road from frustration to hope.

Parent Participant: Kate

Kate is thirty-one years old and the mother of three elementary-aged children. She is White and her husband is Hispanic. Kate is an active member of the PTA and has served as an officer for each of the three years since her children started school. As a PTA activist she has devoted herself to providing funds for new learning opportunities for all of the children at her school, which is located in a low-income neighborhood of her community. I met Kate the year that I taught fifth grade in the same school.

Without even trying, Kate seemed to find herself in the middle of the few moments of tension that occurred between participants during the course of our discussions together. My best explanation for this came from Kate herself in our fourth meeting, when she talked about the fact that she had joined this racially diverse group without previously having examined the privilege that can come with being born into white skin. From my perspective, the moments of racially based tension were some of the most productive ones that we experienced as a group. To Kate's and each participant's credit, these moments were generally negotiated openly and with mutual respect.

The first crackle of tension in the air came during our very first meeting together. It occurred between two parent participants who, until the previous year, had had children in the same elementary school. One of the parents, Tessa, had closed her remarks with, "I don't do PTA, because as far as I'm concerned it just reminds me of high school where you have your little rich ones here and your little I'm going to do this there..." A few moments later Kate introduced herself, in part, by challenging Tessa's characterization of the PTA as an exclusive organization:

> I *am* the PTA. I don't look at myself as the clique. There's only two of us, and I don't even think she sometimes likes me. [Group laughter.] I don't know what represents a clique yet, but I don't think that was it. Obviously I laugh a lot. I make fun of a lot of things that maybe I shouldn't make fun of. But I've found that in being an involved parent, what's sad is that your child is going to get a better opportunity. I've found that through the PTA you do have more opportunities for your children. It's sad that that's the way the system works, but it does.

This small spark of tension between Kate and Tessa was re-ignited during our second meeting by Elena, another parent participant in the group. I had begun the second meeting by asking everyone to talk about what they had taken away from our first session together. Elena, an activist and advocate for students and parents in her community, said that what she took away from our first meeting was appreciation for the fact that Tessa had brought up the issue of parent cliques in the schools. She confronted Kate directly in saying,

> You're very fortunate. You haven't experienced those cliques. We have! Because there's these certain mothers that come in, and they're the privileged mothers, and they're able to give. And I really respected you saying that, Tessa. Because there is that clique. And I think that that's the way it's looked upon, even at school. That you guys are the privileged parents and we're no better than anybody because we can't give as much as you can give. Do you understand what I'm saying?

"To a degree," Kate replied. The terse edge in Kate's voice seemed to echo in the stillness that had crept up on our group while Elena was talking. Other participants stepped in to ease the moment and our discussion moved on; but that disruption in the atmosphere lingered—at least for me—in the form of a little knot of hyper-awareness that I could feel in my stomach, awareness of what I was reading as quiet waves of resentment coming from Kate. She had been publicly charged as an elitist, a member of the privileged class. A phone call from her that night confirmed resentment as an accurate perception of her response to Elena's comments. "She doesn't even *know* me!" she said. Kate felt disrespected and judged by a woman who didn't know the circumstances of her life: that she worried about whether her bi-racial children would face discrimination, for example, and that she had to make sacrifices in her work, a business that she ran out of her home, in order to devote the time she did to the PTA at her school.

A productive result of these tensions wasn't revealed for another two meetings. Toward the end of our fourth session together as we were debriefing our discussion from that night, Kate said to Elena,

> When you said that, that day, that I was privileged, it really made me look back! And say, okay, *am* I privileged? Because you didn't know anything about what I do or how I would be privileged. But after talking with a couple of other folks, I think being white *is* privileged! And I'm starting to appreciate that, by reading *High Stakes*.

> What scares me, though, is that this barrier that we're both speaking of? How do you ever get past that? And how do you jump over that? Because what if I'm a white girl who wants to come to your school and help change *with* you? I will never be accepted! Our school is predominantly Hispanic, but how do I reach out to the Hispanic community? When I'm the only parent who's willing to go against it, and they say, 'Well, look at this privileged white girl who's coming up here trying to tell me what I'm supposed to do with my kids?' How do you change that?

> That's the part that scares me the most, in talking about change and in talking about accountability. Is, wow. It's all race! And the fact that you felt that, from me! It, it... I was hurt. I was totally devastated. I couldn't believe it. But I think the other thing of it is that you could say that, and you were comfortable enough to say that. And that's got to mean something, somewhere.

The fact that members of this racially-diverse group were able to participate in this kind of exchange after having known each other for about ten hours recalls the potential of that matchbook-cover finding. Through Elena's willingness to name privilege and Kate's willingness to examine her reality in light of it, our group was able to touch on some core-level issues early in our process. I think that this made our work together feel real and significant. The sense of genuine significance that our discussions took on was manifested in other participants' responses to Kate's frustrated realization that "It's all race!" and her observation that Elena's ability to say what was important to her "has got to mean something, somewhere."

> Boyoyo (teacher participant): It is just incredible that we can talk that way.

> Julia (teacher participant): I think our state is very unique in that we can have that conversation and start saying it is not acceptable that we have this barrier. And we need to start working on taking it down. No, we won't be able to get rid of all of it, but tonight, I think tonight we removed a brick off that barrier! By saying, 'This is how I feel.'

> Elena (parent participant): And I think that was good of you, Kate. Because how do we learn from one another? I mean, it's just a learning process that we go through every day.

In my initial interview with each participant, I asked what each person felt responsible for when they thought about their role in the public schools. In almost every case, participants understandably talked about their responsibility to their students, their children, their neighborhood. Kate's response, however, was unique in its perspective that moved beyond the boundaries of immediate family and neighborhood concerns. When I asked, "When you think about your involvement with your school, what do you feel responsible for?" she said,

> Making sure that all the children have the same opportunity. My idea last year was that we could give $20,000 to a sister PTA in another school that is either just beginning or to one that is floundering and needs help. But when it was brought up at our PTA meeting, it was, you know, no, they don't want to do that. These parents from this school put their money into *our* school.

> And then we had an excess of school supplies, where I thought we could just donate the school supplies. But when I put it out there, there again! The money that is earned to purchase all these school supplies is meant for *our* school and *our* community. And not for all children. Which is *sad*, because as a PTA it's supposed to be, 'Every child, one voice.' So you *should* be touching every single child, whether we raise it here or whether we raise it there. But it's hard to feel responsible for that over there and not somehow feel like you're being disloyal to over here.

Where I saw Tessa's struggle as one of learning to find and use her voice in order to resist feeling victimized by those who had the power to leave her "out in the cold," I saw Kate wrestling in other ways. As an action-oriented person with a strong voice and strong opinions, it was hard for her to understand why teachers would put up with accountability mandates that contradicted their own professional values and expertise. "The more now that I know," she said in her final interview, "the more I've just lost respect for a whole bunch of teachers that I had a tremendous amount of respect for, before. They're not fighting! I tend to lose my respect for them, that they have no backbone! You're allowing this system to happen! So if you allow this system to happen, how can you possibly bitch about it?" Kate's harsh critique of teachers' lack of resistance is tempered somewhat in the recognition of her own unwillingness to stand alone against the "huge problem" that she learned to see through reading and discussing critical texts on the accountability movement.

> The positive impact of the study is that it educated me thoroughly, that there is a huge problem. The negative side would be, what the hell do you do with it? What do you *do*? I feel like, well, now I know this and I'm still not doing anything about it and my child is still going to test in third grade! And I'm still living with the system. I mean, I'm not bucking it yet. And I think the biggest reason for *not* bucking it is there's not enough people that will buck it with you! And I know I could buck it! I have no doubt. But when you're making waves and nobody's standing behind you to ride the wave with you, it's no fun.

Kate's struggle seemed to be with the problem of her own and others' impotence in making change. I take this, too, as a hopeful and productive frustration because it indicates belief in the idea that things could—and should—be otherwise. As Maxine Greene would say, recognizing and naming the problems in our lives are simply the first steps that must be taken before we can release our imaginations and begin the work of bringing other possibilities into being. As Kate put it during one of our final group meetings, "I feel empowered. And I feel like once you get educated, you feel like you can maybe at some point make a difference."

Parent Participant: Elena

I met Elena in 1999 when I heard her speak to a group of student teachers at the university about the importance of family and neighborhood involvement in schools. Her passion on behalf of the marginalized parents and children in her community left an impression. Four years later when I began thinking of potential participants for this study, I remembered her.

Elena is forty-seven years old and the mother of four children, one of whom is still in high school. Another of her children is studying to become a teacher. Elena is Hispanic and a long-time community organizer/activist. Her husband is African American. Elena's passion lies in the development of Family Centers— parent-run centers for student and family advocacy within the schools in her local district. Says Elena, "Some of the parents don't even feel they have a right to voice their concern about their child's education, much less the testing part. You know what I'm saying?" First through her work as a founding member of Barrios Juntos (an alliance of Hispanic women from various neighborhoods in her city whose primary goal is to improve educational experiences and opportunities for Hispanic youth) and then through Enlace (an alliance between Barrios Juntos and the major university in her community), Elena spearheaded a campaign that to date has created Family Centers in four local schools.

Our first interview took place in the Family Center at her child's high school. We had to pause periodically so that Elena could hug and talk to the stream of students who stopped by to see her. After one small group left, Elena helped me to understand her depth of passion for the Family Centers:

> These kids are so good. But people tell me, 'Oh, those kids at Lincoln High are bad.' And I say, 'Don't you even go there.' These kids are *so* kind-hearted. They come from a lot of incredible issues. I mean, barriers and anything you can imagine. And the bottom line is they don't have that support. I'm there to support my children. They know that. Whatever they need. But these kids are just walking through school by themselves, from the minute a lot of them get into elementary. I'm serious. They are by themselves.

Elena describes herself as a "true community activist." While today she says, "I'm involved in everything that happens in my neighborhood," this wasn't always the case. She remembers the incident that launched her role as an activist fifteen years ago when her children were elementary-, middle-, and high-school aged. When school administrators were considering the idea of moving to a year-round schedule without thoroughly soliciting the ideas and concerns of the families, Elena took action. She went door-to-door in her neighborhood, asking parents if they knew that this decision was being made without them. The shocking discovery that she made during those home visits sealed her transformation from "enchilada mom" in her children's schools to "true community activist."

So then, by me going out into the community and letting parents know, 'Do you know this year-round schedule can happen?' That's how I found out. Parents would tell me, 'Well, you know what? The principal came to our home. And he said that if I gave him something from our house, he would make sure my child would pass elementary.' And then the word got out into the community.

Elena estimates that this principal successfully extorted family heirlooms and other valuables from at least 200 newly immigrated Hispanic families over his decade-long tenure at that elementary school. Her accidental journey toward community activism officially began in this way, when she and thirty other parents from the community met with the district superintendent to demand the principal's removal.

We met, I think it was on a Wednesday. Thursday they sent out a memo to the whole community that the principal would no longer be there because of an illness. And I'm like, yeah, right. But see, I was learning. I told the superintendent, 'Okay, you don't want me to say a word? I want to be on the hiring committee for the next principal that comes in.'

From discovering and helping to eliminate corruption in her child's elementary school to realizing her dream of having Family Centers in the schools, Elena's fifteen years of activism make her a force to be reckoned with. "I have history with a *lot* of people. You know what I'm saying? So they definitely know who I am," she says with a grin. When Elena puts a call in to her superintendent, who heads up one of the largest school districts in the country, or to the chairman of the state House of Representatives Committee on Education, it is returned. Her friend, Selena, is another parent participant in the group who described Elena's influence by saying, "People know who Elena is. She says, 'I get things done because I know a lot of politicians.' I said, 'No, Elena. Politicians know *you*. It's not who you know. It's who knows *you* and what you do!'"

Elena's participation in this research project contributed to her continuing growth and development as an advocate for the children and families in her community. Because of her participation, this already-powerful activist discovered an entirely new avenue for learning.

You guys probably are going to think I'm a psycho, here, but this *High Stakes* is the first book I've actually read! [Group exclamations of 'Wow! Congratulations!'] I swear to you! It's the first book I've ever read. So my family is like, 'Mom!' They're really proud of me. Because I'm one of those people that, my parents never read to me and then reading was a struggle for me. I hate reading. But I told Selena, I'm so proud of myself! I was reading and reading! I sit in a little room where I have my chaise set and my dictionary and I'm reading.

While one effect of participation in the study for Kate was a loss of respect for teachers whom she had previously held in high regard, the reverse was true for Elena. Reading about an accountability movement that is being imposed on schools from above and discussing the realities of working in the public schools with the teachers in our group gave Elena a sense of connection with teachers—both with those in our group and with educators in general—where previously she had mostly felt a sense of alienation.

But the thing that I appreciate, and I do want to say, is that you've got teachers in this group and then you've got parents. And I firmly feel that we are all just *one*. Nobody is, like, the little educator there and we're the little parents here. I feel so much support from everybody. I just love this group. I think a lot of parents need to go through this. It just gave me a different level of respect for the teachers. Because we've been on the other end, basically saying, 'You need parent involvement. We need parent involvement.' I've never really disrespected the teachers, but I haven't had the respect that I'm starting to get.

Elena's struggle is an active one. She values education highly and she wants to have faith in teachers and the schools. Her experience, however, has taught her that the system is not set up to value all children and parents equally. "We have not been educated, as minority parents, to be involved in our children's education. We *haven't*!" she said. "We have been told from the get-go that this is as far as you go." Her own experience in feeling dismissed and devalued as a child ("going to school and having the teachers telling you that you aren't going to amount to *anything*") is relived at times through her work in the Family Centers. "We had a girl that said the teacher had told her that she's better off staying home, having babies, and not coming to school. Because he said she wasn't going to amount to anything, the way she was going." The frustrations are personal and the anger is white-hot. But because Elena's struggle is an active one, daily frustrations are transformed into hope.

We have *definitely* made a big change in this school, with the Family Center. We have. Just us being here! Like, the counselors? The moment they know one of our kids are down here, the attitude changes. That's how they're treating our kids. And *why*? Because they know we're here, and we'll go down there and raise hell with them. That's all it takes, is for them to just be aware.

Parent Participant: Selena

Selena is Hispanic, as is her husband. She is a forty-eight-year-old mother of four, all of whom are out of high school. One of her daughters is studying to become a teacher. Selena is another person who lives the ideal of democratic citizenship in her neighborhood. She is a dynamic activist in the Hispanic community and serves as the president of her neighborhood association. (The majority of our group meetings were held in that neighborhood's community center because of her access to that facility.) I met Selena through Elena, who recommended her as a potential participant for the study.

Selena is also one of the founding members of Barrios Juntos. "*Juntos* means together," Selena explained to me. "And *barrios* is, basically, your Hispanic communities. They're coming together, crossing barriers. We knew every neighborhood that was involved with us had a gang problem, and we wanted to bridge with each other. We really wanted to bridge, and overlook the whole gang territorial issue. We are moms, grandmas, and aunties, and that's how we came about." It was through the forming of this organization that Selena and Elena first met.

> Elena was a community leader on her side of the tracks, I was on my side of the tracks, and we met together at a big meeting they called the Collaborative at Lincoln High School. And we didn't like the way things were going so we teamed forces. There was a group of us, of women who did that. And we started questioning the school district and the city government. Suddenly we were told the Collaborative was disbanded. Then we were told the district didn't want us, we were told the city didn't want us. We said, 'That's okay. We're here forever.' [Laughs.]

Through Barrios Juntos, Selena and Elena joined forces and worked together on the project of creating parent-run Family Centers in the public schools in their district. Their goal in this was to provide in-school support for students and to help educate the parents in their neighborhoods about how to take an active role in their children's education. Selena described her perspective on the need for Family Centers in the schools:

> All parents care for their kids. Every parent wants the best for their child. No one wants their kid left behind. So what if there are some parents who don't . . . I can't say they don't *care*. But this is where people like Elena and I come in and pick up the ball. And should we pick up the ball? You know, it's tiring, and emotionally it's draining. But why not, if we can break that cycle? I think Elena told you this story, about that one girl who was the first one in her family to graduate. She wanted to walk that line so bad, but she couldn't afford the cap and gown. We broke her cycle! We gave her the money and she got to walk the line. She *broke* the cycle. And *that's* what we're hoping to do. Break the cycle.

Selena's experience leads her to believe that the cycle of school failure for Hispanic students is systemically perpetuated. She awoke to this conclusion when her own children reached middle school. They attended a middle school that serves the university-area neighborhoods, which meant that the student body was far less diverse than their elementary school population had been. According to Selena, the middle school that her children attended was "the coldest school to break through," and those were the "most devastating" school years that they experienced.

> You were not welcome there. It was really hard to break the block walls there. The only way I broke them was when I was complaining. I'd complain about this and that, or how *dare* you put my daughter in a special needs class without my consent? That's when I started to see true colors. Black and White. There *is* a difference as to where you live and how you're taught. When one of your own teachers from the middle school confides in you, and she was an Anglo teacher who confided, 'Selena, there *is* a difference. They treat the kids from your neighborhood different than the kids from up here.' And I saw more kids in special ed. that were brown-colored kids, or African American kids. In this middle school it was more your Latino kids who were in special ed., because it's basically a university junior high. That's when I started seeing it.

> And when I saw the statistics of the dropouts, that scared me. It really did. And then I saw who was in the Honors classes, in high school, where it was like, you'd have to wear your sunglasses in there. And I don't want to sound racist, but it was like that.

Selena's road to activism began as an Hispanic mom in a predominantly White middle school, where she believed her advocacy for Hispanic families earned her a special status in the school. "I'm convinced that at the middle school I was dragon lady," she laughs. "Here I was, the Lone Ranger at this school, predominately a white school. And, you know, you can't do that."

Despite her experience of what she saw as institutionally sanctioned discrimination, Selena's belief in "the system" remains strong. She values education, teachers, and the public schools highly. She believes in the ideals of democracy and participatory citizenship, which she describes in this way:

> Democracy means that there's equity, all the way across. It's freedom. Freedom to choose, freedom to express, freedom to make change. And *that's* really important. You have that right to make a change. But one person can't do it alone. It takes a group. And I think you need to be astute enough to know what's wrong. Like looking at, when you go to a special ed. class and you notice the certain color of faces there, or just stuff like that. It starts there. It starts with questioning! It's all an awakening process. It's like the science theory. You know, you start with a question: what's the problem?

Being astute enough to see a problem and then acting on her freedom to choose an alternative, express her views, and make a change is Selena's formula for democratic citizenship. I watched her put this formula into action a few months after we first met. Selena invited the members of our group to attend a community meeting that she had organized in response to the school district's announcement that her neighborhood school would be closing the preschool that she had helped to establish years before. This magnet dual-language school that served both an affluent, downtown population and a poorer neighborhood community was experiencing an upsurge in kindergarten enrollment, in part because of federal legislation that allows parents to transfer children out of "failing" schools. The increase in kindergarten enrollment meant that two classrooms could no longer be devoted to the preschool program. In addition to opposing the loss of the preschool, Selena's protest was also motivated by the fact that parents were being notified of the change in August, just weeks before the start of the new school year. The meeting that she organized allowed me to see her in action as a community leader.

The preschool's double room in which we met on that hot, August night was packed with parents, school district officials, school board members, and state legislators. I asked Selena later if the district and state hierarchy were there, at least in part, because it was she who had called and asked them to come. A quick grin was her only response. As I watched her facilitate discussion among the people assembled there, I realized that I was seeing a powerful model of democratic citizenship in action. She believed that she could make a positive difference in her community, and she did. The eventual outcome of that initial meeting was that barracks were brought in (where it had previously been deemed impossible to do so) and the preschool program was saved for at least one year, during which time the district and parents would be able to explore their options.

When Selena talks about how her participation in the study impacted her, she uses the language of a citizen-activist.

All in all I think I'm reading books I would never pick up. I mean, mine are mystery books. I love to read mystery books, or women's biographies. But I would never read an educational book. In reality, this whole thing, it's challenging the way I think. And I think if you were to ask me those first questions you asked me before we started this project I'd be lost. What is education? What is democracy? What does this mean? And I'm just wondering, what are my words going to be after I've left here? Because everything's changed now.

On a personal level, it's opened my eyes to all of the hard work you guys do, as teachers. You know, just a lot more respect. [The chair of the state's House of Representatives Education Committee] and I have been talking. I've been telling him about our books, and he says, 'Selena, let me borrow one of your books.' And then when I saw the president of the school board, once again I was telling her about our class. And she gets all excited.

See, one of my dreams or visions is maybe those of us who are interested could get together and format some kind of talking points, to speak with [our legislators] and say, 'These are our concerns about testing. This is what's going on. And have the school board president there. We could all develop some general talking points and just hit them. 'This is what's going on. This is my fear as a parent. You know, with the testing and whatever, the restrictions for teachers.' That's why I want to continue meeting, maybe once a month or every other month. But that's what I want to see. Start getting the word out to the higher ups. I think it will happen, but it takes more. It's more of us that need to get out there.

Parent Participant: Sarah

Sarah is forty-five years old. She has two boys; one attends a private middle school and the other attends a public elementary school. She and her husband are White. Sarah identifies as a parent now, but she was an elementary teacher before her sons were born. She taught for five years in the school that her youngest son attends, the same school in which another participant, Mariela, now teaches. She also taught in suburban Tucson, inner city Baltimore, and Austin, bringing her total to eight years of experience as a classroom teacher. "Then I had my kids and I've never gone back," she says. I met Sarah through Mariela, who recommended her as a potential participant for the study.

Sarah wrestles with the fact that she and her husband have chosen private school for their older son. "I keep trying to justify for myself why I was sending my older boy to a private school, frankly. Because I'm a big public school advocate, and I always am arguing with myself. What are you doing here?" Sarah's sense of loyalty to the public schools is compromised by her belief that they cannot serve all of society's children and maintain the kind of academic focus that she wants for her son. "I think the private school I'm sending him to can spend more time on habits of mind kinds of things, and expand and deeply enrich them," she says. "And I'm afraid that if I send him to the public school, he would be dragged down and interrupted by the amount of time that would have to be spent on remedial skills by his peers. And I don't want that for him! Because I think it would make him less optimistic about feeling good about school."

In our initial interview I asked Sarah why she had accepted my invitation to participate in this study. I think her response is important, because it points to a certain void in the lives of many people like Sarah who are passionate and articulate about issues like education, democracy, and social justice, but who have not found a public avenue for exercising that passion. She joined the group, she said,

> Because these are big questions. These are important questions that I want to think about! And reading a book independently, at 9:00 at night, and talking to my husband about it isn't quite the same as talking with other parents and educators that are anonymous to me. I wanted to talk about these kinds of important educational issues with people who are not moms, necessarily. Who are

coming to it from a different perspective. Because I think that's broadening for me.

I appreciate the fact that Sarah specifically addressed the importance of having the opportunity to talk about ideas with people she didn't previously know. This same idea has been addressed by the likes of John Dewey, Hannah Arendt, Jean Bethke Elshtain, Maxine Greene and others who have argued for the essential role of public discourse for citizens who are striving toward democracy. In our fifth group meeting, Sarah described the value of participation in the study unfolding for her in terms that were consistent with her initial decision to join the group.

> I sure think it's good that you've got all these people from all these different ethnic and, and just, different backgrounds here. That's very good for all of us. Because change only happens when you work at it all together. And I think until people really spend time together and hear each other's ideas . . . you can speculate about what other people think and how other people have lived their lives, but if you don't spend time with them and hear them, hear them talking, it's just what you think they think. And it's easy to condemn people, or praise people, based on what you think they think. And so I think this discussion, altogether, is really very good for all of us. You know, that's a very empowering democratic value. The fact that you, as a lonely individual, bonded with other lonely individuals, could be a force in the world that the powers could fear. That's true in a democracy.

Opportunities to engage in this kind of critical discourse have not been part of Sarah's experience with the public schools, even in her affluent community. The open and healthy exchange between teachers and parents that she remembered in the elementary school in which she had taught in the 1980s was not something she enjoyed as a parent in the same school a decade later. She described her first experience as a public school parent in the place where she had once held authority as a teacher. Since her first child was to start kindergarten the next year, she had scheduled an appointment to speak with the principal. There is an edge of anger in her voice now as she describes how that initial school meeting went eight years ago.

> I felt really comfortable going in to the public elementary school, thinking that I had an 'in.' And that sense of empowerment was very important to me because when you're a parent, you're afraid all the time. You want to make the right decisions for your children. And so I felt like I had this sense of power!
>
> So I strode in to the principal, saying, 'You know, I would really like to be able to see the environments that you offer here for kindergarten! I want to go in there and see how those kindergarten teachers are teaching!' And she said, 'Oh, we don't do that here.' And that's exactly how she said it. 'We don't do that here. You can make an appointment to visit with the teacher, but we don't . . .

let parents just go in and observe what goes on in the classrooms. That's too intrusive. Too disruptive. That doesn't go on here.'

Boy! That was such a contrast to what had happened when I taught at that school, where we welcomed strangers, parents, everybody into the classrooms. And she didn't care who I was. You know, I tried to use my little 'in' of, 'Gosh, I used to teach here! This is *my* place.' No, no. That didn't work. So immediately, I was confronted with a door as a parent. That this isn't your place. I don't care who you think you are. You're just one of, like everyone else. You take what you get. You don't get to choose.

Well, as a parent involved in this school, to the point of being PTA president and playing that whole game of trying to empower myself, to make decisions, to have control over whether my kids get the rotten teachers or the good teachers, all of those kinds of little doors that you push, as a parent—when you're an aggressive parent, and feel like you *can* be an aggressive parent. I've learned to play the game, as a parent. Now, the line is, 'It is district policy that you can't choose your kid's teacher.' But you *can*! You just play the game. So you go and you slither in to the counselor, and you say, 'You know, I really want my son to have so-and-so, because she would be good for his self-esteem.' You have the catchwords, the words that are the politically correct issues of the day. You know, 'She would support his interest in math.' So you play the game! And you tell all your friends, who have had a crappy year this year, how to play the game for next year.

I asked Sarah what the name of the game was, and she replied, "It's empowerment. That's the name of the game. How you *empower* yourself. Because in the end, it is true. You are the only advocate for your kid. Teachers can't be the advocate for your kid, because they're just trying to survive every day. And they have everybody's kid. And your kid certainly is not as needy as some of the other kids that these teachers encounter, who have no support at home. And so in the end, you're your kid's only advocate. So you play the game."

A parent with enough financial, social, and cultural capital can find an alternative route when "confronted with a door" in the schools, even if it does mean having to learn how to "slither" her way through the empowerment game. It would be easy to judge Sarah harshly for having essentially stated that the students in her child's school who have no support at home are not her concern, but the problem is too complex to allow a simplistic response. The terms of the "parent involvement" discourse have been cast in such a way as to encourage amoral familism as a way of life. Parent involvement as a necessary component of school reform is generally accepted to mean involvement on behalf of one's own children or one's own school. There is no social movement afoot under the rubric of accountability in the schools that encourages parents to engage themselves on behalf of the "other." What might the accountability discourse sound like if this *had* been the thrust in defining parent involvement when it was identified nearly twenty-five years ago as a crucial school reform strategy in *A Na-*

tion at Risk? Sarah learned and played the game in order to empower herself as an advocate for her own children, just as she has been encouraged to do. But it doesn't sit easy with her.

Sarah, who calls herself "a White woman of privilege," consistently allowed me and the other members of our group to see the conflict that seems to rage inside of her: her public and private values seem often to be at odds with each other. She is genuinely and deeply concerned about "everybody else's kids," but in the end she finds that she has only enough energy to take care of her own. In our final group sessions, I raised the question of what, if anything, did we want to do about any of the things that we had read about and discussed together. Sarah's response was, "What you're essentially asking, to me, is how do we all become active rebels? And I don't know whether I want to be an active rebel for anybody except my two kids! And I know that's morally bankrupt, but I don't know whether I have the energy to be anything but morally bankrupt. And I think that that's probably true of a lot of other parents." Sarah consistently demonstrated a remarkable ability and willingness to not only speak her truths, but to refuse to shield herself from others' judgment in light of them.

Sarah's willingness to name the social impotence that can accompany privilege made hers a particularly intriguing voice in the context of this study. During our final interview I asked her what she felt responsible for. Much of her reply to this question came through tears as she talked her way toward naming and explaining the source of her own impotence.

> That is a big, guilt-ridden question, right there. That's the big G. That's the scarlet letter. Is, who's going to be responsible if not *you*, Sarah? And then I want to go take a long, hot bath and drink a glass of wine and say, 'I don't know! But you know what? I'm really comfortable right here, right now, and I'm not going to think about it.' You know? It's so big. But then there's everybody else's kids. That's why it's so big. Because there's everybody else's kids. [Sarah is crying now, and speaking in a very small voice.] I'm afraid for our society. Because there's everybody else's kids. And it's crushing. It really is. And if it's not you...

> You know, I don't know what it takes. I keep reading these things, after 9/11, when we all said, well, everything's changed! And yet, nothing has changed! We're back to watching our stupid surface TV, and being consumed by all the worthless things. And yet, in that moment after 9/11 we all felt vulnerable together. And it was that shared sense of vulnerability that empowered us to make a change. For all of us to buy into that idea that we are all responsible! To make a change! And I wish that everybody could feel vulnerable enough in this dilemma of education to buy into the idea that we are all responsible to make a change. Because even with 9/11 it was fleeting! It's gone! It lasted while we watched the people cry about their lost relatives, and then two weeks later when we were told to go out shopping to save the world, it disappeared. The thing that makes you want to take responsibility is a sense of vulnerability. And, we just don't feel vulnerable enough! *I* don't feel vulnerable enough. It's that same

thing of Selena and Elena saying to me, 'Your kids aren't vulnerable. You can't even begin to imagine our sense of vulnerability.'

You know what makes a renaissance? A revolution? The idea that you are vulnerable, and your children are even more vulnerable than you. And if you don't take responsibility, they're going to lose.

I will return to Sarah and her willingness to allow me and other group members to see privilege confronting, examining, and challenging itself. Because I think she is right: I think a lot of us privileged folk don't have "the energy to be anything but morally bankrupt." Like Sarah, though, I think many of us want to ask more of ourselves than that. We just need help getting there. My hope is that what Sarah and the other participants in this group shared will help those of us who want more from ourselves to get a step closer to "there."

Parent Participant: Ana

A final parent participant, Ana, is Navajo. She is the mother of three sons, two out of high school and one in middle school. Their father is White. Ana grew up on a reservation in the Southwest but is raising her family in an urban environment. She is now an activist in the Native American community, working on behalf of the 5,000 urban Indian students in her school district. One of the problems she is currently addressing with other activists in her community is ensuring that federal funds that the district receives for improving Native student achievement are actually applied in a focused way to serve the needs of Native students. "Indian children here are supposed to be getting extra money to help them with their education," she says, "but it's diluted throughout the whole school system. You have to keep on the school district all the time because if you don't, they just ignore the issues of Indian children. It's just the fact that we want our Indian children to get an education, especially when there is extra money coming in *for* them, and the district is not being accountable for that."

Ana's frustrations are remarkably similar to those expressed by other minority parents in the group. When Elena introduced herself at our first meeting together, for example, she said, "I've *always* been frustrated because the schools are just so dysfunctional. And our kids, especially the Hispanic kids... the parents aren't involved. I think our cultures are somewhat the same, Ana. Because our parents are raised that you respect people in authority. You respect people that are higher up. So whatever they say is law." Ana's frustrations echo Elena's. These two women speak from different cultural places, but with consistently similar language and concerns.

From my experience, a lot of the Indian parents don't realize that they have the power. That they have that right to go to the school and fight and say what they want for their children. I keep stressing in my community, to Native parents, that they need to be aware of their rights. That they have the power to tell the principal or district administrators that their children have that right, to have an education. And it's kind of hard to make them think that, I think, because of how they grew up. They were taught that the teachers and administrators are way up here, and they're down here. So to convince them that they *have* that power, you know, how do you do that? I go to pow-wows and I talk to the parents. But they're just too busy working and trying to survive. Period. They're just trying to survive.

The parent participants in this group represent a broad range of racial, cultural, social, and socioeconomic realities that influence children's experience of school. Their words indicate the striking differences that exist within the category of "public school parents" in terms of the varying degrees of entitlement that they bring to the project of having a voice in their children's lives at school. At one end of the continuum are the parents who, in Elena's words, "don't even feel they have a right to voice their concern about their child's education." At the other are those who understand that they can effectively improve their children's learning opportunities by being involved in the school; but if the experience of parents in our group applies in a broader sense, even these parents may see their involvement as a strategic exercise in gamesmanship rather than as the exercise of genuine power in partnership with their neighborhood schools.

In our tenth group meeting, the distance between positions on that continuum of entitlement was illustrated in an exchange between two parents, Sarah and Selena. As we began discussing the question of what, if anything, could be done about changing an accountability system that effectively perpetuates class differences through the schools, Sarah said, "What about the idea of a group saying, 'These tests and their implementation in our district are damaging to our children!' And get the ACLU or some free lawyer source to *sue*! Why hasn't *that* been done? Why haven't parents whose children deserve the best education they can get, get the backing of some legal operation?" The simplicity of Selena's reply as she described the reality for parents in her neighborhood had a sense of resigned weight to it, a weight that grew heavier through repetition. "Because we don't know," she said. "We don't *know*. We take what's presented to us as gospel. It's gospel."

Helping Native parents to *know* is part of Ana's mission. "We keep trying to emphasize to the parents that you have that power! You have that right! You need to become more involved in the school and the whole school district. It's not that hard." Speaking as a mother herself, she says, "When I go to my school, they know who I am. They know I will tell them what I feel. They know that I know my rights."

Ana attended the first three of our twelve group meetings, and then stopped attending without explanation. I tried contacting her by telephone and by e-mail to learn why she had quit the group, but after four attempts I stopped for fear of being intrusive. The loss of her voice was a blow to this study. Of three Native American people who had tentatively agreed to participate, Ana was the one who had gone so far as to allow me to interview her at the start and to attend the first few group sessions. We did enjoy a degree of racial diversity in the group, but in losing Ana we missed the presence of a crucial perspective on the accountability discourse.

Teacher Participant: Julia

Julia is forty-two years old and a middle school teacher. She works in a large, urban school district in a probationary school, designated as such by the State Department of Education because of students' low standardized test scores. The school serves a predominantly Hispanic population—85 percent, compared to the K-8 state average of 50 percent. The remainder of the student body is 8 percent White, 3 percent American Indian, 3 percent African American, and less than 1 percent Asian. 90 percent of the students qualify for free or reduced lunch, where the K-8 state average is 65 percent.[30] Julia is in her fifth year of teaching and in her nineteenth year as a public school parent. She is the mother of four children, two of whom are still in high school; one attends a public school and the other, private. She is conflicted over the fact that her son goes to a private high school. "There was no way that this kid was going to go to Washington High School as a thirteen-year-old. I had teachers warn me. 'We'll lose him. There's no way he'll stay here. He's too smart for this group.' And that irritated me, too, because then on top of that they were saying that the rest of the kids, whom I helped educate before they got there, were too stupid to be with my son. So that bugged me."

Julia describes herself as White on the outside but Hispanic on the inside because she grew up and has worked in the Hispanic community her entire life, and her husband is Hispanic. I met Julia through another teacher-participant in the study, Boyoyo, her teaching partner who recommended her as a potential member for the group.

Julia wears her heart on her sleeve when it comes to caring for the children in her neighborhood. This was evident from the beginning of her participation in the study. I met her after school one day in late April for our first interview, and some of her sixth graders were still in the classroom when I arrived at 4:00 p.m. Julia had to finally shoo them out the door, teasing and hugging each one in turn. She is deeply angered by the fact that the students in her school are being judged deficient because of their performance on standardized tests, which she believes have effectively taken over the educational agenda at her school. I asked her what evidence she had to support that observation, and her reply was edged with fury.

> Because we're told at every staff development, we're told at every staff meeting. Because we are on probation. It's, we've got to get those scores up. We've got to get those scores up. I would say, if they want me to get my test scores up, they need to come to my classroom and find out my odds. You know? I have behavior issues with some gang kids. I have issues of starving kids. Some kids

who may not have gotten breakfast that morning. You know, they tell me my own child is very smart because she can do well on the tests. Well, I feed her every morning. She gets a good night's sleep. She goes to bed at 9:00 every night, not just on test nights. You know, she has a great life at home. My child is very lucky.

"I have a passion for children!" she said, stating the obvious. She shared some of the details of her own childhood story with me; they help to explain the depth of her devotion to working with kids, especially those who are neither academically nor socially privileged.

I'm a child of abuse. I'm an adult child of abuse, and I survived. It was very, very difficult. I was never hit, but I was very severely emotionally abused. And then there was sexual abuse. But I survived, in the best way I could. If I had one wish it would be to clean out all the abuse of children in the world. That's my only dream. Let's wipe it all out, and love children. Because you know what? We are *not* going to solve the problems of this world until we start loving our children.

I have a learning disability. I found out when I was doing my student teaching. I went through my accounting degree and never read a book. Not one of my textbooks, nothing. I just conned my way through. I got a 2.7 GPA, which isn't bad for somebody who didn't read! But it caught up with me when I was doing my education classes because they were actually asking real questions. And that's when they figured it out.

For Julia, the problem of accountability in the schools is manufactured, designed to ensure that a social hierarchy based on race and class is maintained in America. She is able to describe the very moment that she first became personally and viscerally aware of that social hierarchy. "I knew that this difference was there between the white schools and the minority schools," she said. "But I really figured it out a few years ago when my daughter was in high school. We'd show up at track meets, and the kids from the white school would have matching bags, matching uniforms, matching sweat suits, matching . . . *hairstyles.* And our kids would just come with Wal-Mart bags, and no water bottles. And their uniforms were tattered. That's when it *really* hit home. That's when I started getting *really, really* angry." At one of these meets, her daughter, one of the best Open 400 runners in the state, was forced by track officials to exchange lanes with a runner from an elite school who happened to be White. Luck of the draw had put Julia's daughter in lane three, one of the best lanes for the race. After the other runner's parents (who were Olympic athletes themselves) complained about their daughter's unlucky draw of the outside lane, officials simply had the two girls trade places. Julia cried as she described her daughter's last-place finish in lane eight. "She came over, and she was in tears. And she said, 'Mom, this is the first time I've ever felt like a dirty Mexican.' Because they were ugly to her. She ended up getting a letter of apology from the school district. But she goes, 'Mom, I've never been talked to like that.' She was devastated."

The social hierarchy that Julia saw on the track is one that she believes is intentionally perpetuated by the accountability movement in schools. There is a helpless rage in her voice as she describes the role that she believes standardized tests are intended to play in her students' lives.

Our administrators are panicking because we *are* going to go on Corrective Action next year, if our scores don't go up. They're not *going* to go up, I don't believe. My students can pass the *Supera*, which is the *Terra Nova* in Spanish, but they won't let us give it to them unless they speak only Spanish, or have been here less than two years. Last year our students took the *Terra Nova* and the *Supera*, with the exception of some of the kids who couldn't speak any English at all. And they didn't do bad on the *Terra Nova*, but of course they didn't do as well as they did on the *Supera*. Some of these kids blew it off the charts, on the *Supera*. And I think that's the reason that they took it away from us.

I don't believe that the state department *wants* us to succeed. They're setting us up for failure. I don't know why. I don't understand their motivation, other than that maybe it is political. In my opinion, a piece of it is that if we teach our Mexican kids to read, write, and become educated, we won't have anybody to clean our houses. We won't have anybody to dig our ditches. We won't have anybody to lay our cement or to wait on us at tables, in restaurants. That's my personal opinion. But then, I've been there. I've seen it happen to people. And my daughter even said that. When she first went off to college she called me and said, 'I've never seen so many White people in one place.' And then she called me two weeks later, after she'd been there awhile, and she goes, 'Mom, the only brown people around here, other than me and a handful of other students, are the ones who have the mops.'

My participant group was intentionally diverse. I believe this contributed to the fact that the issues of race and class became threads in our discussions that were ultimately inseparable from the overarching issue of accountability that had brought us together to begin with. Whether it was Sarah and Mariela marveling at the fact that the PTA had provided free breakfast for all of the students at their school throughout the month of testing, or Elena and Selena still seething over the story of an out-of-town track meet the previous year (when the school district housed athletes from their high school at Motel 6 while those from an elite school in the same district were put up at The Hampton, protested after the fact by the former school's principal), or Julia describing her experience of administering standardized tests, when "I just sat there and bawled for an hour and a half, literally wiping the tears from my face, after watching these kids being forced to take a test in English"—class and race played essential roles in our discussions as participants worked to make sense of the idea of what accountability means in the schools. They evoked frequent expressions of disbelief, frustration, anger, and even despair, at times, around our table. As Julia put it, "To work so hard with kids and to not be validated for that makes me really sad. It hurts so much. I feel so hopeless sometimes." But having that table to gather around made a difference, a difference that was empowering for Julia.

I want to keep talking because I'm learning more. It makes me see through the stories. And it's really opened my eyes. It's just really opened my eyes to what teachers have been through. I have known that what we are doing [with the standardized tests] is wrong but I haven't had the educated part of me to be able to articulate it. And now I think I do. Now I can stand up when district office people come to our staff meetings, and I can say, "Excuse me! You're not making sense!" I can say to parents, "You know, you can sign 'refused' on here."

Teacher Participant: Boyoyo

Boyoyo was the lone male in our group. While I was able to achieve my goal of creating a diverse group in many ways, I was unable to balance the group's gender profile. (See Appendix A, Methodology.) While it is certain that our group discussions were impacted by this predominantly female perspective on the accountability movement, I am not aware of any tensions or frustrations that occurred in the group due to the fact of this gender imbalance.

Boyoyo is 55-years old. He is the father of four children, all adults now. Boyoyo teaches math and science in Spanish, his native language, in a dual-language program. He is in his sixth year as a middle school teacher, working in the same school as Julia. Their school, which serves a predominantly Hispanic population (85 percent) and in which 90 percent of the students qualify for free or reduced lunch, has been designated as probationary by the State Department of Education. Before coming to the United States, Boyoyo taught veterinary science at a university in Mexico. He and his wife, who is also from Mexico, came to the United States in 1986 so that Boyoyo could pursue graduate studies in Educational Administration. "My idea was that if I learn about education I will improve as a teacher, and in Mexico I will improve the curriculum. Because we never studied to be teachers." He decided not to return to Mexico at the end of his graduate studies in America, however. A new political administration in Mexico had devastated the economy and destroyed the middle class. Friends there who had gone from teaching at the university to driving taxis told him, "If you can stay, don't come back."

I met Boyoyo in 2000. He was a student in a teacher licensure program that I coordinated for a year. I valued his participation in the group not only because I knew that he was a talented and thoughtful teacher, but also because his perspective on education had the benefit of comparison with his experience as a teacher and student in Mexico. In our initial interview, Boyoyo said of the United States, "I think this country gives more opportunity than other countries, to be honest. But that doesn't mean we are just perfect. That means that, probably, we are helping a little more. So I think that is something very positive in this country. But still, we are so far from giving the equal opportunity to everybody. We are still far from that. But there is more opportunity, definitely." This appreciation for opportunity in the United States was shared by everyone in the group. However, in reading the texts for our discussions together, some members were as surprised as Boyoyo to learn how greatly varied children's access to opportunity can be in America.

> I knew that there were some problems in education. But to be honest, I never thought there was so much poverty in the United States. It was a big surprise for me. When I started reading that, I was thinking that in our countries, in Latin America, that's very common. I didn't know it was that bad here! It seems like this is not true. *High Stakes* seems like a fiction book.

Boyoyo is one of those teachers who is able to not only look with a critical eye at his own classroom practice, but to talk about it in a way that creates connections to the broader topic of accountability in the schools. Boyoyo makes himself vulnerable by sharing his critique of his own performance in the classroom, but in doing so he ultimately empowers himself by creating strong connections to the bigger picture of what it means to be accountable as a teacher and as a learner.

> I think the way we assess kids, we are really, *really* behind, to be honest. I can see it when I talk with other teachers. We are working to prepare our lessons and all that, but when we talk about evaluation, we really don't put that much time on how are we going to evaluate this? Usually we are going to finish with a regular quiz or a test, but there are so many ways we could do it! And we go to classes and we discuss these ways of evaluating. We know them. But at the end, because of time issues sometimes, we don't do a good assessment. There are so many students, and we have to go so fast. We are always very superficial. I think I'm like that. I don't think I'm getting deeper in my evaluation.

Boyoyo's criticism of his own assessment and evaluation practices with his students usefully informs his view of standardized testing as the singular means of determining whether students, teachers, and schools are achieving the goals they have been charged to meet. In our fourth group discussion, he laughed as he shared his view of the ridiculousness of this narrow determiner of accountability. "It's kind of stupid, that they want to measure all the kids with the same ruler when their situations are completely different!" Earlier in the study, during our first interview, he had addressed the same narrowness metaphorically.

> They want to measure something only using one lens, when we know we need to use several lenses to be able to see the picture right. They're taking one picture! When you know you have to take pictures from different angles to really catch everything. So in other words, they take the picture from the top, and they use one lens to capture the whole picture. And the whole picture has a lot of different angles, so you have to take different pictures with different lenses.

Boyoyo's perspective offers an opportunity to look at some of the layers of accountability in more complexity. As I read and re-read his initial interview transcript, I discovered a link between Boyoyo's critique of his own assessment and evaluation practices and his snapshot metaphor for standardized-test-based accountability measures: he was critical of superficiality in both contexts. To me, his willingness to critically evaluate his own classroom assessment and evaluation strategies helped him to bring a strong, authentic voice to the critique of the standardized-test-based accountability discourse. His ability to see the need for asking the hard, essential questions in light of his own professional practices demonstrates the kind of acceptance of responsibility that genuine accountability demands.

The impact that participation in the study had on Boyoyo was what initially led me to formulate and believe in the matchbook-cover version of this study's findings. During our twelfth and final group meeting when he described how our readings and discussions had affected his sense of authority as a teacher, Boyoyo named his findings in this way:

> You know, without this information I would still be very clueless about what's going on with the standards. Because I didn't know about a lot of these things, about standardization and the tests. Before, probably I would be like, 'Uh-oh.' It's like somebody is saying, 'No, this is the way you have to work.' Okay. And I do that. And then they say, "No, now you have to work this way.' Oh, okay. Because I was not completely sure. And now I feel more secure in myself that what I am doing is, probably is not perfect but it is not that wrong. And that I don't have to follow the direction that is coming from the top when I see it is wrong. I don't need to follow that. Now I feel more secure about myself and in what I am doing. Probably that is the best thing I can do as myself, with my students, instead of trying just to follow what they are saying at the top. Because they don't know my students as I know my students.

> Talking is what this has been all about. We've had the chance to talk and express our ideas. If you don't talk, then it's for sure that *nothing* is going to happen. Talking is a wonderful tool, and it helps you to feel better! But we don't do it a lot of times because we don't have the time. So let's keep talking! Let's keep getting together, even if it's just once a month. You never know when one drop is going to make a big lake.

Teacher Participant: Alex

Alex is twenty-eight years old and she teaches in an elementary school. She is the mother of one, an infant son who was only a few months old when we began this project. She and her husband are White. I met her in 1998 when she was a student teacher and I was an instructor in her degree program. In addition to her meeting the basic criteria I had established for selecting participants, Alex brought an additional attribute to the group that I saw as beneficial for the study. She had recently earned a Masters degree in a department whose program of studies favors the use of critical theory as a lens to explain how power operates in and through institutions to reproduce social patterns. Since she came to the group already understanding the postmodern critique of "hidden" power arrangements, I saw her presence as a kind of check on my facilitation of the group process. My intent was to practice transparent facilitation by making my biases and values an overt part of our discussions; having Alex there helped me to ensure that the topic of power itself was always on the table.

Alex is in the fifth year of her career. She is now working half time, since the recent birth of her son. Alex is in her fourth year of teaching in the same full-day gifted education program that she attended as a child. She laughs in telling of this full-circle journey in education. "I always told my gifted teacher that I was going to be just like her when I grew up. And now I work with her at the same school!" That school is part of a large, urban school district. It is located in an affluent neighborhood where only 11 percent of the students qualify for free or reduced lunch (the state K-5 average is 68 percent); 77 percent of the student body is White, compared to the state average of 31 percent. The remainder of the student population is 16 percent Hispanic, 4 percent Asian, 3 percent American Indian, and 1 percent African American. At Alex's school, standardized tests are "certainly not anything that anyone really worries about that much." This is a source of conflict for her. She struggles with her sense of place and responsibility as an educator.

> While I challenge myself all the time in wondering what type of school I should work at, I often think, well, I need to be at a school where I am working with the doctors and the lawyers of the community. I need to figure out a way to educate them so that they can be... I mean, they have that voice already. People listen to them because of the color of their skin.

Frustration is a familiar feeling for Alex, because her vision of what children could and should be experiencing in school is so far away from the reality that she sees. "There are a lot of really lousy teachers out there," she said with a sigh during our tenth group session, as participants were discussing the need for genuine and meaningful measures of accountability in education. "And there are a lot of lousy teachers at my school. And so it's frustrating to me that there isn't any type of accountability for that. Because I wish that people *were* visiting them and saying, 'This is not acceptable to have your first graders in rows, listening to you talk 90 percent of the day and they're only seven years old.'" Alex's school has been labeled "exemplary" by the state, but that is not a word she uses to describe what education there has looked like to her for the past twenty years.

> So that was very hard for me, when I first got there. Just walking down the halls and seeing the cutouts up on the walls of, oh, we're learning about Africa. The *whole first grade* is learning about Africa. So there are African pots *all* over the first grade hallway, and every pot looks pretty much the same. And the desks are all in rows, and the math books that they're using are just like the math books they were using when I was there. I mean, you see very little sign of any type of progress in education since I was in elementary school.

Her vision of what school should be about is a far cry from a hallway full of identical pots and classrooms arranged in orderly rows. She credits Maxine Greene for helping her to articulate her own philosophy of what education is for.

I believe so strongly in the power of imagination and creativity for children, so if I could create one change at my school it would be to throw away this traditional approach to education—where everything has to fit in certain boxes, and we do math for an hour, and then science for an hour, and we do every single subject in one day so that everything gets so compartmentalized and watered down as a result. And try to create more of an environment for kids to create their own knowledge and to create their own understandings, rather than having their teachers tell them what those understandings are and what knowledge is.

I think when we just tell them that this is the way things are, then they grow up accepting it. And I think that's why we have such an incredible population of adults now who can't think for themselves and who don't participate whatsoever in their society, because they don't think they have any power over anything in their lives, and so they just accept what's handed to them. They don't know how to challenge it, because they've never been taught. If we want to see anything different in our society, whether that's on a micro- or macro-level, you have to be able to imagine it first. And I think kids are *capable* of it.

Frustration edges Alex's voice when she reflects on how far away the majority of her colleagues are from the arts-based model of constructivist teaching that she envisions. "The teachers at my school are stressed at the beginning of the year! 'Oh, I'm so behind, and school just started!' Well, how is that *possible*? You *know*? I mean, if you're really paying attention to where the kids are and what they bring *to* you, the idea of getting behind couldn't *exist*." This frustration with other teachers is something Alex struggles with. She describes it as one of the most challenging aspects of her professional life—the struggle to invest her faith in her colleagues and to relate with them in a respectful way.

I've only been extremely, extremely disappointed by my fellow colleagues as I've existed in my district the last five years. I felt like they were very, just, ho-hum, hum-drum, had been doing the exact same things in their classrooms that they had been doing for the last twenty-five years. And I felt, after being at this particular school that I'm at for the first year, and loving my students and loving the type of kids that I was getting to work with? That if I was going to stay there that I needed a major attitude change. Because I was just really separating myself from the other people that I was working with.

And I think about the statement in here [from Lummis's *Radical Democracy*] where it talks about this idea of radical faith, that it is at once the most natural and the most difficult thing to achieve. It's natural in that it's just, for me, getting to a basic level of just being kind! And accepting. And recognizing that the other women that I work with are there because they have really good hearts. And yeah, maybe they haven't been to school lately to have heard what the latest ideas on progressive education are, but they're still there because they're good people! And so, it's natural on that level. But then it's so difficult because I take it so seriously! And because when it comes to children I feel like they deserve *so much*! And when I see teachers sitting in the teachers' lounge, getting more worked up about who's going to bring what to the potluck next week than they are about the fact that they're spending more and more time getting ready for standardized tests, just as one example, it's *hard* to be accepting of that.

So, for me, I think the sacrifice in terms of my lack of democratic faith is that I don't get to be close to a lot of people who really are good people. And so I try every year at the end of the summer, as I get ready to go back and spend a whole year with these people, to just *soften my heart* to them. And to just remind myself that they're there, working with children, for only good reasons. They wouldn't do it otherwise!

Participation in the study appeared to be a more frustrating experience for Alex than for other members of the group. This had to do with the approach that I took with the study, an approach that Alex called an "anti-orientation" rather than a more proactive one that she would have preferred. Since my research project was to discover how parents and teachers would make sense of the accountability movement as they read and discussed critical texts and perspectives that are generally unavailable in the popular media, my first four book choices for the group focused on exploring what is happening in schools in the name of accountability. In short, I chose texts that I thought were both accessible and effective in providing a critical perspective in defining the accountability movement in education and its effects. Alex wondered if our group's time would have been better spent had we started rather than closed with Kohn's *The Schools Our Children Deserve*. She wished that our orientation had been toward reading texts for the purpose of informing our imaginations about what we did want in our public schools, rather than learning about what we didn't want—that is, about the terms and effects of the accountability movement.

How are you oriented to the subject? Orienting only in a, 'I don't want this, and I don't want this . . .' It's like an anti-orientation. Or are you looking at, 'Okay, so then what *do* I accept and what *do* I embrace? What do I believe in?' Because I know what I don't believe in. And that becomes tedious, then, when you're with kids all day, every day, because you know what you believe in and that guides your day! But that piece hasn't been explored.

I just wonder, sometimes, how necessary this kind of knowledge is. Because I feel like there's always going to be this kind of knowledge out there. So that when I've been teaching for thirty-five or forty years, there's going to be a new *Nation at Risk* letter. I don't feel like the government or the administration, especially in a school district like mine, they're never going to be the ones that take us where we need to go. And so I wonder if, by paying so much attention to them, if that's almost making it worse? Because instead, what if we would've spent the last however many months that we've been meeting together, what if instead we had started with *The Schools Our Children Deserve*? And approached it from that vein, recognizing that this is all out there, and the standardized tests are out there, but there's always going to be that something, out there.

I include Alex's critique of the process I facilitated because I think it raises an essential question. In the absence of knowledge about how accountability is currently being defined in education and about how that definition is impacting our society at micro- and macro-levels, *can* new possibilities be imagined and brought into being? It is a question I can't answer definitively, and it's one that deserves consideration. My study was built upon my personal belief that effective solutions require an intimate understanding of the problem, and that building a knowledge base for the purpose of accurately defining the problem is therefore the first step toward making change. At the same time, I appreciate Alex's readiness level for imagining other possibilities for how things like *education, achievement,* and *school success* might be defined. Indeed, her frustrations help to define the implications of this study in terms of the new questions and directions for continued research that it suggests. "So then what *do* I accept and what *do* I embrace? What do I believe in?" I can already imagine the outlines of a new research project involving community meetings in which parents, teachers, students, administrators, and other members of a community explore such questions with one another. In such an environment, words like *education, achievement,* and *school success* could be defined from the ground up.

What Alex did take away from her experience with the group came from a place that surprised her.

> The biggest thing for me has been learning from the parents. And I wasn't expecting that because I didn't know what I didn't know! I didn't know about how involved parents are, and their perspectives regarding teachers and schools and standardized testing. I was expecting more to learn just in the way that I'm used to, which is from texts. I'm so used to burying myself inside of a book and learning just through that connection. Instead, it's happened more through the human element, which is much, much more fun in a lot of ways.

If it is true that Alex's greatest professional struggle is to effect "a major attitude change" and make genuine connections with other adults in her school, this effect of participation seems significant. An experience in learning "more through the human element" from the parents in the group rather than in the text-based way she was used to strikes me as a step toward hope because it illustrates the impact of connecting in genuine ways with others. It is a step toward believing in the idea that we can and must learn from and develop trust in each other. "I was just really separating myself from the other people that I was working with," Alex had said. Yet she knows the power of connection and the impact that others' investment of faith has had in her life.

> We wouldn't continue to be teachers if it weren't for every now and again getting those thank-you letters from parents. Or from kids who are in high school now and are sending the letter back to you as an elementary school teacher. I

mean, we wouldn't keep *doing* it if we didn't see signs of that faith in us as people who are contributing to their lives! We wouldn't be going back, day after day, not with everything else that we put up with. But when we do see signs of this, it's *so beautiful* and makes you feel like you are important, and that you are contributing. That makes it worthwhile.

Teacher Participant: Mariela

Mariela teaches in an elementary school and is thirty-eight years old. She is bi-racial; her father is Hispanic and her mother is White. She is the mother of three boys, only one of whom is still in high school. Her partner, the boys' father, is Native American. All of her boys went to the same private high school, "And it's not because I'm not an advocate of public education. I'm a public school teacher. I just wanted them to go to a school where they can have faith and believe in God, and that it's okay to do that." I met Mariela through a university colleague who recommended her to me as a potential participant for my study.

Mariela is in her twelfth year of teaching in a wealthy community where "the kids do well. They'd do well if they gave them whatever program because they're very privileged kids." The typically affluent students that Mariela and Alex teach belong to the same large, urban school district as the poorer students in Julia's and Boyoyo's school. 23 percent of the students in Mariela's school qualify for free or reduced lunch, compared to the K-5 state average of 68 percent; 60 percent of the student population in this school is White, roughly twice the K-5 state average of 31 percent. The remainder of the student body is 36 percent Hispanic, 2 percent American Indian, 1 percent African American, and 1 percent Asian.

Like Alex, Mariela struggles with her sense of place and responsibility as an educator. Of her current teaching assignment, she says, "I teach a primary grade where I don't have to give these kinds of high stakes tests. I still can teach. I can be innovative and creative and do what I feel passionate about in my classroom, with my own children." She wrestles, though, with a sense of obligation to work elsewhere, with underprivileged students. At the same time she fears having to give up too much in order to do so. "Sometimes I feel like I really need to teach in another school. I have felt guilty. I still feel guilty. I feel guilty on one hand, and then I think, why would I set myself up for that disrespect and blame?" Mariela knows that teachers who work in "failing" schools don't have the freedom to teach that she currently enjoys. "As a professional I don't want to teach in a school where I have to do Four Block, and they tell me 'It's 9:06, read page...' I don't want to do that!" She exemplifies the dilemma that teachers are left to negotiate on their own: the system has created a situation in which teachers who want to work with our society's least privileged children must often do so at very real and significant cost to themselves.

The weight of responsibility that Mariela feels to children who are less privileged than the students she teaches represents the most obvious source of conflict that I could detect in her. The guilt that accompanies her decision to remain in a school where she "can be innovative and creative" seems to be rooted in personal knowledge of the realities that are experienced in some of the less affluent schools in her district. After graduating from college in December of 1990, Mariela spent a semester substitute teaching. That semester gave her a picture of public schools that contrasts sharply with the one she has developed over the past twelve years while working in her current school.

> It was interesting to see how inequitable it was. Because I subbed at a lot of the poorer schools, and... [Mariela sighs audibly]. It's just things like, 'No, you can't have paper.' There's teachers that don't have *paper*. Or one of the schools at that time was flooding with sewage. I cannot imagine that happening at *my* school! You know? That kind of stuff. And it seemed like the poorer the school was, the poorer the quality of the teachers, too. Either they get moved there, or they're just new, you know, or inexperienced. And that's not fair to say. I mean, I think you see very good things, as well. But it just seemed like there's a lot of that.

While tensions between teacher-participants in the group were not overt (like the few that had occurred between some of the parent participants in our first two meetings), there was a brief moment when Rachel, a high school teacher, laid bare a nerve for Mariela during our ninth group session. Rachel said, "How come at my school more than half of our kids are reading at a fifth grade reading level? What happened? I mean, if I get them in high school in tenth grade and they're at a fifth grade reading level, at some point they did not reach a standard that was necessary to move on to the next grade. It seems to me that a fifth grade reading level means that they were socially promoted when they shouldn't be." Mariela responded by saying,

> I think sometimes it has to do with the blame thing. In elementary school, if you're failing it's because the teacher is doing something wrong. In high school, the teacher calls you and says, 'Your kid's failing because your kid's doing something wrong.' In elementary school, if a kid hasn't learned how to read by the end of first or second grade, it's because the teachers have failed them! You know, *we've* done something wrong.

Mariela had raised this same issue months before with me, during our initial interview before the group sessions began. We had been discussing the idea that perhaps the success of the accountability movement in defining the agenda in public schools has been successful, in part, because of a predominantly female, typically compliant workforce. Mariela's comment then about how accountability is construed at different levels of schooling was a preview of the exchange between her and Rachel that would occur in the group four months later.

It's funny. Because I think that as you get older and higher in education, [the teaching workforce] shifts toward men. And the accountability shifts toward the student, rather than the teacher. If I don't teach the kids to read, it's my fault. If a high school teacher doesn't teach, then the kid didn't study hard enough. And in college, even more so.

In the context of the accountability movement, this reality—in which the perception of an educator's power and authority is gender related, increasing with the grade level that s/he teaches—is ironic. Rachel herself named that irony in the course of that same discussion during our ninth meeting. Her revelation came just a few moments after she had wondered, "What happened?" to the idea of teachers' accountability for students' learning in the years prior to high school.

Students are not assessed at a high school level. You know, you [elementary teachers] assess your kids when they come into first grade. I can tell you that in high school, we don't assess kids. We don't know what level the kids are when they come in or when they leave us. *You* do that. You assess them at the beginning and again at the end. We don't. *We* don't. We give *grades*, but what does that mean when everybody grades in a different way?

In light of Rachel's comment, it could be argued that genuine accountability for students' learning fluctuates in a directly inverse proportion to the socially-perceived degree of power and authority that a teacher enjoys: the lesser the degree of socially-perceived power and authority that a teacher enjoys, the more genuinely accountable is that teacher for students' learning, and the greater the degree of socially-perceived power and authority, the less accountable s/he is for students' academic achievement. Future research is necessary for exploring the question of whether genuine accountability for students' learning is perceived as a gender-related responsibility. "What happened?" is a wonderful and potentially productive question in the context of the accountability discourse, illuminated by that exchange between Rachel and Mariela.

Mariela was a unique participant in that her outlook on the state of education in America was almost always optimistic. She was the sole participant in the group who consistently spoke well of her school; perhaps not coincidentally, she was also the only teacher participant who reported feeling consistently respected and empowered by her administration. "I don't feel that I have to follow what somebody else is feeding to me. My own professional experience and judgment, what I've learned is taken into consideration," she said of her experience at her school. This optimistic outlook is reflected in her commentary on what she took away from participating in the study.

I think for me our readings have given me something to stand on. I think it's reaffirmed what I have always believed. You know, we're bad-mouthing public education so much that we're failing to see all the good that it does, and the good that it does in spite of everything that's handed to us all the time. So it gives me ammunition to talk. It gives me something to back up what I have seen. So, you know, I feel more confident. And it comes up a lot!

Teacher Participant: Rachel

Rachel is forty-nine years old and teaches in a high school. She is a single mother of two, with one child still in high school. Rachel is White. I met her through a colleague at my university who recommended her as a potential member for my research group. Rachel is in the seventh year of her career in teaching in the same large, urban district that employs all but one of the other teacher participants in the group. She teaches in a "failing" school that follows a predictable demographic pattern: 88 percent of the students are Hispanic, compared to the state average of 51 percent for grades nine through twelve. The remainder of the student body is 7 percent White, 3 percent American Indian, 1 percent African American, and less than 1 percent Asian. 58 percent of the students qualify for free or reduced lunch, compared to the state high school average of 38 percent.

Rachel's school failed to make "Adequate Yearly Progress"[31] during the previous school year, so the threat of some day being placed on "corrective action" by the state is one that could be realized. To Rachel, however, the threat itself is an ambiguous one, perhaps made all the more powerful for the fear of the unknown that it engenders. She gives voice to the sense of uncertainty and powerlessness that teachers face who work in "failing" schools. "The state will *take over*, and nobody knows what that means! Does that then mean that they give us to Edison? To a private . . . ? That's the great fear." The language that Rachel uses here is similar to the words Julia used to describe a recent experience at her "failing" middle school. She said, "We were told this week that they're thinking of bringing in a whole new staff if they're not pleased with us by the end of the year. Of taking us and putting us somewhere else." Teachers who have internalized the possibilities of being "given to Edison,"[32] or of being "taken" and "put" somewhere else, are clearly not speaking the same humanizing language as Mariela, whose administrator recognizes her status as a professional. "I don't feel like I have to follow what somebody else is feeding to me," said Mariela. "My own professional experience and judgment, what I've learned is taken into consideration." It is difficult to imagine a teacher who is treated as a professional ever having to voice the fear of being "given" to Edison, or being "put" at another school.

Judging from participants' experiences in this group, teachers in "failing" schools know well that their professional experience and judgment are of less value than their obedience. The truth of this in Rachel's case was demonstrated when she shared her fear of being publicly affiliated with our study group. When I asked participants in our first meeting to name any potential risks to themselves that they could imagine resulting from their participation in the study, Rachel was quick to respond.

I think that there definitely is a risk for a teacher, if you start doing something. That's been my personal experience. When you in any way rock the boat, or fragilize an administrator? Yes. You risk letters of reprimand in your files. You risk being branded as a negative person, as somebody who's not a good team player. Those are the kinds of catchwords that I've encountered. And so I think that is a risk for a teacher, at least in my case. There would be a danger if anything said here left this room.

"You risk being branded." Rachel later described the experience of having an institutional mark seared into her identity at school. "Last year I tried to go up to the administrators and talk about the ludicrousness of certain things, and I got a letter of reprimand in my file. So now, I'm quiet. I don't open my *mouth*!" The impact that this institutional rebuke for challenging authority had on Rachel explains her fear and continues to catch her off guard.

What never ceases to surprise me is how naïve I was about the system. About human nature. I mean, I should know this. It's in the books! [Laughs.] It's what makes great literature. You read about greed. You read about people's incompetence. You read about higher-ups scapegoating lower-downs. But when it happens to *you*, it's a whole different story. It never ceases to amaze me, how upset I get.

Rachel's daughter attends an "exemplary" high school in another part of town. In her school, 3 percent of the students qualify for free or reduced lunch, and the population there is 78 percent White (compared to the state high school average of 32 percent). During the course of our first interview I had quietly wondered to myself whether the discrepancy between her daughter's and her students' experience of high school posed a problem for Rachel. Finally, feeling like an intruder, I asked. My sense that this could be a tender subject for Rachel was confirmed by her response.

My kids ask me that, and that is one of the biggest problems I have at my high school. Is when my kids ask me, 'Why doesn't your daughter go to school here? Why don't you live here, Mrs. R? Why don't you send your daughter here? You don't like this school, or what?' And I tell them it's because that's where we live. That's where we bought a home. That's where she's grown up now. If it were to do over, I might do it over . . . [sighs]. But I'd never put my daughter there. [I asked why, and Rachel paused for a moment. Then she sighed again, deeply.] This is cruel. This is cruel.

Because the chances of her getting a rigorous education are higher where she is now. I think the standards are higher where she is. Undoubtedly. The standards that most of the teachers have, and just the standards set by the kids! It's not being elitist, but I'm sorry. You go to Yale or Harvard where the competition is tougher and you're going to be surrounded by more motivated, smart people than at a less competitive school. The number of people who might potentially drag you down is greater at the less competitive schools.

A few months later, during our seventh group meeting, Rachel brought up the problem of this discrepancy again. For that session participants had read the first third of Berliner and Biddle's *The Manufactured Crisis*. Rachel's unique perspective on that text was informed by her position as a teacher in a "failing" school, operating in the same district as the "exemplary" school that her daughter attends. Her perspective causes her to yearn for real accountability on behalf of her students.

> These are wonderful books, but my experience would lead me to say that the manufactured crisis exists in certain schools. I can guarantee you that it exists at my school. I live this on a daily basis. And standards . . . the school that my daughter attends doesn't need standards. It's got its standards in multiple, various other ways. But my school desperately needs standards because it's such a chaotic environment where nobody knows what anybody's doing. And the kids deserve more than that. They deserve more. The manufactured crisis and the savage inequalities in our schools reflect the inequalities in our society. I don't think we say that enough. That's the bottom line, for me. Is that the manufactured crisis exists in our lousy schools, because we have lousy schools. I mean, I teach in one. And it's not a manufactured crisis. It *is* a crisis. Because it's a crisis when kids are denied an education that they are entitled to.

Rachel's frustrations are deep, and they seem compounded by a sense of utter loneliness that she feels at her school. She called me, sounding very upset one night after having attended a professional development day at her school at the start of the school year. She shared her perspective on the day, describing the "charlatan" who had been brought in from the Midwest to motivate the teachers at her school on the topic of teaching to the state's standards and benchmarks. He was an entertaining speaker who had his audience hooked, she said, but from her perspective his message was without substance. She later went to his Website and found "antiquated" standards listed for her state and lesson plan samples for the high school that she thought were appropriate for fifth or sixth grade. "And we spent tons of money on this guy!" Rachel laughed disbelievingly. "And we bought assessment tests from him, so we're locked into him." She told me about the wave of sadness that crushed her as she sat in the audience amongst laughing colleagues, looking in vain for another face in the crowd that might tell her she wasn't alone in hearing the hollow sound of nothing coming from their motivational speaker. She said that she felt so alone. Rachel shared this experience with other participants, too, during one of our group meetings a few months later. She ended the story by asking with a desperate intensity, "With whom can you talk about reality?"

The loneliness in that question is as profound as the depth of Rachel's frustration from seeing the gross inequities that exist for the students in her district. This combination of frustration and loneliness could explain why participation in this study seemed more personally significant for her than for some of the other participants. In her final interview, when I asked if she intended to continue with the discussion group, Rachel didn't hesitate. "Yes! I have to! This is *food* to me."

> I think what's so strong about this group is that alliance between teachers and parents. Get the parents and teachers together? Oh, man! It's given me hope. That concerned people—teachers, parents, neighbors—can get together and at least talk about what's going on. Truthfully. In a dedicated, concentrated, organized fashion. Because I don't see that happen in my school community. I don't see that happening nationally, at a state level. Not real people, community people, the people who are in the schools and directly affected by this. I don't see that happening. And so it gives me hope!

Teacher Participant: Peyton

Peyton is a thirty-two-year-old elementary school teacher in her tenth year in the classroom; she has also worked at local, state, and national levels for the past six years as an education consultant. I first met Peyton in 1998 when she mentored student teachers whom I was supervising for the university. Several years later she and I taught next door to each other; her K-1 students were my fifth graders' reading buddies. In addition to meeting my selection criteria for participants, Peyton brought another attribute that I believed would enhance the trustworthiness of the study. Her expertise with group processes and with conducting text-based discussions meant, to me, that I would have a built-in check on the appropriateness of my facilitation of our group discussions.

Peyton works in a different school district than the other five teachers in the group. While her district serves an affluent community, her school is located in one of its lower-income neighborhoods. Unsurprisingly, it is one of the lowest-performing schools in the district as measured by students' standardized test scores. 58 percent of the students in her school qualify for free or reduced lunch, less than the state K-5 average of 68 percent (but over three times greater than the average number of poor students attending schools in that district's more affluent neighborhoods). 47 percent of the student body is Hispanic, compared to the state K-5 average of 52 percent. The remainder of the student population is 41 percent White, 6 percent American Indian, 4 percent African American, and 1 percent Asian.

Peyton has taught at the same school for ten years. For the first seven of those, she says she was lucky to be working with a principal whose vision for the school was firmly founded on child-centered, constructivist principles of education. She also thought that leadership at the district level in those earlier years was innovative. Ten years, however, has been long enough for her to witness what she perceives to be her school's and her district's decline, an unfortunate devolution in progressive and child-centered practices that she attributes to the unrelenting, district-wide emphases on standardizing curriculum and instruction and on producing high test scores. Where once she felt that she was a member of a genuine, vibrant community of learners devoted to the wellbeing of the students and their educational achievement, now she likens her environment to an army base camp in which competition, segregation, and disrespect are the operative norms. In describing how the current culture of her school feels to her, she says, "I envision people marching and being told what to do. Because I think people bark orders now, to the teachers. And the teachers pass it on. I mean, it's *barking* now. It's not people talking."

Her opinion that "It's the emphasis on testing that did it," seems to be borne out in the evidence she cites to describe how her school has changed in the past three years. Where once every teacher in her school spent three days at the beginning of the school year making home visits to every family represented in their classes, now parents are required to make an appointment to bring their child in to the "testing center" (as the principal called her school in a letter to parents) for a formal assessment by their teacher. Where once teachers collaborated with one another across grade levels, now there is tension and finger pointing between the grades. "The other day fourth grade teachers yelled at the third grade teachers. 'What are you doing with those kids? Why are you letting them come to fourth grade? They're not ready yet. They're not doing well on tests. If they don't pass the test, why are you moving them on?'" Where once, community members came to the school to read in the primary classrooms each year on Dr. Seuss's birthday, "We cancelled it this year. They cancelled it this year because the older kids were testing on that day." Where once Peyton felt like she "used to have a role in creating the climate at the school in terms of how teachers work together," now "professional development is all Baldrige, so we don't really have conversations any more about teaching and learning."

In response to my asking her to clarify the term "Baldrige," Peyton said, "I feel like I don't know that much about Baldrige, but it's supposed to be a *quality* way to run a school. Everything's about data folders and graphing *everything*. To me it's a business way of running it, because we call the next year's teachers our customers. We're getting our kids ready for the customers. And they're more of a product than a kid. That's how I see it."

Peyton let out a sad-sounding laugh as she recalled the good old days of her early years in the district and the distance away from children she has seen it travel over recent years.

> I didn't know what I had then. We had new people running the district who were excited about being innovative. And we did a lot of interesting things for kids, and we *talked* about the kids. We used to talk about the Ten Common Principles. People were trying to make district-wide change, trying to get people to have groups in their schools of teachers talking about *kids*.

> I feel like I've lost a school. And I feel like we've lost what was best for kids. I just can't believe it happened. I want my old school back.

She mourns the decline.

Throughout the course of this study, Peyton's anger grew. It seemed that the more she read and thought and talked about the accountability movement, the angrier she became. The growing presence of market values in the public schools (manifested, for example, in the Baldrige-style, total-quality management approach to education) is something that she found particularly deplorable. "School is just not a business!" she raged during our sixth group meeting, after we had read excerpts from Michael Engel's *The Struggle for Control of Public Education: Market Ideology vs. Democratic Values*.

> It's not about putting kids in and shooting them out the other side! But that's what businesses do. They make products and they start here and they put it through a machine and then it comes out and they all look the same! And I think it *is* all market ideology now in school. And it's making people an object versus a mind and a body and a soul and a heart. It's making them just an object.

Through our readings and discussions Peyton became more familiar with the concept of market ideology and the role it is playing in defining the education agenda in schools across the country. She sees the hand of the market in the decline of her own school and district, and it disturbs her. "We don't seem to talk about kids any more. We talk about 'student segments' instead."

The ultimate impact of Peyton's participation in this study may well be that through the processes of learning and connecting with other teachers and parents, she has discovered her anger.

> I was on a plane, going somewhere, and reading *High Stakes*. And I was just enraged. And I am somebody who, 99 percent of the time I'm just this happy person. I find the good in every situation. And I was just *angry*. I couldn't believe that in our country, and across the world, what is happening to kids and to teachers and to parents. It's just completely unacceptable. So I'm excited to talk about it and work together and find a way to do something. There's the idea that maybe just one person can change it. And I'm just starting to think of me as one person. What can I do to change it? Instead of waiting for all the teachers at my school to get lined up, you know? Maybe people will get out there if they see just one. I thought a lot about that.

As Peyton makes clear, hope resides on the other side of anger.

Notes

1. Kimberly Waggoner, and Alison Griffith, "Parent Involvement in Education," *Journal for a Just & Caring Education* 4, no. 1 (January 1998), Ideology and Experience section, ¶1.

2. Michelle Fine, "[Ap]parent Involvement: Reflections on Parents, Power, and Urban Public Schools," *Teachers College Record* 94, no. 4 (Summer 1993); Waggoner and Griffith, "Parent Involvement in Education"; Kathryn Nakagawa, "Unthreading the Ties

that Bind: Questioning the Discourse of Parent Involvement," *Educational Policy* 14, no. 4 (September 2000).

3. Carol Vincent, "Parent Empowerment? Collective Action and Inaction in Education," *Oxford Review of Education* 22, no. 4 (December 1996); Daphna Birenbaum-Carmeli, "Parents Who Get What They Want: On the Empowerment of the Powerful," *Sociological Review* 47, no. 1 (February1999); Linda Miller-Kahn and Mary L. Smith. "School Choice Policies in the Political Spectacle." *Education Policy Analysis Archives* 9, no. 50 (2001).

4. Fine, "[Ap]parent Involvement"; Vincent, "Parent Empowerment?"

5. Vincent, "Parent Empowerment?" Conclusion section, ¶1.

6. Fine, "[Ap]parent Involvement," Introduction, ¶2.

7. Claire E. Smrekar and Lora Cohen-Vogel, "The Voices of Parents: Rethinking the Intersection of Family and School." *Peabody Journal of Education* 76, no. 2 (2001): 75–100; Nakagawa, "Unthreading the Ties that Bind"; Joel Spring in Fine, "[Ap]parent Involvement."

8. Claire E. Smrekar and Lora Cohen-Vogel, "The Voices of Parents," Introduction, ¶3.

9. Vincent, "Parent Empowerment?"

10. Instrumental participation positions the parent as an object, as a means to an externally-defined end; agentic participation would position the parent as a subject, as an active participant in defining the ends and means of education and accountability.

11. In Fine, "[Ap]parent Involvement," ¶1, 3.

12. Vincent, "Parent Empowerment?" Empowerment section, ¶1.

13. Vincent, "Parent Empowerment?"

14. Fine, "[Ap]parent Involvement"; Vincent, "Parent Empowerment?"; Waggoner and Griffith, "Parent Involvement in Education"; Birenbaum-Carmeli, "Parents Who Get What They Want"; Nakagawa, "Unthreading the Ties that Bind"; Smrekar and Cohen-Vogel, "The Voices of Parents."

15. Waggoner and Griffith, "Parent Involvement in Education," Researching Families in Schools section, ¶7.

16. Vincent, "Parent Empowerment?" ¶1.

17. Fine, "[Ap]parent Involvement"; Vincent, "Parent Empowerment?"; Waggoner and Griffith, "Parent Involvement in Education"; Nakagawa, "Unthreading the Ties that Bind"; Smrekar and Cohen-Vogel, "The Voices of Parents."

18. Nakagawa, "Unthreading the Ties that Bind," Critical Discourse Analysis and the Creation of the Involved Parent section, ¶5.

19. Smrekar and Cohen-Vogel, "The Voices of Parents," ¶2.

20. e.g., Michael Apple, *Education the "Right" Way* (New York: RoutledgeFalmer, 2001); David C. Berliner and Bruce J. Biddle, *The Manufactured Crisis: Myths, Fraud, and the Attack on America's Public Schools* (Cambridge, Mass.: Perseus Books, 1995); Michael Engel, *The Struggle for Control of Public Education: Market Ideology vs. Democratic Values* (Philadelphia: Temple University Press, 2000); Stephen J. Ball, "Education Markets, Choice, and Social Class: The Market as a Class Strategy in the UK and the USA," *British Journal of Sociology of Education* 14, no. 1 (March 1993); Fine, "[Ap]parent Involvement"; Vincent, "Parent Empowerment?"; Birenbaum-Carmeli, "Parents Who Get What They Want."

21. Vincent, "Parent Empowerment?" Exceptions section, ¶2.

22. Smrekar & Cohen-Vogel, "The Voices of Parents," Introduction, ¶3.

23. Fine, [Ap]parent Involvement," The Philadelphia Story section, ¶29–30.

24. Robert McChesney and John Nichols, *Our Media Not Theirs* (New York: Seven Stories Press, 2002).

25. Fine, [Ap]parent Involvement," The Philadelphia Story, ¶29.

26. Fine, [Ap]parent Involvement"; Waggoner and Griffith, "Parent Involvement in Education"; Nakagawa, "Unthreading the Ties that Bind."

27. Evon G. Guba and Yvonne S. Lincoln, "Competing Paradigms in Qualitative Research" in *Handbook of Qualitative Research*, edited by Norman K. Denzin and Yvonne S. Lincoln (Thousand Oaks, Calif.: Sage, 1994), 105.

28. Guba and Lincoln, "Competing Paradigms in Qualitative Research," 113, emphasis in original.

29. Note that participants are introduced in the context of their lives as they were at the time of this study (i.e., ages of children, roles in the schools, etc.) Also, names of participants and their schools have been changed.

30. School demographic information comes from <http://www.greatschools.net> (3 Jan 2003).

31. Adequate Yearly Progress (AYP) "represents the annual academic performance targets in reading and math that the state, school districts and schools must reach to be considered on track for 100% proficiency by school year 2013–14. AYP is part of state and federal statute." <http://www.ped.state.nm.us/div/acc.assess/accountability/index. html>

32. "Founded in 1992, Edison Schools Inc. now serves more than 132,000 public school students in over 20 states across the country through its whole school management partnerships with districts and charter schools; summer and after-school programs; and achievement management solutions for school systems" <http://www.edisonproject.com/ home/home.cfm>.

CHAPTER 5

Research Findings:
Tracing a Path Toward Hope

Through introducing the parents and teachers who were the study group participants in Chapter 5, I simultaneously introduced a simple and fundamental finding: *The energy that is generated when people gather purposefully to talk with each other—to find and to create connections through focused discussion of important texts and ideas—is transformative. This power of focused conversation is potentially revolutionary.* I see this transformative potential manifested in the journey between frustration and hope that the members of our study group helped me to see. Though the reasons for it differed, frustration was a common denominator for every person in the group. Yet because of their experience in reading about aspects of the accountability movement and in discussing ideas about education together, participants were able to say some significant things: *Now I can stand up—It's challenging the way I think—I feel empowered—It's given me hope—It's given me something to stand on—I'm starting to think of me as one person who can change it—I don't have to follow the direction that is coming from the top when I see it is wrong.*

These are important statements because they represent the fact that a difference was made; and the fact that a difference was made means that possibilities exist for redefining reality in our schools. While participation did make a difference for individual members in the group, the broader and deeper value of this study extends beyond the impact that it had in the lives of individual participants. That significance is in how their words reveal the workings of power within what Michel Foucault would call the "panopticon" of the public school system—making it *visible* to those who live and work inside of it. I will reserve the next chapter for defining and discussing both the theoretical lens of panopticism that I am using to explain my findings and what I think of as the larger significance of my research. For now, I will return to participants' experience of the study so that the path toward my findings can be traced, and the journey I have described for each person—from frustration to the hopefulness that I found—can be examined.

That journey is one that becomes more visible from a distance. I am not confident that all participants, for instance, left the experience at the end of our group discussions able to see the reasons for optimism that they helped me to identify. Though my participation in the group allowed me to witness the transformative potential of focused dialogue, the significance of that realization became increasingly clearer over the subsequent months of data analysis. In the next chapter I will return to this aspect of the significance of the study. For now, though, knowing that the optimism of what I learned through this research project is where I arrived, I will backtrack through the themes that emerged from discussions and interviews and retrace the steps that I took in getting here.

Theme #1: Disconnection and Competition
The Accountability Movement as an Instrument of Social Disconnection and Personal Disempowerment

An Absence of Shared Understandings Contributes to a Sense of Disconnection

How do teachers and parents make sense of the accountability movement? This was the question that framed the study. Though their words varied, each member of the group ultimately gave the same answer to it: "sense" cannot be made of the accountability movement. For these participants, accountability in schools is fundamentally without meaning as a concept because it is not grounded in common definitions or understandings of just what it is that Americans value enough to want to account for educationally, through our public schools. "What does accountability *mean*?" asked Rachel. "It's an empty concept. It's just a word. It doesn't mean anything because nobody is really being held accountable to anything! It's an empty concept that doesn't mean anything."

In a number of ways, the members of this group pointed the way to this basic discovery about the accountability movement—that the flurry of activity taking place in schools across the country in the name of accountability is being mandated by those who have usurped the authority to define for the American people what is *good*, educationally speaking. This presumption of what I have come to think of as definitional authority (a concept that I will define more thoroughly later in this chapter) has taken place with neither the input nor the consent of the governed. "We have to *all* define the common good," said Sarah. She continued:

> The question is, what is *good*? What is it that makes a teacher good? What is it that makes a good school? What is it that makes a good place for my kid to be? We all have different definitions of the common good. And I think that's the

difficulty in establishing what accountability is. Is that we all have a different picture of what's good.

Peyton's perspective on this lack of agreement over what is educationally good has to do with what it means to teach. "It's a personal value," she says. "The teacher next to me may not have the same opinion as I do. And so what I value from kids and what I expect to get from kids, what is important to me, may not be the same next door." This becomes problematic when the perception of teaching ability ("goodness") is attached in a way that favors officially sanctioned but not commonly shared values. Peyton explained the problem in this way:

> The teacher next door may be drilling and skilling her kids, and they may be acing the standardized test but arguing and fighting on the playground and being ugly to each other. But some people are going to look at her as doing her job really well because she's meeting the expectations that the businessmen put out. Her kids are doing well on tests. But when I get the kids and they're fighting and being cruel to one another, am I going to trust that she did her job? Well, first we have to define what the job was.

Peyton understands that the assignment of value is the province of those who have presumed the authority to define. With neither a commonly shared understanding about "what the job is" nor opportunities for members of a school community to debate and define what is true of good teaching, "some people are going to look at her as doing her job really well because she's meeting the standards that the businessmen put out." Sarah's and Peyton's remarks about the absence of shared definitions point to the fact that, although local control has been a cherished tenet of ideology in this land since the Articles of Confederation were law, community members do not typically have access to that fundamental right when it comes to defining what is good in education. They are not consulted when it comes to identifying what they want "their" neighborhood schools to be accountable *for*. Mariela illustrated the problem with an example. "I can't draw," she said. "And I try and try, but I'm just not an artist. But that's not important to anybody else. It's not important enough to get assessed by these tests, whether you can draw or not. But I know a lot of kids who can't read very well but are good artists!" The parents of "those" children have not likely been invited often—or ever—to participate in establishing with other parents, teachers, and community members just what it is that they want "their" public schools to do for their kids.

In the absence of shared meanings for words like *education, achievement,* and *school success*—or perhaps more importantly, in the absence of productive public debate over them—parents, students, educators, administrators, and other community members are disconnected at a fundamental level, and not only from each other. Without having participated in the democratic work of debating such concepts and negotiating acceptable compromises over their meanings and their implementation, the people *in* public schools are also distanced from a sense of ownership over their own activities of teaching and learning. The accountability movement, in this light, can be seen as an effective instrument of social disconnection and personal disempowerment. "The reason for learning these basic skills is to create!" exclaimed Peyton. "But there is no connection. We've lost the big picture." Tessa put the problem of disconnection for students in Orwellian terms. "I think they just want to try to kind of program our kids like robots, so that way when they get out in the world, they'll just be, like, 'Okay, tell me what to do. How do I dress?' So that way they can have this perfect world." The accountability movement as an embodiment of totalitarianism in American society becomes an arguably accurate characterization when the experiences of teachers in "failing" schools are considered. During our tenth group meeting in mid-September, Boyoyo shared with the group his experience of an inservice session that his new principal had conducted earlier in the week. His description of the message that his school leader delivered to her staff left others in the group literally gasping in dismay.

> Well, the inservice was just to emphasize that we are on probation and that we are going to receive visits, and that we need to have all the standards, they have to be right there so I can see them. The kids have to know exactly what the standards are for. And they say no free time. There is *no* free time. 'I don't want to hear that somebody is having free time. We don't have time for that. Zero free time. Don't be creative. Don't risk. Just go with what we are saying. This is what we need to do. Period. Don't start to create new things. Follow the rules of the game.'

In the absence of debate and shared definitions for the appropriate ends and means of education in their neighborhood schools, parents are effectively disempowered as the guardians of their children's educational welfare. No parent in our study group wished for their child what Boyoyo's principal had defined as a necessary reality for all of the children in her school. Selena likened the definition of teaching within the context of the accountability movement to factory work, particularly for teachers in schools that serve poor and minority students. "It's going to turn out so that teachers are going to be nothing but piece makers. You do a belt, you do a buckle, you do this, you do that. And that's my fear." Selena's factory metaphor for the work of teaching is similar to Sarah's image, described below, of children who are pulverized with knowledge. Both depict the processes of teaching and learning as beyond the definitional authority of the people doing the work.

> We can smash all the information in the kids at an early age if we want so that they'll test well, or more competitively with other nations that do smash educational goals into them at a very early age. But is that *wise?* That's my big question, as a parent. Is how competitive do I want my kid to be, just for the sake of competition? And is it wise to try to smash stuff into kids when they're not ready to be smashed?

chronic, and pervasive, but occasional and even seemingly unavoidable lateness can also be affected. Ferro (2003), for example, reports on a seemingly innocuous lateness in a normally punctual patient caused by a train delay due to some acting out of a drug addict on the train that caused the delay. Further inquiry led to her fears of her more violent emotions getting out of control. Ferro connected this with her violent reactions to any interruption of the analytic schedule, emotions that could only be contained in her fantasy by a padded cell. Such occasional lateness can often enough provide the context in which transference dynamics first come to light. Kaplan's (1990) patient, arriving late for the first time, explained that he had been delayed by the subway train having stopped for twenty minutes between stations. When the analyst inquired about this delay, it led to a testy and somewhat persecutory protest, that, as it turned out, masked feelings of enjoying the analysis that he fantasized as being contrary to what one was supposed to feel in analysis and, in his transference-based expectation, would draw a negative response from the analyst.

Barrows (1999) likewise reported on her patient who had to travel for an hour on trains and buses to get to the sessions and was usually on time. When, about two-and-a-half years into her analysis, she arrived a few minutes late, flustered and apologetic, she referred to having difficulty leaving her surgeon's office because he might think her ungrateful. The analyst related this to her possible feeling that the analyst might think her ungrateful in relation to missing some sessions. The patient expressed her regret at planning on missing her sessions in the following week because she was going to visit her boyfriend, who had moved out of town for that year. Also, the doctor had been talking with her about possibly having children. As Barrows concluded, "I interpreted that she seemed to think that I might not realise that she felt that she needed to see her boyfriend and to talk to the doctor about the possibility of having children. I suggested that she was afraid that I would be hurt or angry with her for missing her sessions or even for thinking of having children and for leaving me out" (556). I would also suggest that this episode also indicates some problematic aspects of the patient's therapeutic alliance (Meissner 1996b) insofar as her behavior seems to suggest unresolved difficulties in the areas of her autonomy and freedom—she seemed to lack a degree of autonomy to assert herself and her needs (specifically her wish-need to visit her boyfriend and to have children independently of the analyst) and did not allow herself the freedom to express her feelings to either her surgeon or her analyst.[1]

My woman physician-patient (introduced in chapter 4) had the additional burden of having to drive for half an hour to get to my office and was almost always apologetic and remorseful about coming late. When I inquired about ognizes the destructive and disconnective effects of competition, she sees herself caught in the very trap that she detests.

> I don't want to go in [to a parent-teacher conference] and have you tell me, 'Johnny's drawn beautiful pictures and has written many good pieces,' and then hand me a report card on the way out the door. It doesn't give me a reward. I want a reward for him. Isn't that awful? See, I think that's a moral failing on my part.

With unflinching honesty, Sarah time and again laid bare the ways in which amoral familism is manifested in her life. A number of comments and stories from other participants suggests that this self-interested phenomenon is present, in varying degrees, in most people's lives. In my case, I shared with the group my reasons for choosing to teach in the district that I did three years earlier rather than in a "failing" school in my own district: in addition to wanting to teach in a school where I already knew many people (because of my work there as a supervisor for student teachers), the money was significantly better. The presence of amoral familism was also reflected when Mariela said,

> The tests aren't such a big thing for our school! I almost feel like I have the least amount of passion toward this topic of anybody in the group, maybe because I have the least high stakes. But I can see where everybody else is coming from, with your different situations. I just am very glad that I don't have to feel as passionate as some of you, in your situations, have to.

It was present in Sarah's frustrated realization that "I don't know the answer—how, if at all, do we make a difference—except for our own kids." It was present in Ana's activism on behalf of only Native American children, and also in Alex's observation that "As teachers, I think that's what we find refuge in, too. We close the door and we just look out for our own kids." The terms by which school reform has been defined for over two decades encourages a school culture in which parents, teachers, and administrators must be singularly devoted to the project of looking out for their own.

Teachers in our group spoke frequently of "closing the door and doing our own thing" as a form of resistance. From the perspective of combating amoral familism at the level of school culture, however, this is an ultimately misguided and ineffective strategy; it simply compounds the isolation that teachers already experience at school. Whether the words were Rachel's ("So who do you speak with? With whom can you talk about reality?"), Julia's ("It can be a very lonely profession, especially if you don't feel like the support is out there"), or Alex's ("My work environment is so, so lacking in terms of creating any type of space for dialogue amongst teachers"), isolation appeared to be a common trait in the working lives of many of the teachers in our group. Alex's observation about teachers choosing to just close their doors illustrates one way in which teachers themselves contribute to their sense of disconnection and isolation. She names an important problem with the isolation-as-resistance approach, in that we end up "just look[ing] out for our own kids." We end up subscribing ever more thoroughly to amoral familism as the operative norm in our schools. Noam Chomsky's description of the crucial strategy employed by "the world of private power" to correct the problem of excessive democracy is pertinent here, as it was in Chapter 3.

> Much of the right-wing fervor behind the drive to destroy Social Security and public schools, and to block efficient and popular programs of public health care, reflects the understanding that such programs rely on values that must be extirpated: the natural and deep-seated values of sympathy and solidarity, the conviction that one should care about what happens to the child or disabled widow on the other side of town. These pernicious ideas must be driven from the mind. People must be atomized and separated if they are to be ruled by the responsible men, for their own good.[2]

Amoral familism's disconnective, self-absorbed outlook is perpetuated by the competitive spirit of the accountability movement. I recently attended a staff meeting at a middle school in which the principal explained to her teachers why their school had been judged deficient by the state in terms of achieving Adequate Yearly Progress (AYP) the previous school year: they had missed reaching their expected achievement target in one of five areas. Then, this principal—a person who strikes me as being genuinely warm and caring and passionate about students' welfare—quietly said with an exultant grin, "But another school in our district missed all *five!*" While an air of despondency was nearly palpable in the room during the principal's explanation of their own school "failure," this announcement seemed to be received gratefully by most of the teachers. They were eager to know, "Which one?" Their apparent enjoyment of the news about the other school's "failure" struck me as a sad confirmation of the success that the "responsible men" in the accountability movement are currently enjoying. I sat in that meeting, listening to Chomsky's line echoing silently in the laughter around me. "People must be atomized and separated if they are to be ruled by the responsible men, for their own good."

Disconnection Between the Public and Their Schools Is Fostered by the Media

In the context of the accountability movement, it is interesting to wonder just what the "responsible men" are willing to hold *themselves* accountable for. With over nine million children living in America without health insurance at the time of this writing,[3] for example, the concept of accountability appears to be one that has been selectively applied over the years. Kate came to our second meeting outraged at this reality after reading about the punitive effects of high stakes testing on poor, African American students in northern Louisiana. "Where is everyone accountable here?" she demanded. "And *how is it okay* for

Johnny to come in to school with no teeth, or rotting-out teeth? We're not even meeting the basic *physical* needs of the students!" I voiced my own indignation during that meeting in response to the same text. "And the sky falls down because a test is missing. The sky doesn't fall down because there are cockroaches and mice in the classroom. How are we defining 'unacceptable school'? What is accountability? We're closing 'unacceptable schools,' but who gets to define what 'unacceptable' is?"

While the origin of that definition may not lie with the media, it is certain that the mainstream media play a major role in determining popular perceptions of school success and failure. In a journalistic era in which the determination of newsworthiness is often profit-dependant, this is a problematic reality. Boyoyo shed light on that problem when he described the impact that media treatment of the accountability movement had on him, in the past.

> If I would not be here [in this study group], to a lot of things I would say, 'It's not that bad.' It's like you are trapped in these big lies. It's the media, again, is playing with the politicians. It's a game from the power. And the media is playing with us! We are not looking to the reality, because nobody is showing that reality. Nobody is giving that. It's a big lie, and they cover the big lie in a very good way.

The values of disconnection and competition are nurtured through the popular media's treatment of accountability in the schools. Boyoyo's remark that "we are not looking to the reality, because nobody is showing that reality" goes a long way toward explaining the lack of popular resistance to the imposed definitions of accountability under which students, parents, and educators are now living. "If I would not be here, to a lot of things I would say, 'It's not that bad. It's like you are trapped in these big lies." Boyoyo's words are echoed in Rachel's observation that thanks to the media, "we've lost our perception of reality as humans, as a society." This charge has merit, from Mariela's perspective:

> I think it's the media that is making us think that things are falling apart. It's not from personal experience! People rate their own schools, their own teachers very highly. It's the system that they don't rate highly. You do *see* the effect that teachers had on your kid, and the effect the school has had on your own child. And you've *seen* how much they grow, but all you *hear* is how horrible it is out there. And so I think faith seems to be based on what people are *hearing* rather than what they're experiencing.

Score one for the "responsible men."

Theme #2: A Crisis of Faith

People Doing the Work of Teaching and Learning Are Not Worthy of the Public Trust

A second theme emerged through the course of our group discussions that, in addition to the theme of disconnection and competition, also addresses the question of how teachers and parents make sense of the accountability movement together. Simply stated, this theme centers on the idea that children and teachers cannot be trusted. The problem with this, according to Alex, is that faith is the very reason that public schools are able to exist. She explains,

> You have to believe in the goodness of other people if you're handing your children over to them, to spend every day with them! And I think what's threatening public schools right now is a lack of faith. So that they *don't* trust the teacher any more, that they're sending their child off to. And so instead, the state has to come in, or the district has to come in, and say, 'This is how you're going to spend the time with these children.' Because we don't trust. Because we don't have that faith.

Alex's idea that "faith is how public schools are able to exist" represents an end point in our group discussions on the topic of faith. Before getting to that point, however, many participants shared stories over the course of several group meetings about the lack of trust and respect for teachers and students that they were experiencing in their school environments. In discussing the accountability movement as a manifestation of a crisis of faith in children, Sarah referred to the position espoused by Abigail Thernstrom, an "accountability" proponent who served on the Massachusetts State Board of Education. (Her essay in support of state-sanctioned standards and standardized testing is included in *Will Standards Save Public Education?* as a rebuttal to Deborah Meier's critique of them. Because that text includes arguments both for and against standards from a variety of leaders in education, "the little red book" was a favorite for many members of the group.) Sarah referenced Thernstrom's essay in addressing what she sees as a general attitude of disrespect for children in American society.

> Earlier we were talking about, in this book, the red book, that we don't really believe in kids. You know, that woman, the Thernstrom woman, saying that kids really have no value. She said something like, 'Who do they think should control the classrooms? Do you think we should get ideas from even the *students*?' Like that was the most hideous idea in the world! To imagine that any good ideas could come from students. That they're nothing. That they should never play a role in their own education. They're not worth our faith. And to

me, that's what the whole issue is. We don't have faith in our children, who are our future.

An exchange between Peyton and Alex illustrated another perspective on the crisis of faith in children that is manifested in today's accountability movement in education. During our fifth group meeting, I used a series of excerpts from Michael Engel's *The Struggle for Control of Public Education: Market Ideology vs. Democratic Values* as the basis for that night's text-based discussion. In one of these excerpts, Engel had written that "the most creative, challenging, and inspiring visions of what U.S. public education could be have always been rooted in a democratic value system . . . the people were to be ends, not means; subjects, not objects; and creators, not machines."[4] In making sense of the phrase "ends, not means," Peyton said, "What that means to me is that kids now are just there to give us high test scores and to get us funding. It's like kids are working for us to keep our schools at a certain percentile, versus us kind of working for them." Alex added,

> On a larger perspective, also, it's making sure that those kids not only do what they're supposed to do for us in school, but when they leave school that they do what they're supposed to do also, in terms of making sure that certain people stay the garbage truck drivers and the fast food workers and that certain people stay the doctors and the lawyers to maintain the status quo in our society.

I do not mean to suggest here that a crisis of faith in children was precipitated by the accountability movement. That lack of trust and respect is older than the recent emphasis on standardized test performance as our society's method of choice for defining and measuring educational achievement. People who are familiar with the typical middle school and high school arrangement, for example, in which teachers see as many as 150 students a day in classrooms that were designed with efficiency in mind (rather than, say, collaborative exploration), will appreciate Alex's comment about her first year of teaching, five years ago:

> In middle school, what I saw time and time again was, now they're thrown into these classes with thirty to thirty-five other kids, where most days they don't ever hear the sound of their own name. And then they start to understand the bigger picture, that nobody's thinking about them any more. And it's *not* about them any more. And they shut down as a result.

Group members spoke, too, of the evidence they saw that illustrated a crisis of faith in educators. An example that came up repeatedly from the teachers in our group was the existence of "canned curricula" with scripted lessons that communicate on a daily basis the message that teachers are incompetent. This was certainly the idea that I took away from my Everyday Math "training" as a fifth grade teacher, when I learned that the program was organized so well that "a monkey could teach it."

Peyton described another way that teachers get the message that they are incompetent and untrustworthy. In reflecting upon the lack of trust that she has observed at her school, she said, "I was just writing about the idea of trust, and wondering why we don't have it anymore within our schools. I was thinking about the idea that we have to sign in for *every single meeting*. It didn't used to be that way." Peyton finds evidence of the absence of trust at her school in the "policing, literally, of every, little, tiny thing." In addition to being made to sign in at every school meeting that she attends, she notes, "I get these memos that the secretary has to initial my folders, confirming that I've put my students' pictures in." Such monitoring mechanisms make it clear that teachers cannot be trusted to take care of their responsibilities and to perform competently on their own. Administrative efforts, particularly in schools that serve disadvantaged children and families, appear to be relentlessly focused on watching and monitoring teachers, rather than on promoting a school culture in which faith and trust are nurtured, responsibilities are shared, and the challenge of high expectations (a challenge that is complete in its anticipation of mistakes and failures as necessary and natural elements of growth) is welcomed. Like the existence of curricula that render teachers unnecessary, this monitoring focus provides evidence of an assumption that they are unworthy of the public trust. In the discussion excerpt below, Sarah points out the social cost of that distrust; she also suggests a benefit that a climate of distrust may offer the "responsible men" who have defined the terms of accountability in our public schools.

Without that trust in each other, our society is deeply undermined. We have to trust each other. And they *love* that we don't trust each other, because then we trust *them*. It's like a science fiction thing! That we will bow to *them*, and trust *them* to know what's right!

Echoes of Orwell. They begin to make sense when viewed through the perspective of Foucault's theory of panopticism. This will be the focus of the next chapter.

The Addendum: A Conversation about Teachers, Trust, and Totalitarianism in Schools

We heard these Orwellian echoes frequently from each other in our discussions as well as from sources outside of our group. A friend who teaches in an elementary school gave me a copy of the "welcome-back" letter that her principal had sent out in early August, prior to the start of the school year. Attached to the letter was a strip of paper about three inches high, entitled "Addendum." The following text of that addendum is reprinted here as it appeared in the original.

After the convocation, which ends at approximately 10:15 a.m. you will immediately return to [School] where we will go over school business until between

12:00 and 12:30. You will then be release [sic] for lunch and come back to [School] to meet with grade levels to work on your curriculum mapping. Attendance will be taken at the beginning of the meeting.

I was curious to learn what teachers and parents in our group would make of this note in the context of the other texts we had been reading, so I used it as the basis for a text-based discussion in one of our meetings. It sparked a lively and lengthy discussion, much of which I include below for several reasons. One, I want to re-create in a small way the flavor of those twelve group sessions so that readers can more fully envision the context of the study, the dynamic that existed amongst the members of our group, and (for purposes of helping to establish a critical sense of trustworthiness in these findings) my facilitation of these group discussions. Two, I want to remove myself from the position of being "between" readers and the study group members for a moment by allowing these parents' and teachers' words to be experienced in the context in which they occurred. Although my selection of this excerpt still places me in that filtering position, my hope is that an immersion in the group's conversation will invite a sense of vicarious participation so that readers may gain a more intimate, less filtered understanding of our group process and of its members. My final reason for including it is to illustrate teachers' and parents' perspectives on this second major theme that emerged from our discussions: the absence of faith in those who are doing the work of teaching and learning in our public schools. The following excerpt is taken from our study group's eighth session together.

> Kaia: A teacher friend of mine showed me this, and I just thought, you know, I've got some people who should see this. She had received from her principal a back-to-school letter that said, okay, this is the first day back, these are all the things you'll be doing, this is what our agenda looks like for the first week. And then this was included in the packet as an addendum to the letter that had been written. This was re-typed exactly as it appeared in the original.

> *Addendum: After the convocation, which ends at approximately 10:15 a.m. you will immediately return to [School] where we will go over school business until between 12:00 and 12:30. You will then be release for lunch and come back to [School] to meet with grade levels to work on your curriculum mapping. Attendance will be taken at the beginning of the meeting.*

> I'm curious what your response is to that.

> Elena: It's just so cold!

> Selena: And I mean, the next thing is, where's the salute?

> Sarah: Well, it's pretty condescending, too, saying, we don't trust you enough so we're going to take attendance.

Alex: And they didn't even spell-check it! [Laughs.] "You will then be *release?*" [Group laughter.] That's *terrible!* That's so unprofessional! [Laughs.]

Kaia: What else do you see?

Sarah: Well, school business. It's so regimented. So inflexible to allow people to really connect. Like you were talking about, Peyton, really having a chance to connect.

Alex: "You will *immediately* return . . ."

Mariela: And it's not that you will meet with your grade level to work on what you need to work on for your grade, but this curriculum mapping. Whatever the hell that is.

Peyton: I like that they get to be *released* for lunch. Or release. [Group laughter.]

Alex: Right.

Peyton: Like the cages will be opened for the animals to go out. And immediately come back.

Kaia: What is *released* in life? That business about being released just pulled me, too. I mean, I really started thinking, when do we use the word, to "release" something? You know, like you *release* a passenger pigeon.

Mariela: Kids are released for recess. It's, they're free of school. [Laughs.] They're released for the summer.

Peyton: But we're in control of them, to release them.

Mariela: When we release them we don't have them under control any more. Yeah. Control.

Kaia: So anyway, what relationships, what connections do you draw between this little addendum and the things that we've been reading for the past three months?

Sarah: That teachers are looked down upon. They're not respected enough to be considered competent players in the whole game.

Alex: That about sums it up!

Selena: It's like a factory. You know, you do this and that . . . It's all business. It's a factory. You do this, you have your break, then, yeah. This is what you're going to do. This is your goal.

Sarah: Scripting everything.

Selena: You clock in, you clock out. That's what it is! It's a factory.

Mariela: Well, and it doesn't feel to me like there's any, like, whoever wrote this obviously doesn't have any faith in the teachers. You *have* to do this, and we *will* take attendance. If there's something else that's more important that comes up that has to do with your job or whatever, I think we should be trusted to say, 'You know, I *couldn't* attend the meeting. I had to deal with a kid!' Or whatever else there might be that might happen. And then what happens if you're not there and they took attendance? Are they going to dock you?

Selena: See, and I don't even like the word *work* on your curriculum mapping. It's, once again, my factory. I don't like the word. I would like the word plan, because plan involves discussion, dialogue. This is work. You know, get that doggone hammer and . . .

Peyton: I was just thinking about the person who wrote this, how much leeway they left themselves. That the convocation will end at *approximately* 10:15. [Someone gasps, someone laughs.] And the business will end somewhere between 12:00 and 12:30. So *we* get to determine and have all the leeway we need. *But,* we'll take attendance the second we decide we're starting. And we'll make sure that you come back as soon as we are done.

Kaia: Immediately.

Peyton: Yeah. Immediately. After we're done. *Around* whenever we feel we're ready to be finished.

Mariela: I wonder if you'll have time for a pee break before you have to leave the school, to get to wherever else you have to be. [Laughs.] My son's in the army, and this is *exactly* the kind of document you get from them. [Laughs.] 'Today *this* is what you'll . . .' You know, they sound exactly the same. 'Deal with it.'

My suggestion that totalitarianism has replaced local control as the operative organizational structure in education appears to have some merit in a variety of school settings. The school context for this addendum is in a middle-class community where extremes of wealth and poverty are not typical; parent involvement is relatively strong in the forms of volunteerism in classrooms, attendance at curriculum nights and parent-teacher conferences, and the existence of an active Parent Teacher Association. In this solidly middle-class environment, a totalitarian presence in the school is illustrated in the example of an addendum pronouncing that "teachers will be release[d]" and "attendance will be taken." That presence is more strongly evident in the "failing" school in which Boyoyo and Julia teach, however. There, the principal has the authority to declare, apparently without consequence or concern for backlash from her community, "I don't want to hear that somebody is having free time. We don't have time for that. Don't be creative. Don't risk." It is hard to imagine the same admonition being so blithely delivered to the teachers of society's most privileged children.

Still, even those teachers are not exempt from the imposition of externally derived mandates. Mariela (who teaches in a school that serves an affluent community and who enjoys a level of autonomy and respect beyond that of most other teachers in the group) spoke of controls being dictated from above that influence her autonomy in being able to decide how to best spend the time that she has with the students in her classroom.

> Sometimes I'm forced to do things with students that take up so much time, and I have to do them to be accountable to somebody. And it's hard for me to give up the time that I would rather be using to give *myself* information. But to gather some information for somebody else that I'll never see again, never use again, it won't be useful to me to teaching these students or to finding what their next step is. So *time* is a big problem for me because people don't have faith in what I'm doing.

The degree of external control over teachers' decisions about how to spend time with their students appears to be linked to the degree of affluence that exists in the communities they serve. At least, this was the case for the teachers in this group. The phenomenon that these participants revealed from a variety of socioeconomic perspectives is the inverse relationship that exists between faith and control. The lesser the faith that we have in teachers' and students' abilities to do their work well, the greater the need to impose external definitions and controls on the processes of teaching and learning. Selena illustrates this relationship with her factory metaphor, through which she envisions school workers being told, "This is what you're going to do. This is your goal." Sarah's perspective on the relationship between faith and control prompted her to comment on the existence of prescribed standards for teaching and learning.

> I think that with the whole idea of having standards, the implication is that we don't have faith in the abilities of our teachers—and our school system in general—to be able to do good for our students. So we have to bring in standards from outside, to tell them what is good. Because they're not well-educated enough, committed enough, willing to sacrifice enough to be able to establish standards independently.

This comment points to an important issue: the accountability focus in public schools is on standards, testing, and other means of surveillance, not on the underlying lack of faith in children and teachers that is manifested in that surveilling gaze. Even resistance to the accountability movement has followed this pattern. Across the country, parents, educators, students, and other community members have mobilized under the banner of organizations like fairtest.org and the Educator Roundtable to protest the inappropriate uses of standardized tests; professional associations as diverse as the National Council of Teachers of English and the American Psychological Association have issued position statements on the topic of fair testing practices. These kinds of protest and activism are essential. My point here, however, is that both advocates and opponents of the accountability movement have tended to focus their attention on promoting or critiquing strategies of control and coercion rather than on examining the underlying condition of distrust identified by these participants. As a result, there appears to be a near-exclusive focus on extrinsic motivations and justifications for teaching and learning in today's public schools.

Control/Coercion vs. Trust/Faith: The Impact of Extrinsic Motivators on Performance

Decades of research findings about the detrimental impact of an extrinsic orientation to motivation make it clear that the "responsible men's" approach to school reform by means of control and coercion effectively prescribe school failure as the result of their accountability efforts. It is worth taking a moment to consider here, in the context of participants' exploration of the lack of faith in teachers and children that the accountability movement evidences, what decades of research reveal about how extrinsic motivation strategies affect performance in the classroom.

Alfie Kohn[5] presents compelling evidence regarding the detrimental effects of extrinsic motivators on intrinsic motivation. Extrinsic motivators in schools (that is, externally imposed rewards and sanctions for children's and adults' performances in classrooms and administrative offices) take a variety of forms: from letter grades, gold stars, and pizza parties to bonuses for "exemplary" schools and designations of "corrective action" for others. The following are a few of the findings summarized by Kohn regarding the impact of extrinsic motivation on school performance:

- People (children and adults alike) who receive an extrinsic motivator for doing something they initially found interesting become less interested in the activity itself and require more and better rewards for subsequently engaging in the activity.
- Extrinsic motivators are very effective in the short term at producing compliance. They are ineffective at making any long-term difference in attitudes and behaviors.
- Extrinsic rewards usually improve performance only at very simple tasks, and even then they typically improve only quantitative performance.
- Anything presented as a prerequisite for something else comes to be seen as less desirable. Writes Kohn, "'Do this and you'll get that' automatically devalues the 'this.'"
- People who participate in an activity where the stakes are raised (i.e., when extrinsic motivators are used), are less creative and do work of poorer quality than do those who participate in an activity for its own sake.
- Intrinsic motivation is eroded not only by the use of rewards. Our internal motivation suffers when we are threatened, watched, forced to work un-

der a deadline, controlled, made to compete against other people, and expecting to be evaluated. "In fact," writes Kohn, "any time we are encouraged to focus on how well we are doing at something—as opposed to concentrating on the process of actually doing it—it is less likely that we will like the activity and keep doing it when given a choice."[6]

It is instructive to contrast the list of demotivators above with another list from Spence Rogers. He names five things that human beings must feel in order to be intrinsically motivated: we must feel safe; we must feel valued; we must feel smart, capable, and creative; we must feel autonomous; and we must feel enjoyment.[7] Rogers' list is related to Abraham Maslow's theory of a "hierarchy of needs,"[8] which states that individuals do not perceive the presence of a "higher" need until the demands of the prior level have been satisfied. Peyton voiced this reality in explaining why she thought more teachers were not actively resisting harmful accountability mandates.

> It feels *hard* to go bigger when our basic needs aren't being met, when every time we talk about this we can put it within our own context. Because *we're* not being trusted. *We're* not safe. We're not any of those things. So if we're not working safely within our own school and in our own *classroom*—which is the teaching, as hard as that is in itself—how do we go big?

It would seem that students and teachers are not in a position to *care* about achieving "academic excellence" unless they feel that they are safe, valued, capable, autonomous, and able to enjoy their work. In light of what has been known for decades about the effects of extrinsic motivators on human beings, it would seem that the distrust, coercion, and control that characterize the accountability movement in education are prescriptions rather than cures for the school failure that it ostensibly set out to rectify. According to Kohn, our internal motivation suffers when we are threatened, watched, forced to work under a deadline, controlled, made to compete against other people, and expecting to be evaluated. Perhaps the "responsible men" read Kohn's *Punished by Rewards*, too. It seems as logical an explanation as any to explain the dovetail fit between this list of demotivators and the defining features of the accountability movement.

How might the concept of accountability be construed in schools today had the National Commission on Excellence in Education found in 1983 that it was a crisis of faith that imperiled the nation? What if, for the past twenty-five years, the "responsible men" had been pursuing (with the same degree of fervency with which they have pursued simplistic, quantifiable measures of achievement) ways to help children and parents and educators live up to a public expectation that they are smart, capable, and creative?

I can convince myself that all of this makes sense, that the accountability movement and its mechanisms of control and coercion are fundamentally and profoundly misguided. And then I listen again to the words of parents and teachers, and I remember: it's not a simple problem.

"There Are a Lot of Really Lousy Teachers Out There!" (Alex)

> This teachers' union? It's driven me and a lot of other parents really nutty. Because we *do* have a lot of teachers that are really dysfunctional with our kids. Some people go into this profession and the desire is not there. And you can have that staff development, you can have all this crap going on, and the teacher is still going to be the *teacher*. They're just *there*! So, when we confront the union about how do you get *rid* of these teachers? I mean, they're *hurting* our children! Well, the administrators have to go through this whole red tape. They've got to write them down, they have all this documentation. Then when we finally do get rid of them, they go to another school. (Elena)

Elena's frustration over the harm that bad teachers are doing to children points to an interesting complication in this discussion about the accountability movement in education. "There are a lot of really lousy teachers out there!" as Alex put it. I think every member of our group struggled with the hard truth of that statement. Several participants shared their dilemma of wanting to believe in public schools and wanting to be advocates for teachers, but at the same time having to acknowledge the reality that not all schools and teachers are doing right by their students. Just what "right" means, of course, is a relative judgment—a point that harks back to the theme of disconnection due to the lack of shared definitions described earlier. Still, it's easy to agree on the extremes. Elena's example of the high school student whose teacher had told her that she might as well stay home and have babies rather than come to school "because she wasn't going to amount to anything, the way she was going" corroborates the existence of at least a degree of verifiable lousiness in the public schools. An honest critique of the accountability movement requires an exploration of this reality.

Several participants spoke about their conflicted attitudes toward public schools and teachers. Peyton's conflict stems from the changes she has observed in her working environment that she believes were caused by the intensification of accountability mandates in recent years. She has modified her answer to the question of what it means to be "doing right by students" since watching her school's and her district's approach to education devolve, in her view, from a child-centered to a performance-centered orientation. She says that in the early years of her career she thought that "traditional" teachers were the ones to look out for, that the teachers "who still had their kids in rows" were not the good ones. A change that she has perceived in colleagues' attitudes and behaviors in recent years, however, has caused her to revise her own definition of *good*.

> Every year I want to go to the next grade because I don't consider anybody else good enough. And I hate saying that, but . . . And it's not even about how

they're *teaching*. When I think of the teachers [in the next grade], I don't think about whether or not their class is set up traditionally, which is what we used to be told to worry about. I don't even *worry* about that. I just worry about who's compassionate, who's going to hug this child, and who's going to just talk to them like they're real people. And there are, like, *two* in the next grade that somewhat meet that requirement. And before, I *never* worried about placing kids. I *never* used to worry.

Alex is another participant who is deeply conflicted in her attitudes about public schools and teachers. She debates the need for externally defined standards and measurements that define a common content agenda for all teachers and students at every grade level. Her conflict in this area is between her philosophical rejection of imposed uniformity on the processes of teaching and learning and her recognition that without some kind of an organizing framework, "every child would learn about Egypt almost every year in elementary school." In response to the reality of "lousy teachers," Alex yearns for more accountability. "There are a lot of teachers out there who can't, by the sixth week of school, tell you even their students' names! There has to be something in place where teachers are held more accountable." The problem, of course, is in figuring out how to define and measure accountability in ways that are authentic and meaningful to the people in our classrooms, schools, and neighborhoods.

A problem that participants identified is that the current definition of accountability in schools reinforces rather than rejects a daily diet of rote learning for students and what members of the group believe is bad teaching—"if you can call that 'teaching,'" as Boyoyo said. "It's very easy to standardize," he continued. "It's so easy. You just make worksheets and then you say, 'Okay, practice these and you're ready.'" According to these participants, the accountability movement itself is compounding the problematic reality that there are, indeed, some bad teachers in the public schools. This idea came up in a brief exchange between Elena and Kate, one that is all the more interesting because Elena had originally come to the study with a fairly negative attitude toward teachers in general.

> Elena: That word, *teaching* . . . I think you all don't just teach. I think you guys truly impact a human being's *life*. And you impact it from the moment they enter to the moment they leave. And to just say *teaching* . . . That just sounds like, blah! I think that people need to really look at what you teachers do. Is that you have such an impact on these kids' lives. It's incredible!

> Kate: But I think there *are* teachers who only teach. And so that's what the system is creating, is teachers that just teach. Or it's taking unbelievable teachers that are so good at what they do, and making them be just drill people.

Other participants agreed with Boyoyo's and Kate's opinion that the accountability movement's emphasis on standardization and test performance is encouraging a thoughtless, lazy style of "teaching." Alex, for one, said she thought that if teachers were freed from focusing on the standards and tests, she wasn't sure "that they could create something that looks any different" in their classrooms. She continued, "The main reason why I say that is because they are so willing to accept whatever it is that they're handed, and I think that's because that makes things easier for them!" Julia echoed Alex's concerns. "What the heck would some of these teachers *do* if they took the test away?"

Rachel's perspective on the need for accountability and standards extends beyond the existence of "lousy teachers" to the existence of "lousy schools." After reading a portion of David Berliner and Bruce Biddle's *The Manufactured Crisis* for our seventh group meeting, Rachel remarked, "The manufactured crisis exists in our lousy schools, because we have lousy schools. I mean, I teach in one. And it's not a manufactured crisis. It *is* a crisis. Because it's a crisis when kids are denied an education that they are entitled to." Because of what she has learned from eight years of teaching in a "failing" high school, she yearns for a definition of accountability and the means for measuring it that will make a positive difference in the lives of her students.

> Every year we graduate so many kids who have not been given the opportunities that they deserve. And I deal with that *every day*. It's *terrible* that we start with a class of 900 kids [in ninth grade] and we're graduating 270. And so when books are written about our failing schools I go, 'Yes! Yes!' [Laughs.] 'Somebody recognizes it because I'm living this every day!' Six hundred-something kids are just, pssht! Down the drain!

> And in a way, standardization, I mean, I know all the horrors of it. But you know, I see a value in standards, because it's such a *mess* where I'm at, and *nobody's* accountable for *anything*! The kids, the teachers, the administration. And, you know, this is one school, but there are thousands of schools like that out there. And so I had to say that, because in many schools you don't need those standards and procedures, but when you're in a failing school . . . You lose six hundred kids in four years? There's got to be something . . .

> So they're starting, at my school. Now they're starting to get scared. The standards and the benchmarks, the accountability and the testing, so something at least is happening and it's getting a little bit better.

Rachel was unique in the group for her advocacy of "the standards and the benchmarks, the accountability and the testing." Other participants were more aligned in their critique of these things. Rachel's perspective pushed other participants' thinking, however. A comment that Sarah made during our eighth meeting (which Rachel wasn't able to attend) points to the importance of that fact.

> I wish that old Rachel were here! She was real honest. She was the first one in this whole group who said, 'Yeah, we really need standards! Because I have these colleagues who are sitting around doing nothing with kids and they're

getting away with it! And we need some standards!' And I *liked* what she said. I was *shocked*, frankly, to hear her talk that way. Because I thought we'd already negated all that crap. [Group laughter.] She was willing to make those kinds of statements, and I thought they were actually very refreshing. Because they made me question again, well then what *is* accountability?

Faith: The Core Democratic Virtue

Participants struggled during the course of this study with their own lack of faith in public schools and teachers. To a person, they believe in the ideals of equality and freedom of opportunity for *all* children, ideals that they think the public schools were created to achieve. They want to believe in the public schools and teachers in their communities, but their experiences caused them to say otherwise. *What the heck would some of these teachers do if they took the test away? (Julia); I don't have faith in my fellow colleagues (Alex); What would they do without these sets of pre-printed and distributed curricula placed in front of them? (Sarah); I am having a hard time having faith in the adults I work with (Mariela).*

On more than one occasion I sat in our group meetings, listening in full agreement as participants discussed the problem of poor teaching, yet wondering whether "those" teachers were sitting somewhere else, discussing the problem of "lousy teachers" from their perspective. A certain sense of elitism crept into our conversations on occasion, and the tacit presumption prevailed that we who were teachers in this group were not part of the "lousiness" problem. (If there were reservations about the teaching abilities of the people sitting around our table, they were not publicly shared, understandably, allowing that tacit presumption to stand.) The introduction of an excerpt from C. Douglas Lummis's book, *Radical Democracy*, powerfully impacted our group's conversations about the problem of bad teaching; it caused many participants to challenge their own seemingly elitist assumptions about what it is. This short text affected several participants in significant ways. I will return to those effects after I briefly summarize the content of the two-page excerpt that we read and discussed together, during our seventh group meeting.

Lummis argues that the core democratic virtue is faith. This belief is rooted in his view of democracy, which presumes that it is a phenomenon that is often in the making but seldom achieved. However rare, those moments of achievement in which the people's power has sparked to life have occurred in countries all over the world—specific moments in time when people rose up together to fight for a change in the social fabric of their lives. In order for democracy-in-the-making to have a chance, though, what is essential is that people have faith in the idea that change is possible, and that every human being is capable of making a difference in the world. This is what Lummis meant by saying that the core democratic virtue is faith. "Faith in human beings is the hardest faith," he wrote, "yet we all have it in some degree. We have to, to live. It is the very stuff out of which our personal lives are shaped; it is so common we barely notice it."[9] Democratic faith is the hardest kind of faith to have, according to Lummis, because it's not a sure thing. He explains that it's not like the kind of faith that Abraham, the "father of faith," had in his god—a faith so certain that he was prepared to kill his son over it, to prove it. So while investing faith in "we, the people" is a prerequisite for democracy-in-the-making, it is a very difficult thing to do precisely because it *is* an act of faith. There are no certainties. Putting our faith in other human beings comes with no guarantees.

I include an extensive quote from Lummis below because this is the very text upon which the hopeful outcome of my study hinges. Judging from our group discussions and the individual exit interviews, this is the text that had the strongest impact on the lives of many participants.

> The naturalness and the difficulty of democratic faith are rooted in the essential paradox of trust. The only proper object of trust is people, *because* people are capable of untrustworthiness; only people are capable of untrustworthiness, *because* they are trusted. We do not trust a rock to be hard or a hen to lay eggs . . . Trust—and untrustworthiness—was invented as a way of dealing with the uncertainties of human beings, who are free. It does not change the uncertainties into certainties. Trust is not a proof but a judgment and a choice.
>
> Democratic faith is not simply trusting everybody equally; it is not sentimental foolishness. It is grounded on a lucid understanding of the weaknesses, follies, and horrors people are capable of. It is precisely because of those weaknesses, follies, and horrors that something as weighty as faith is called for. Democratic faith is the decision to believe that a world of democratic trust is possible because we can see it in each person sometimes. It is the decision to believe in what people can be on the basis of what they sometimes are. . . .
>
> So the democrat is not impressed with the Abraham who puts his faith in God the Omnipotent, the Omniscient, the Unchangeable, the Eternal, as against the little boy who, for all we know, sometimes steals cakes from the kitchen, dreams forbidden dreams, and is now wishing he had any other father in the world but this one. Obeying the omnipotent is no great feat compared with gambling on the boy.[10]

The impact of Lummis's ideas about democratic faith was such that the concept became a central theme in our subsequent group discussions. A simple count of the number of times that the word "faith" appears in transcripts prior to and after the introduction of this text is a revealing indicator of the significance of that impact. In the first six group discussions, "faith" was used three times, each time in reference to a participant's own religious beliefs. In the five meetings following our seventh session during which we read and discussed the Lummis text, the word appears 122 times, never in reference to an individual's religious beliefs. The concept became a vehicle for participants' work not only in making sense of the accountability movement, but in clarifying and articulating their own conflicted relationships with public schools and teachers. While the conceptual impact of democratic faith on our conversations has already been evident in my presentation of this "crisis of faith" theme [*I don't have faith in my fellow colleagues (Alex); I am having a hard time having faith in the adults I work with (Mariela); That lack of faith in teachers for my kids is a hard thing to deal with (Sarah)*], I have reserved until now my treatment of its more positive effects.

Being able to identify and name such things as teacher-proofed curricula and faculty meeting sign-in sheets as specific examples demonstrating the lack of democratic faith being placed in them was an empowering experience for some of the teachers in the group. Peyton described an effect of this new feeling of empowerment that she was experiencing at her school. "I'm just not wanting to take it any more in little doses all of the time," she said. "Now, for me, it's more of wanting the administrators to know what that feels like, so I've been kind of pushing that more so that they understand what they're asking. And I didn't expect that to happen, for me." Reading and discussing critical texts on the accountability movement helped Peyton to see the constant "little doses" of disrespect and the various mechanisms of control and surveillance that she had been experiencing in her school and district as evidence of the lack of faith in teachers that is effectively perpetuated by various accountability mandates. An increased consciousness of this lack of democratic faith has caused her to "push" her administrators, she says, toward seeing and understanding the damaging effects of the disrespect and distrust that she believes are now common in her school.

Equally significant for several members of the group was the experience of examining their own relationships and attitudes toward public schools and teachers through the lens of democratic faith, as some participants questioned the degree of faith that they were capable of placing in others. In our eighth group meeting, after several people spoke about their lack of faith in other teachers, I asked, "What do you sacrifice because of that lack of faith?" Mariela answered, in essence, that what is at stake for her is the opportunity to honor diversity in terms of making multiple ways of knowing and being available to the students and teachers at her school.

> I've thought a lot about this. I was *sure*, when I started teaching, that every-thing I was doing was just right and so, by default, anything anybody else was doing *couldn't* be right. [Group laughter.] But I see a lot of different styles at our school, and I think that that's one of the things that gives our school strength. Kids *need* different things! There's kids that I reach, or kids I *don't* reach that would've just done so much better with this other teacher who *I* don't think is as good of a teacher [laughs], but this certain kid would've done so much better. You know, they'll say, 'I *loved* so-and-so.' And I think, god! What was there to love? But they *do*! And who am I to say that what I'm doing is the right thing, and what somebody else is doing is the wrong thing? It works different for different people. And I'm trying to be more proactive in talking about the good things about other teachers because I think it's really easy to

just say the bad things. So I just am trying to be more faithful about how I think about other teachers.

Boyoyo offered a theory as to why this kind of democratic faith is such a difficult thing to achieve among teachers. "What I think is, we are with the kids six hours a day. But we never meet with our colleagues! As teachers we don't have the time to get together to discuss!" Boyoyo's comment raises the question of what happens when teachers are kept so busy that they do not have opportunity for conversation with one another. One effect certainly seems to be the creation of a school culture in which teachers simply do not know one another. And in a culture in which people do not know one another, it seems likely that democratic faith would have a hard time growing. Alex talked about this in terms of the understanding and the faith she is able to invest in her students. She attributes her generosity of belief in them to precisely this: she knows them.

> It goes back to the idea of understanding. I'm sure that if I got to know [my colleagues] better and understood where they are coming from that it would help soften my heart a lot. Since I know the kids so well, I'm going to always give them the benefit of the doubt and continue to always greet them day after day after day with more ideas for how to help them, and more ideas for how to meet them where they're at. I don't know my fellow teachers as well.

Seen through the words of these teachers and parents, it seems reasonable to believe that democratic faith cannot thrive in a context in which people do not have the time to get to know and understand one another. Furthermore, it seems reasonable to believe that people who neither know nor understand one another are compromised in terms of their ability to reach their potential for being intrinsically motivated to do their best. Without knowing and being known, it seems likely that people may not feel safe or valued or find enjoyment in their work— three of the prerequisites for intrinsic motivation that Rogers names. Finally, when this exploration of a crisis of faith in the public schools is seen through Michel Foucault's theory of panopticism (the focus of the next chapter), it seems reasonable to believe that democratic faith may not be *intended* to thrive in a school context, and that the people in our schools do not have the time to get to know and understand one another because workforce solidarity is not a desirable phenomenon, from a systemic perspective driven by market ideology. From that perspective, democratic faith may be perceived as a dangerously volatile idea.

Theme #3: Definitional Authority

After our group's eighth meeting, the term "definitional authority"[11] occurred to me while journaling about my experience with the study group. It came up in my writing as a way to name the phenomenon that participants had been talking about in a variety of ways for the preceding several weeks: the lack of power that students and teachers have to define their own reality at school. This is the third major theme that emerged through analysis of interview and discussion transcripts. It is a connective theme, linking the two that came before:

- The crisis of faith described in the preceding section indicates a general lack of trust in students' and teachers' abilities to competently direct their work of learning and teaching, revealing the limited degree of definitional authority that they enjoy in the immediacy of their own classrooms and schools. (If the experiences related by the teachers in this group are typical, it is safe to say that this lack of definitional authority becomes increasingly evident as neighborhood income levels decline.)
- The theme of disconnection and competition described at the beginning of this chapter indicates the problem of alienation that exists in the absence of common agreements over the appropriate ends and means of education in the public schools. The fact that teachers, parents, and students are not typically offered opportunities to engage the debate addresses the reality that definitional authority over the nation's public school system tends to be reserved for the kinds of people who attend education summits rather than PTA meetings.

I referenced the concept of definitional authority in our group's eighth meeting. In response to Boyoyo's argument that assessment of student achievement should not be predicated on the idea that all students will—or should—develop identical academic strengths, I said, "I always come back to definitions. Who has the authority to define the words that we use? What *is* education? What is assessment?" A week after that meeting, a name for this concept occurred to me, prompted by stories from two other teachers in our group. This time, though, they were stories about participants' decisions to lay claim to definitional authority in their lives at school. The following is an excerpt from my journal, written after receiving a telephone call from Rachel. She had called to describe the inservice day at her school that she had just attended which, in her opinion, lacked depth and substance and was an insult to her as a professional.

She said she looked around for someone to talk to, 'but there was no one,' she said. 'I cried all afternoon. I have no one to talk to!' I asked Rachel what she thinks she can do about this. She had talked back in May about making a Michael Moore-style documentary about education, and she's revisiting that idea now. She feels like she needs to *do* something. She is taking the authority to define her own reality. . . .

I think of all of the stories I've heard from participants . . . So many stories about teachers' lack of autonomy and authority to define their own realities. No definitional authority! . . . Peyton plans to keep a book of stories like these this year. I hope she can pull it off, on top of everything else she has to do. There's a book I would like to read. There's power in the details of real stories.

It is worth noting that the idea of definitional authority occurred to me while I was reflecting on its presence—in the context of two participants' decisions to claim it—rather than in the context of the preceding weeks of group discussions in which its absence was often described. This strikes me as significant because it points to the possibility that the concept of definitional authority offers a solution at the same time that it names a problem. The problem is clear in the many examples I have cited that illustrate the lack of authority and autonomy that many teachers and parents experience in their classrooms and schools—a problem that can be more fully appreciated when research on the effects of extrinsic motivation is considered. A potential solution is suggested in the fact that, for several participants, the opportunity to engage in focused discussions with other teachers and parents positively impacted their own determination to have greater access to definitional authority in their lives at school. This impact is evidenced in the words they used to describe some of the effects that participation in this study had on them: *Now I can stand up—It's challenging the way I think—I feel empowered—It's given me hope—It's given me something to stand on—I'm starting to think of me as one person who can change it—I don't have to follow the direction that is coming from the top when I see it is wrong.*

Defining Public School Accountability: Participants' Perceptions of Authority

It was during our seventh group session that participants read the excerpt from *Radical Democracy* in which Lummis suggests that maybe Abraham (the Old Testament "father of faith") had actually failed his god's test of faith. In Lummis's alternative interpretation of the sacrifice of Isaac story, Abraham was stopped from killing his son by a horrified god who realized, just in time, that Abraham couldn't see that it was Isaac who actually *needed* his father to be faithful to him. In facilitating a discussion on the excerpt, one of the questions that I asked participants was if they could find any parallels between that story and the story of accountability in the schools that we had been reading about and discussing together. Rachel responded immediately. "I think we're all Isaacs," she said. "I think the teachers and the students and the parents, we're all Isaacs." Mariela asked her, "Who's holding the knife?" And Rachel replied, "The system! The businessmen and corporations. The legislatures. The politicians. The corporate power. *None* of us are running any of this!"

Following up on Rachel's suggestion that "we're all Isaacs," I asked, "What are we bound with, then? What are the ropes themselves? Why are we unable to resist?" In exploring an answer to that question, Julia said that she feels like she actually alternates between playing the roles of Isaac and Abraham in the accountability drama.

Sometimes I feel like Abraham in that I just do it because . . . [sigh]. I just don't
have any power, and I just do what they ask me to do. But then I feel like Isaac,
in that . . . You know, I'm so *sick* of it! I get very, very frustrated. I'm tied by
standards that the businessmen have created. And they keep yelling at me. I got
a letter yesterday about how our school is failing, and the union is doing something for us because we're going to have to work so many extra days. And
they're saying they're not going to pay us for it! I'm like, you wanna make a
bet? [Laughs.] But there I am. I'm tied by that.

Throughout our discussions, group members were united in the perception
that the power to define the public school agenda currently resides in elite corporate and political realms of life in America, beyond the sphere of influence for
most parents and teachers. This perception was consistently reflected in participants' comments throughout the time that we spent together. "The business en-
tity is taking over. It is a commodity," said Selena. "And the whole idea of education and life is being eased out, because business people run it!" Peyton made
the same point in saying,

Having standards isn't about who gets to decide them. It's not about us talking
together. It's about what the business sector wants from our kids! As a teacher,
I *want* accountability. But I want accountability for things that we can't measure easily. And so it's not about us all making these decisions. It's about somebody out there who has more power than I, and the rest of us, making them.

Perplexity as to how this political and corporate presumption of definitional
authority in the public schools was accomplished filled Kate's voice when she
exclaimed, "Somehow it's become okay that if your kids aren't 'smart' enough
you can't have good schools! And some of us bought into that, or we all did, or
we didn't do something about it at some point when we had the . . ." At this
point Kate stopped abruptly. Then she continued, "I don't know if we ever had
an opportunity. I don't know." Sarah voiced the same concerns about a corporate takeover of the public school agenda. Her comment introduces the relationship between the concept of definitional authority and the responsibilities of
citizenship in a society that lays claim to the ideals of democracy.

What this whole market ideology tries to drill into us is that business knows
how to do it. Public entities *don't* know how to do it. They are unsalvageable.
And it's always been my premise throughout this whole thing that the whole
testing phenomenon is to get rid of public education, because 'public' is no
good. And that is the undermining of our democracy, for me. The public good
is what democracy *is*, and if we undermine that to please the businesses, then
we are lost.

I have previously described Banfield's term of amoral familism as pure self-
interest. On a continuum depicting an orientation to being in society, it would be
located on the opposite end of the position entitled "concern for the public
good." It was clear throughout this study that the parents and teachers in our

group believe that the authority for defining the public school agenda in the United States does not currently reside with citizens who are concerned about the public good. They believe, instead, that definitional authority in the schools is currently in the hands of an elite body of corporate and political leaders whose interests do not extend beyond the purview of amoral familism.

During our ninth group meeting, the week after I had written about definitional authority in my journal, I introduced the idea to participants and described it in this way:

> I came up with a phrase, 'definitional authority,' that I think I'm going to be writing about. And what I mean by that is, who do we give authority to for defining the words that are important in our lives? When I think about what 'education' means, and 'achievement,' and 'success,' and what it means to teach— who has definitional authority for those words? Do we demand those rights for ourselves, to define them? Who has definitional authority for deciding what parent involvement is? And then what are the consequences of that?

When I asked for responses to my thinking along these lines, Rachel described her reaction to having read *A Nation at Risk* for that evening's group discussion. She spoke to the issue of definitional authority in her critique of the authors' perspective in that document. She challenged the section entitled "A Word to Parents and Students" as an egregious misplacement of focus, given what she sees as the media's power to define reality in America.

> The guys have the *nerve* to have a *word* to parents and students . . . What *I* wanted to say was, 'Hey, Government! When are you going to speak to the media?' Because when you really look at television in particular, the media does *not* support and respect intelligence. The media does *not* respect achievement. Learning, *certainly* not. So when I got to that, my response was, 'Hey! Please speak to the media, Government. Board of Education, State Board, speak to the media! Because the media is shaping our culture.'

Boyoyo's comment, which I have quoted before, reinforces the same idea: virtually unchallenged authority to represent reality resides with the corporate mass media, which is problematic in that "the media is playing with us!" according to him. "We are not looking to the reality, because nobody is showing that reality. Nobody is giving that. It's a big lie, and they cover the big lie in a very good way." Citizens who are not shown a variety of perspectives on reality by their media system are ill-equipped to participate meaningfully in conversations about school reforms that are desperately needed if equality of educational opportunities for all children is the goal. If that is *not* the goal of accountability measures in our schools, then promoting the official authority of the corporate voice in America and discouraging the people's access to their own definitional authority appear to be effective strategies for thwarting that democratic ideal.

Definitional Authority as the Democratic Challenge

> Democracy? It's full of crap. I just really feel that it's a word that's used
> loosely. It's used when it needs to be used, to where people need to fall in line
> toward that direction. Do you know what I'm saying? They use it when they
> want to bring people together to do something that some person wants to be
> done. Not in the benefit of *everybody*. They pull that word just to bring people
> together, that this is the *right* thing you've got to do, and this is the thing for us
> as *Americans*, and . . . Which is a bunch of bull. It's just full of *crap*. (Elena)

The majority of the people in this study group spoke with me during their
initial interviews about the meaning of democracy in ways that communicated
varying degrees of skepticism regarding its status as the operative governing
framework in America: "Indigenous people don't have that democracy. They're
not treated equally. It's kind of like a farce, but [the equality of all people in
America] is what we're brought up to believe" (Ana); "I think it's an ideal now,
rather than a practiced thing" (Sarah); "Somehow along the line it got really,
truly corrupted" (Tessa); "Democracy. What it's *supposed* to mean, or what I
think it means? Democracy is, I don't know, getting buy-in. How's that?" (Peyton); "We can talk a lot about democracy. The other thing is, are we doing that
or not?" (Boyoyo); "What *is* democracy?" (Rachel); "Democracy in the purest
sense is that each of us is equal. Unfortunately, we see through human eyes, and
we don't all see each other as equal" (Julia).

Although their conceptions of democracy varied, the teachers and parents in
this group believe to a person in the ideals of equality and freedom that they
associate with the concept. Selena's definition of democracy effectively summarizes those ideals.

> I think democracy means that there's equity, all the way across. It's freedom.
> Freedom to choose, freedom to express, freedom to make change. To me that's
> part of it, you know? And *that's* really important. You have that right to make a
> change.

Alex also focused on the possibility of change as the defining feature of
democracy. She described democracy as a way of life "where you are open to
change." Alex, like Selena, conceives of democracy in terms that are active and
local rather than abstract and distant. For her, the idea of democracy is manifested not only in being open to change, but also in a commitment to be "constantly just trying to make things better than what they are for the people that
live in any given community." In writing of the relationship between education
and democracy, Michael Engel promotes the same kind of local, action-oriented
view.

> The most creative, challenging, and inspiring visions of what U.S. public edu-
> cation could be have always been rooted in a democratic value system. . . . That
> discourse promoted the idea that the schools could enable citizens to take an ac-

tive and positive role in shaping their society. In this way, the people were to be ends, not means; subjects, not objects; and creators, not machines. They were to be valued in and of themselves, not for what they could do to suit the purposes of others. They were to own U.S. social and political institutions, which they would control for their own benefit rather than having the institutions own and control them. And the purpose of the public education system was to help make all this possible.[12]

Our public education system is not consistently engaged in helping to make all of this possible, according not only to the authors that we read, but also according to the discussions that those authors' texts launched about teachers' and parents' own experiences in the schools. The idea that students are rewarded more for compliance than for critical and active engagement in their classrooms was often repeated by many people during our group discussions. Sarah was one who described that phenomenon. In doing so, she made it personal.

> Somehow, somewhere along the line, being compliant and doing the things that my teachers always told me to do became the most important feature of who I was as a learner! And maybe part of it is because I'm a woman. And now as a mother, I oftentimes find myself saying to my boys . . . and because they're boys, to a certain degree they rebel against doing homework. They rebel against sitting and doing the crap that they bring home. 95 percent of which is crap! At least for my younger boy. 'Just do it. Get it over with! Just do it, Jamie! You can do it! It'll only take you six minutes. Whip it out. Just get it done.' And I kind of feel like that's a metaphor for a lot of the whole day that they spend. Just get it done. Just do it. You'll be rewarded for just doing it!

The empowering and humanizing ideal that Engel summarizes—that public education exists, in part, to "enable citizens to take an active and positive role in shaping their society"—is effectively contained by a definition of accountability that reinforces rather than corrects the lessons of compliance-as-virtue that Sarah began learning in childhood. The problem of lessons in compliance learned in childhood is evidenced in Peyton's description of working conditions for adults in elementary schools, an environment that is commonly recognized as peculiar for its lack of gender balance in the workforce.

> In elementary school we have an hour of planning time a week, not a day. And that's just what we do. And so I think it's almost, you're *used* to it. Nobody's questioning why middle school and high school teachers have daily preps, why they can get paid extra for working during their preps and then have a higher salary than any elementary teacher [in the same district]. And for whatever reason, nobody's fighting for it. Not unions. Not principals, not teachers, not superintendents. It just, unfortunately, *is*. And we talk about it [laughs], *every day*, at elementary schools. I mean, if our P.E. teacher is sick, P.E. is just cancelled that day and half of your weekly planning time is *gone*. Or if your P.E. lands on a Thursday and there's no school some Thursday, because of whatever reason, you don't have your planning time that week. And I think, for whatever reason, it's just different!

The topic of female compliance was a common one in our group, whether the discussion context was the lack of union activism in elementary schools or the lack of resistance to accountability mandates that some participants described as ludicrous. "Whenever there's extra paperwork, we just keep *doing* it!" Mariela exclaimed. "We just do it." (Interestingly, while stories of boys' rebellion against homework or school rules were occasionally shared, I heard no stories from the parents of girls describing their rebellion against homework or anything else. In fact, the daughters of two participants are in college, preparing to become teachers. No one in the group had a son who was planning to teach.)

The usefulness of definitional authority as a concept may be in the challenge it offers each citizen to reject amoral familism as a way of life and to shoulder, instead, the responsibilities of democratic citizenship. Ironically, it was Selena, one of the most active democratic citizens in the group (as defined by Engel) who identified the inherent problem in this challenge of claiming definitional authority.

> Nobody encouraged me to take control of my world. Everything was planned out. And I don't see it! How do we help these kids let their voices be heard if we as adults, parents, teachers are struggling with our voice being heard? How are we going to pass that skill on to our younger rascals?

Selena's question points to the importance of attending to first things first, and to the ability to identify just what those priorities are. The "first thing" that occurs to me in light of Selena's comments is a quote from a book that was published in the same year as *A Nation at Risk*, the same year that I began my career in education. "To have a voice is to be human," wrote Carol Gilligan. "To have something to say is to be a person."[13] In my mind, I equate the ideas of "having a voice" and claiming definitional authority. So the "first things" question that occurs to me in the context of Selena's quote is this: if it is true that teachers and parents have, by Gilligan's definition, relinquished a degree of our own humanity by relinquishing our definitional authority in the public schools, by what authority would we presume to engage the questions that Sarah had posed regarding the definition of the public good? She asked, "The question is, what is *good*? What is it that makes a teacher good? What is it that makes a good school? What is it that makes a good place for my kid to be?"

Michel Engel's words suggest an answer. That authority to debate the public good is attached to what Thomas Jefferson described as "the office of citizen," and it is developed by means of education. In the United States, Engel writes, education has been conceived as the means by which citizens learn how to take "an active and positive role in shaping their society." In this conception of education, "the people were to be ends, not means; subjects, not objects; and creators, not machines. . . . They were to own U.S. social and political institutions, which they would control for their own benefit rather than having the institutions own and control them."[14] We who have relinquished definitional authority over our neighborhood schools have abdicated, or perhaps have never assumed, the office of citizen. The hopeful reality that Engel's words illustrate is that education that is rooted in the discourse of the democratic value system is both humanizing and empowering, making the office of citizen newly available.

The project of engaging parents and teachers together in conversation about the accountability movement in our public schools was both educative and rooted in the discourse of the democratic value system. It was a humanizing and empowering experience for several participants, as Boyoyo demonstrated in saying,

> I think that we as teachers, I think a lot of us, we are not aware of all these things. I'm starting to know more because of these readings . . . Now I feel more secure in myself . . . I don't have to follow the direction that is coming from the top when I see it is wrong. I don't need to follow that.

In this chapter I introduced and described the three large themes that emerged in helping me to answer the question of how teachers and parents would make sense of the accountability movement together. Those themes were: (1) disconnection and competition; (2) a crisis of faith; and (3) definitional authority. I indicated at the beginning of the chapter that these themes represent significant aspects of my findings. Individually, they contribute direct answers from different perspectives to the question of how teachers and parents would make sense of the accountability movement; together, they represent the material with which my conclusion about the power of focused dialogue between parents and teachers is woven.

In large ways and small, these participants' words testify to the personal power that is generated when people get together for a common, focused purpose. Even after arriving at this basic finding, however, I keep having to learn the truth of it. I was recently complaining to a friend, in private, about the fact that even though half of the teachers and parents in our group asked if we could continue meeting on a monthly basis after the formal study concluded, and even though they would commit to attending these meetings when I contacted them, the majority never actually showed up. Yet every time I brought up the idea of stopping, everyone protested. They said that they wanted and needed this discussion group to continue. I knew that their intentions were good, but I kept organizing monthly meetings that were not well attended. As I shared my disappointment, I said that maybe I needed to just stop investing energy in the group since it didn't seem to be making a difference any more, anyway.

At that point my friend, who I thought had been listening sympathetically, said, "How *dare* you?" I looked up in surprise, blinking at the suddenness of having surfaced so quickly from the self-absorbed hole I had been digging. She continued. "You've told me that Julia has said the continued support of the group helps and validates her. That she can stand up now in a staff meeting and challenge what district office people are saying about the tests. You think that's nothing? And that Peyton has said she's speaking up more at her school now and arguing against things like her principal's proposal to track students into reading groups! That's *nothing*? Those things are *huge* for them! How dare you?" A blaze of anger from a friend I'd never seen get really angry at anyone, much less at me. She had me pinned.

It may fit on a matchbook cover, but the simplicity is misleading. After spending two years learning it, I had to be taught again that *it matters*—that the simple act of participating in purposeful conversation with others can make a measurable difference in our lives and in our society. This time around, though, I got a bonus lesson in humility. "How dare you?" was a gift from a friend who taught me that *it's the difference itself that matters*, no matter how large or small, no matter how long-lasting, because the fact that the difference exists at all is what possibility is made of. It's the tiny sprout growing in the blackened aftermath of a forest fire. Any difference that results from the energy generated through focused discussion is a sprout of audacious possibility.

"It's given me hope," said Rachel. Sprouts of possibility are growing.

Notes

1. Edward Banfield in Walter C. Parker, ed., *Educating the Democratic Mind*. Albany (New York: State University of New York Press, 1996), 8–9.

2. Noam Chomsky, "Renewing Tom Paine's Challenge" in *Our Media Not Theirs*, by Robert McChesney and John Nichols (New York: Seven Stories Press, 2002), 18–19.

3. <http://www.childrensdefense.org/childhealth/default.aspx/> (8 Dec 2005); <http://www.amsa.org/cph/CHIPfact.cfm> (22 Sept 2007).

4. Michael Engel, *The Struggle for Control of Public Education: Market Ideology vs. Democratic Values* (Philadelphia: Temple University Press, 2000), 1–2.

5. Alfie Kohn, *Punished by Rewards* (New York: Houghton Mifflin Company, 1993); Alfie Kohn, *The Schools Our Children Deserve: Moving Beyond Traditional Classrooms and 'Tougher Standards'* (New York: Houghton Mifflin Company, 1999).

6. Kohn, *Punished by Rewards*, 80.

7. Spence Rogers, "Increasing Student Motivation to Learn" (Presentation at the National Schools Conference Institute's *Effective Schools Conference*, Phoenix, 1998).

8. The five basic human needs that Maslow identified are: physiological needs; safety needs; needs for love, affection, and belonging; needs for esteem; and needs for self-actualization <chiron.valdosta.edu/whuitt/col/regsys/ maslow.html>.

9. C. Douglas Lummis, *Radical Democracy* (Ithaca, New York: Cornell Univ. Press, 1996), 151.

10. Lummis, *Radical Democracy*, 153–154.

11. I have not found this term referenced in searches through databases of education journals, but it does appear in the medical and legal fields.

12. Engel, *The Struggle for Control of Public Education*, 1–2.

13. Carol Gilligan, *In a Different Voice* (Cambridge, Mass: Harvard Univ. Press, 1983), xvi

14. Engel, *The Struggle for Control of Public Education*, 1–2.

CHAPTER 6

The Inversion of Visibility

In Chapter 5, I presented the three main themes that emerged through discussions among the parents and teachers in our study group: disconnection/competition, a crisis of faith, and definitional authority. These three themes, which essentially describe various aspects and ramifications of the people's typical lack of power and solidarity in their own public schools, serve as the backdrop for this chapter in which the exercise of modern power is examined. In this chapter I will use Foucault's theory of panopticism not only as an explanatory framework for contextualizing the three themes of the previous chapter, but also as a means of making the goals and the instruments of modern power in the public schools *visible*. If the pattern established by the parents and teachers in this study group holds true, this expanded field of visibility in the accountability discourse will lead to stronger local access to definitional authority in our schools and classrooms. Explaining and exploring the issue of visibility in the context of the public school panopticon will be my focus in the remainder of this chapter.

Spotlighting Accountability, not Possibility: Perfecting the Inversion of Visibility

Perhaps the biggest problem that Americans are facing as a society is that we have a hard time believing in possibility, imagining that things could be otherwise. As a society we have accepted as natural, even inevitable, the hegemony of capitalism and the value of corporate over public welfare. Accountability in education, defined in such a way as to cast children and teachers as workers for the corporate-state, has achieved the status of being a natural, even inevitable lens to use when looking at schools, teachers, students, and families. Accountability, not possibility, is the ruling paradigm in the lives of children and teachers in America's schools. The public spectacle of the corporate-state's noisy demand for all students to be held accountable to the same high achievement standards—regardless of the little-known yet profoundly differing access that children in these United States have to adequate food, shelter, health care, teachers, instructional resources, school facilities, and other opportunity-to-learn variables—is in perfect symbiosis with the quiet business of its abandonment of countless numbers of children and their families. Behind the public furor of political rhetoric and legislation and education summits to which CEOs rather than public school teachers or parents are invited, is the discreet activity of corporations going about their business—basing their operations outside of the country, exporting jobs, evading taxes and responsibility for environmental health and any number of other obligations to the public welfare.

When it comes to education, the corporate-state has perfected the trick of what historian-philosopher Michel Foucault has called the inversion of visibility.[1] In earlier times, Foucault explains, power was manifested in the visibility of the ruling class. The crown, the throne, and other displays of ostentatious finery served the purpose of making power visible. The modern exercise of power, however, is manifested in the ability to avoid being seen, to control what is and is not visible to the public eye. The inversion of visibility is a phenomenon of what Foucault calls disciplinary power, by which the subjects rather than the rulers are illuminated. He wrote,

> Disciplinary power . . . is exercised through its invisibility; at the same time it imposes on those whom it subjects a principle of compulsory visibility. In discipline, it is the subjects who have to be seen. Their visibility assures the hold of the power that is exercised over them. It is the fact of being constantly seen, of being able always to be seen, that maintains the disciplined individual in his subjection.[2]

From the perspective of inverted visibility, then, "accountability" as a spotlight is perfectly controlled—steadily and brightly illuminating those things that serve the corporate-state in their visibility, diverting attention from those behind the spotlight whose hands are directing its beam.

I have suggested that the biggest problem we are facing as a society is that we have a hard time believing in possibility and imagining that things could be otherwise. This certainly seems to be the case for the people who are living and working under the imposition of externally defined accountability mandates in our public schools. In fact, teachers' lack of resistance was a common topic of discussion for the participants in our study group. "I'm having a hard time now with the teachers. Why are they letting this happen?" said Kate, a parent participant in the group. Rachel, a high school teacher, concurred. In frustration, she exclaimed, "I don't understand why teachers put up with what they put up with! We're intelligent, educated people. I just don't understand why we put up with it!"

I believe that in describing the phenomenon of the inversion of visibility, Foucault offers a viable explanation for this apparent inability to resist the status quo and to see the existence of alternatives. Perhaps other possibilities for defining accountability in education are hard to imagine for the teachers in our nation's public schools because they have been pinned to the wall with the accountability spotlight, caught in the path of its one-way beam. It could be that other conceptions of accountability are simply hard to see for people who have become accustomed to squinting into an incessant glare, habituated over the decades to the "natural" belief that it is *their* visibility that matters.

Breaching the Parent-Teacher Divide: "What's really going on" in education?

What the teachers and parents in this study group did with me, in effect, was to step into a backstage room for a while, closing the door on the accountability spotlights that were trained on them. In this quiet space, parents and teachers sat as equals around a table and engaged in the democratic work of citizens looking back at power. They broke the unwritten rule that has existed in every school in which I have ever worked, that teachers and parents are not to talk with one another about "what's really going on" in education; they are not to talk, that is, about their personal interpretations of and attitudes toward policies and politics in their schools and districts. In that restful room backstage, beyond the reach of spotlights that had previously defined the parameters of acceptable discourse between parents and teachers, these participants dispensed with the veneer of false neutrality and they read, talked, argued, and learned with one another about the history and ramifications of the accountability movement that have been censored by the corporate media. (It is worth noting that these conversations took place beyond the boundaries of any particular neighborhood school. Teachers and parents coming together from a number of schools felt safe in the context of relative anonymity to engage in honest critique and conversation. Whether parents and teachers from the same school would be able to accomplish the same level of safety and solidarity is open to question.)

Participants agreed that what made their experience in this study group powerful was the intentional bringing together of parents and teachers for dialogue about education. As Rachel said, "I think what's so strong about this group is that alliance between teachers and parents. Get the parents and teachers together? Oh, man! It's given me hope." This perceived potential for power in the joining of teachers' and parents' voices addresses one of the underlying questions I had brought to this study. Prior to the start of this research project I had wondered, how will participants' identities as parents and teachers influence group discussions and participants' experiences of those discussions? The answer that I found is reflected in the title of this book. In reading, talking, arguing, and learning together, the participants in this study were engaged in the mutual project of what I now think of as *volatile knowing*. Together, teachers and parents have the potential for disrupting the influence of corporate power in their neighborhood schools. That, I think, is a very good thing. I join Michelle Fine in

believing that the historic separation of teachers' and parents' interests effectively serves the interests of "the very bureaucracies that are underfunding and
overcontrolling public education."[3] What possibilities might exist for children in
neighborhood schools if parents' and teachers' interests were successfully
joined? In the microcosm of our little backstage room, the beginnings of such a
joining were evident. Elena, a parent participant, put this to words when she
said, "The thing that I appreciated, and I do want to say, is that you've got
teachers and then you've got parents. And I firmly felt that we were all just
one."

So in the end, while it is true that participation did make a difference for individual members in the group (described in Chapters 4 and 5), the broader and
deeper value of this study extends beyond that personal impact. The larger significance is in how these participants' words reveal the workings of power
within what Michel Foucault would call the "panopticon" of the public school
system—making *it* visible to those who live and work inside of it. In effect, it is
the *re-inversion of visibility* that I am after, making the means of control by the
ruling classes visible for the purpose of inviting teachers, parents, students, administrators, and other community members to demand greater access to definitional authority in their own schools. I also want this re-inversion of visibility to
serve the additional purpose of problematizing amoral familism (described in
Chapter 4) as the operative norm in our public schools, inviting a sense of responsibility to be felt in every school and neighborhood for children whose local
advocates are without the cultural, social, and/or financial capital to facilitate,
through education, their access to the promise of a hopeful future.

The theoretical lens that I will use to explain and explore this concept of re-
inverted visibility is Michel Foucault's theory of panopticism. His famous use of
Jeremy Bentham's 18th century plan for creating the perfect prison—the panopticon—is a model for explaining what Foucault refers to as the modern technologies of power. What I have called the accountability spotlight is an example
of such a technology. In Foucauldian terms, then, the accountability spotlight is
an instrument of power used by the ruling classes to control their subjects in the
public school panopticon by maintaining them in a state of compulsory visibility. From a systemic perspective, the subjects' ability to see and understand the
accountability spotlight as an example of a modern technology of power would
represent a particularly volatile form of knowing. This kind of knowing would
have the potential for disrupting power in our neighborhoods' and our nation's
public schools by making its exercise visible and understandable to those who
have been subjected to it. This kind of knowing, I argue, in serving to re-invert
visibility, would make the exercise of modern power and access to definitional
authority in the schools available to people who see the concept of "excessive
democracy" as an oxymoron, not as a threat.

An Introduction to the Panopticon: A Metaphor for the Modern Exercise of Power

In *Discipline and Punish*,[4] Foucault explains that as populations grew and the old technologies of power (beating, maiming, killing) were no longer adequate for controlling "the multiplicities," more sophisticated methods became necessary. Enter Bentham's plan for controlling large populations of prisoners with minimal resources: it's all in the architecture, as long as the design is such that the prisoners are always visible and the guards are not.

Imagine the panopticon as Bentham designed it. The cellblocks are arranged in a circle, with all of the cells facing inward. In the center of the circle is a very tall tower that rises up into the sky, and at the very top of the tower is the area where the guards are located. The layout of the cellblocks and the prison yard allows the guards to see all of the prisoners, all of the time, from this vantage point. Since the prisoners can't see into the guard tower from below, though, they never actually know if there is anyone watching them. Because there *might* be someone watching, however, they must always behave as if there *is* someone watching—or suffer the consequences if they misbehave and are caught.

The genius of the panopticon is that architecture itself, the very structure of the system within which people live and work, can be manipulated in such a way as to foster uncertainty and fear. Surveillance and the ambiguous threat of consequences for misbehavior effectively cause the prisoners to police themselves, leading to their eventual internalization of the expectations and values of the system. When the prisoners have accepted systemic values and expectations as their own, guards become superfluous. This modern technology of power is all about efficiency and the utilization of fear. A very large prison population can thus be effectively policed by a very small number of guards if the inmates can be manipulated into policing themselves. An entire workforce of teachers and an entire population of students and their parents can be domesticated if they can be taught to internalize the competitive, capitalistic values of the corporate-state.

Foucault adopted the panopticon as a paradigm for explaining what he called "disciplinary technology." He defines a discipline as "a 'physics' or an 'anatomy' of power, a technology,"[5] and as "the unitary technique by which the body is reduced as a 'political' force at the least cost and maximized as a useful force."[6] The accountability spotlight, my abbreviation for that aspect of the accountability movement in education that is motivated by private interest rather than by a genuine commitment to the public welfare, is an example of a disciplinary technology.

Observation and visibility are primary concerns in the modern technologies, or disciplines, of power. The end goal is efficient control of the multitudes. Whether the disciplinary system is to regulate a prison, a social ideal of femininity, or a school, its purpose is to control from within by encouraging the people inside of it, at every hierarchical level, to internalize and enforce the values and norms of that system. Those whose behavior is regulated by the system thus become, at the same time, the enforcers of compliance. Mexican educator Arturo Ornelas put it another way when he said, "Teachers are the guard dogs of the ideology of the ruling classes."[7] Regarding students' experience of any particular school or classroom, the degree to which top-down accountability mandates overshadow possibility as an educational value indicates the amount of truth in that hard statement.

I refer once again to my suggestion that the biggest problem that Americans are facing is that we have a hard time believing in possibility and imagining that things could be otherwise. When most of us in the public school system, from superintendents to students to everyone in between, are going along with the idea that some invisible, unscrutinized, unaccountable force from above has the right to hold us accountable with neither our consent nor our input, and when this arrangement is broadly accepted as both natural and inevitable, it is easy to see why other possibilities for defining education, achievement, and success may be hard to imagine. If we have accepted the conditions of our own objectification as natural and inevitable, we will have relinquished our authority to define the world otherwise. We will have lost the ability to look back, having ceded our own definitional authority to those who own the spotlight.

A Framework for Panoptic Control:
The Continuous, Individualizing Pyramid

Looking back at the modern exercise of power and fighting for a degree of definitional authority in our schools matters, particularly for those of us in the system who do not subscribe to the idea that competition and capitalism should be its driving values. In the absence of a media system devoted to the ideals of comprehensive and balanced reporting on issues of public concern, however, the realization that the goal of visibility should apply to every hierarchical level in the system—not just the lowest ones—may not come naturally. As Boyoyo, a teacher in our study group said, "If I would not be here, to a lot of things I would say, 'It's not that bad.' It's like you are trapped in these big lies. It's the media, again, is playing with the politicians. It's a game from the power. And the media is playing with us!" With the assumption that the kind of enlightenment that Boyoyo described here is a desirable thing, the necessity of learning what does not come naturally to well-disciplined individuals then becomes clear. In order for everyone in the public school system to escape the trap of "these big lies" and to gain a degree of definitional authority in their lives at school, the ability to look back at the workings of power in public education must be developed. A beginning step toward achieving this goal is to work toward a more intimate understanding of the goals of modern power, or what Foucault calls the functions of discipline.

The Functions of Discipline

According to Foucault, any panoptic system that regulates the behavior of a large population serves the same common goals. In his essay "Panopticism"[8] he describes four basic functions of discipline, four large purposes that are served through the exercise of modern power:

> Discipline fixes; it arrests or regulates movements; it clears up confusion, it dissipates compact groupings of individuals wandering about the country in unpredictable ways, it establishes calculated distributions.

> Discipline must master all the forces that are formed from the very constitution of an organized multiplicity; it must neutralize the effects of counterpower that spring from them and which form a resistance to the power that wishes to dominate it—agitations, revolts, spontaneous organizations, coalitions—anything that may establish horizontal conjunctions.

> [The disciplines] must also increase the particular utility of each element of the multiplicity, but by means that are the most rapid and the least costly, that is to say, by using the multiplicity itself as an instrument of this growth.[9]

> [The disciplines have to] bring into play the power relations, not above but inside the very texture of the multiplicity, as discreetly as possible, as well articulated on the other functions of these multiplicities and also in the least expensive way possible.

In summary, the overarching purpose of a discipline or a modern technology of power (metaphorically known as a panopticon) is to decrease the people's political power while maximizing their productivity and utility in efficient, cost-effective ways. In order to accomplish this, discipline functions in four specific ways: (1) it defines, organizes, and regulates "reality"; (2) it separates and neutralizes people; (3) it finds efficient ways to utilize people and maximize their productivity; and (4) it infiltrates, studies, and documents everything and everyone that is subject to its power.

The panoptic linchpin is in the second function named above: in order to achieve its overall goal of decreasing the people's political power while maximizing their productivity and utility in efficient, cost-effective ways, those people must be separated and neutralized. After all, workers who have the time and energy to organize will work at cross-purposes to the panoptic vision of utility and efficiency. Discipline, wrote Foucault,

> must master all the forces that are formed from the very constitution of an organized multiplicity; it must neutralize the effects of counterpower that spring from them and which form a resistance to the power that wishes to dominate it; agitations, revolts, spontaneous organizations, coalitions—anything that may establish horizontal conjunctions. Hence the fact that the disciplines use procedures of partitioning and verticality; that they introduce, between the different

elements at the same level, as solid separations as possible; that they define compact hierarchical networks; in short, that they oppose to the intrinsic, adverse force of multiplicity the technique of the continuous, individualizing pyramid.[10]

In order to understand how control in the public school panopticon is achieved, picture the education system in these terms, as a "continuous, individualizing pyramid." Imagine a pyramid that is divided into a series of hierarchical rows. Next, imagine that each row is divided horizontally so that each side of the pyramid itself looks like a triangular brick wall. Each brick is an individual cell, and each cell is occupied by an individual person in the system. The highest tier in the pyramid is composed of only one cell, while the bottom tier has been divided into the greatest number of cells. There are so many cells and so many hierarchical levels that there is a place within this pyramid for everyone who has anything to do with the public schools: principals and parents, students and politicians, administrators and educational assistants, elementary teachers and university professors, student teachers and school board members, governors and CEOs.

Where would each of these players be placed within the public school panopticon? Who occupies the highest and lowest tiers in the pyramid? Which cell would a Kindergarten teacher occupy? a high school principal? a state legislator? an educational assistant? a university professor? Now, add a wrinkle. Instead of lumping parents, for instance, into one undifferentiated group, add socioeconomic descriptors. Where would middle-class parents belong in this pyramid? wealthy parents? poor parents? Next add other descriptors like race and gender. Where would the Native American female student go? the White male? the Hispanic female? the African American male? How about the socially-connected mother whose son is autistic? The homeless dad whose daughter has Down Syndrome?

The pyramid doesn't exist so that we can imagine that each category of participants is fixed in their "correct" space; obviously, variables like race, class, and gender complicate the assignment of hierarchical positioning. The pyramid is simply a metaphor for illustrating the continuous, individualizing hierarchy of the public school panopticon. The system only works if the people are individualized, fragmented, and atomized—that is, effectively contained in their cells. To that end, measures are taken to ensure that the cell walls themselves are impermeable, discouraging sustained and meaningful interaction between the people in the system. Not only is vertical movement in the panoptic pyramid made difficult in this way (some educational assistants, parents, and teachers would feel out of place talking with the superintendent about district policies, for example); horizontal movement must also be constrained to protect the interests of the elite tier that currently directs the system. After all, if teachers, much less students and parents, had the time and the support to engage regularly with each other in spirited, focused discussions about education, the very concept of school as we know it would be forever changed. And that, from the perspective of that top cell in the panopticon, would not be good, literally, for business. Children growing up with the daily experience of witnessing their parents and teachers talking, arguing, and making decisions together—even participating in those arguments and decisions themselves—would probably not become the gullible and voracious consumers they are currently groomed to be.

When the cell walls of "the continuous, individualizing pyramid" are constructed solidly, people are indeed *individualized* rather than encouraged to develop a sense of collectivity or solidarity. The continuous, individualizing pyramid serves the goal of the "responsible men." As Chomsky said (with sardonic tongue in cheek), "People must be atomized and separated if they are to be ruled by the responsible men, for their own good."[11] Isolation and individualism—the stuff in which the social condition of amoral familism is brewed—represent ideal operating conditions from the perspective of the elite tier in the system. Conversely, in the case of the public school panopticon, what *threatens* the elite who are guiding the accountability spotlight are "agitations, revolts, spontaneous organizations, coalitions—anything that may establish horizontal conjunctions."[12] People joining with one another to pursue common interests do not serve the interests of the ruling class. Horizontal conjunctions, therefore, are systematically discouraged through the use of what Foucault calls the modern instruments of discipline, that is, through "the use of those overall methods known as timetables, collective training, exercises, and total and detailed surveillance,"[13] thus creating optimal conditions for the trouble-free and efficient utilization of the system's workers.

I want to be clear about my position: I support the concept and need for accountability. What I challenge is the version of one-way accountability in which those who occupy the elite tiers of the hierarchy presume the right to define the ends and means of accountability for students, teachers, and families without ensuring that their own roles and responsibilities are equally well-defined and visible. My purpose is neither to suggest that the hierarchy itself should—or could—be done away with. Nor is it to decrease the need for accountability in the public schools. My purpose is to argue for a healthier system in which definitional authority is more evenly distributed and in which the essential demand for accountability applies in equal measure to all of the participants in every tier of the system. My findings support the idea that one way to improve the health of the public school panopticon is for workers in the system to both reject on one hand the idea that *they* are the only appropriate focus for the accountability spotlight, and on the other hand to claim the right to help guide the direction of that beam. Finally, I argue that one effective way to create a hunger for this kind of definitional authority in the "lower" tiers is through the purposeful and diligent cultivation of both horizontal and vertical conjunctions. By this I mean that the concept of volatile knowing—the joining together of people from similar (horizontal conjunctions) and dissimilar (vertical conjunctions) hierarchical levels for the purpose of broadening access to local definitional authority in the schools—must be intentionally nurtured.

The seemingly simple goal of connecting with other people in the system will be an extraordinarily difficult thing to accomplish, however. The applications of the modern instruments of power (e.g., timetables, collective training, exercises, and total and detailed surveillance) are entrenched in our minds, invested with the status of common sense, of normalcy. A next step toward claiming definitional authority, therefore, is to examine and interrogate the instruments of discipline themselves. In making them visible, we may be able to reach an understanding of just what it is that we in the "lower" tiers of the system might wish to have the authority to define.

Notes

1. Michel Foucault, *The Foucault Reader* (New York: Pantheon Books, 1984).

2. Foucault, *Foucault Reader*, 199.

3. Michelle Fine, "[Ap]parent Involvement: Reflections on Parents, Power, and Urban Public Schools," *Teachers College Record* 94, no. 4 (Summer 1993), The Philadelphia Story, ¶29.

4. Michel Foucault, *Discipline and Punish* (New York: Vintage Books, 1977).

5. Foucault, *Foucault Reader*, 206.

6. Foucault, *Foucault Reader*, 210.

7. Arturo Ornelas, personal communication, April 1, 1999.

8. In Foucault, *Foucault Reader*.

9. Foucault, *Foucault Reader*, 208–209.

10. Foucault, *Foucault Reader*, 209.

11. Noam Chomsky, "Renewing Tom Paine's Challenge" in *Our Media Not Theirs*, by Robert McChesney and John Nichols (New York: Seven Stories Press, 2002), 18–19.

12. Foucault, *Foucault Reader*, 209.

13. Foucault, *Foucault Reader*, 209.

CHAPTER 7

The Instruments of Discipline

In order for the ruling classes to achieve the panoptic goal of decreasing the people's political power while maximizing their productivity in efficient, cost-effective ways (that is, in order to control them profitably), it is essential that appropriate steps are taken to ensure that those people are isolated to the greatest extent possible. Of ultimate concern is the prevention of "horizontal conjunctions" that would threaten the power structure of the public school panopticon. In two essays, "Panopticism" and "The Means of Correct Training," Foucault names a number of specific tools that are employed for the purposes of separating and neutralizing the people. Through the course of our group discussions, the use of each of these instruments of discipline could be identified, in varying degrees, in all of the schools represented in our group: (1) the timetable, (2) hierarchical observation, (3) normalizing judgment, (4) the examination, (5) collective training, and (6) superficial exercises. Beyond the six specific instruments of discipline named by Foucault, three additional disciplinary tools were described by these teachers and parents: (7) the expert, (8) the memo, and (9) control of mainstream media. In a later section each of these instruments of discipline will be described and illustrated.

These disciplinary tools were not the subject of discussions in our study group. It was actually through the processes of analysis that I discovered their presence in our transcripts. Two things led to this discovery: one was the identification, through my initial analysis of data, of the three themes that I described in Chapter 5 (disconnection/competition, a crisis of faith, and definitional authority). Foucault's perspective on the modern disciplines of power provided an explanatory framework for those themes. The other incident that led to my analysis of transcripts through the Foucauldian lens of discipline was a comment that Boyoyo made in our final meeting together. Toward the end of that meeting, he asked what sense I was making of our study group's conversations. I responded by briefly describing Foucault's theory of panopticism. I drew a picture for participants of his "continuous, individualizing pyramid" to explain his view of how control is maintained in any system by creating a hierarchical network of individual cells for the people to occupy. Boyoyo looked at the picture I had drawn and said, "That's a problem that we have as humans, that we always like power. So everybody has a little fault. Some more, some less. We even apply that kind of stuff even in the classroom, sometimes." I responded by saying that I was thinking that we needed to figure out how to make the boundaries between all of the levels in the hierarchy a little less solid. "You know," I said, "if those boundaries could be made with dotted lines instead of with hard and fast lines like these..." Boyoyo interrupted me then with a mind-turning thought, exclaiming, "Osmosis! There is no osmosis. We need to make the membrane of the cells more permeable."

It was Boyoyo's connection of panopticism to osmosis that sent me back to re-examine some of Foucault's essays that I had read several times during previous years. While my interpretation of the panopticon then had led me to the conclusion that a healthy hierarchy would be constructed of cells with dotted lines for walls (an image that was, in fact, partially responsible for my idea of designing a research project with teachers *and* parents as participants), Boyoyo's introduction of osmosis made me want to take a much closer look at the internal structure of the panopticon. This time around, I read Foucault with the ideas of cell wall composition and permeability in mind. This time, when I read that the disciplines "use procedures of partitioning and verticality" and that "they introduce, between the differing elements at the same level, as solid separations as possible," I was actively imagining the composition of the barriers that tend to prevent me from connecting in meaningful and critical ways with others, within and between every level of the system. So it was that on this sixth or seventh reading of "Panopticism" I was ready to connect with Foucault's description of the modern exercise of power in a way I hadn't before. Now, with Boyoyo's analogy of osmosis to guide me, I thought about systemic health and disease in association with Foucault's introduction of the instruments of discipline.

> Hence, in order to extract from bodies the maximum time and force, the use of those overall methods known as timetables, collective training, exercises, and total and detailed surveillance.[1]

Through analysis of group discussion transcripts, I identified many examples from teachers' and parents' stories illustrating the use of these and other instruments of discipline that effectively create "solid separations" between people in the public schools. These separations between cells are constructed with the instruments of discipline, and their composition is so solid as to prohibit the metaphorical functions of osmosis. I will return to the concept of healthy osmosis in the panopticon. For now, it is enough to say that disease rather than health appears to be the more prevalent condition in our schools. This conclusion resulted from the ease with which I discovered, through analysis of group discussion transcripts, that Foucault's "procedures of partitioning and verticality" are abundantly evident in the public school panopticon. In large ways and small, these procedures impede the people's free exchange of ideas, questions, criticisms, and dreams for new possibilities. If such things as these can be taken as nutrients in the context of schools—where education and learning and growth are the goals—it is reasonable to conclude that as an organism, the public school system is dying. While public school opponents may be undisturbed or even unsurprised at this effect of heightened discipline in the name of accountability, the possibility of public education dying at this pivotal moment in history bodes ill for the ideals of democracy and social justice. The more hopeful perspective on the flip side of this coin is that the cure for starvation is obvious. If the free exchange of thought within and between the hierarchical levels of the system can be seen as analogous to food for the people within the public school panopticon, then every person with an idea, a question, a critical perspective, or a dream for new possibilities already possesses the means for reviving the people's definitional authority and the public ideal for our schools. The key is in realizing that our cell walls are constructions created by means of the instruments of discipline; as such, they are subject to deconstruction. The individualizing walls of our public school panopticon are only as solid as we believe them to be.

In the next section I will describe and illustrate the nine disciplinary instruments evidenced in discussion transcripts as being in use in participants' neighborhood schools: (1) the timetable, (2) hierarchical observation, (3) normalizing judgment, (4) the examination, (5) collective training, (6) superficial exercises, (7) the expert, (8) the memo, and (9) control of mainstream media. (A summary of these disciplinary instruments and their correlation to the functions of discipline is provided in Appendix B, *Discipline in the Public School Panopticon*.)

It is precisely here, in making the names and the applications of these disciplinary instruments visible, where I believe the ultimate significance of this study lies. These simple, familiar mechanisms represent the means by which hierarchical control is accomplished. They are the means by which "the maximum time and force" is "extracted" from the bodies of all who live and work within the public school panopticon. In making these familiar exercises of power strange by describing them in the context of panopticism, I hope to prompt an expanding conversation and ongoing study of the ways in which definitional authority in the public schools can be both lost and found.

The Re-inversion of Visibility:
Shining the Light on the Instruments of Discipline

1. The Timetable

This is one of the most powerful and effective instruments of discipline that Foucault names. I interpret "the timetable" as a mechanism of power to mean that those in the upper tiers of the panopticon reserve for themselves the authority to control how time is spent throughout the system. The power to control time and to dictate schedules is one that increases in an inverse proportion to the number of cells that exist at each panoptic tier: the fewer the cells there are on any given level, the more control do the individuals in them have over their own and others' time.

Control of time figured prominently as a topic in many of our study group's discussions. One example I have already described is in the "addendum" to a principal's back-to-school letter in which elementary teachers were brusquely informed of how their first day of the new school year would be spent:

> After the convocation, which ends at approximately 10:15 a.m. you will imme-
> diately return to [Name of School] where we will go over school business until
> between 12:00 and 12:30. You will then be release [sic] for lunch and come
> back to [Name of School] to meet with grade levels to work on your curriculum
> mapping. Attendance will be taken at the beginning of the meeting.

In Chapter 5, I briefly raised the issue of female compliance in the elementary school. Gender dynamics may again be present in the context of discussing the disciplinary strategy of controlling timetables, as time appears to be more tightly controlled in elementary schools than at any other educational level. Peyton, Mariela, and Alex, the elementary teachers in the group, discussed their reality of having one hour a week to prepare for all of the different content areas they are responsible for teaching, in comparison to the daily preparation periods that their colleagues in middle and high schools enjoy—despite typically having fewer subjects to teach. Other teachers and the parent participants in the group were shocked to learn that neither the elementary teacher's weekly hour of planning time nor her legal right to a duty-free lunch period are guaranteed. Peyton explained, "If our P.E. teacher is sick, P.E. is just cancelled that day and your prep's *gone* for that half-hour!" Mariela added, "And if the wind blows at lunch, which just happened at our school, we go back to class! We come back in! So we didn't get lunch." To this, Peyton and Alex nodded along in agreement. "Right," said Alex. "So you don't get to eat lunch."

Control of timetables is a powerful and effective instrument of discipline because people whose time is tightly controlled cannot organize. If you're kept busy all day long, even to the point that "during your lunchtime you're with the kids," as Rachel said, "it becomes *very* difficult to organize. That has been the problem of working class people throughout history!" When workers "just don't have the physical time to organize," as Rachel pointed out, it is more likely that the panoptic goal of "increasing the particular utility of each element of the multiplicity, but by means that are the most rapid and the least costly" will be achieved.[2]

A final example that I will cite of how time is controlled in public schools is in Boyoyo's description of his principal's message to her teachers that "I don't want to hear that somebody is having free time. We don't have time for that. Don't be creative. Don't risk. Just go with what we are saying. Follow the rules of the game." The prescription of "zero free time" for achieving school success is a clear indicator that the values in Boyoyo's corner of the panopticon have nothing to do with the human needs that children and teachers bring to the work of teaching and learning. On the other hand, this principal's prescription for success couldn't have served the values and interests of the elite more perfectly. In admonishing teachers not to take risks, not to be creative, and not to allow students a single moment of down time in "their" studies, she identified herself as a thoroughly disciplined individual—a true guard dog of the ideology of the ruling classes.[3] If the elite tier were to sponsor competitions for their amusement, this would qualify as a show-dog caliber performance.

Clearly, control of time is a powerful disciplinary instrument used freely in, and on, schools. Teachers use it, too. While an administrative version of this power may be to say, "There is no free time," a similarly autocratic teacher's version might sound more like, "No, you may not (go to the bathroom, sharpen your pencil, get a drink of water)." Though the scope of their power varies, the tools of discipline work in all levels of the hierarchy.

The teachers in this study know at an experiential level what Foucault meant when he observed that "in order to extract from bodies the maximum time and force," certain strategies are effective, including the use of such things as "timetables, collective training, exercises, and total and detailed surveillance."[4] They know that they are not in control of their own time, and they know how effectively this reality works to constrain any potential for "horizontal conjunctions" in their professional lives. They may not be imagining "agitations, revolts, spontaneous organizations, or coalitions" as the activities they would indulge if they had the time; just being able to talk every day and share ideas with other teachers in their schools would be revolutionary for people who currently can't count on the privilege of getting to eat lunch.

2. Hierarchical Observation: Total and Detailed Surveillance

From the perspective of the ruling classes, all of those in the lower tiers of the panopticon must be visible at all times in order for the panopticon to function correctly. The lower the tier, the more visible they must be. This degree of visibility is accomplished through the disciplinary instrument of hierarchical observation. The key to the successful use of this mechanism of power is that it must function internally at every level of the system, since external surveillance of the people at every hierarchical level would be both clumsy and costly. Hierarchical observation that functions well from the inside requires the existence of people at every level who have accepted and adopted panoptic values, like the ideals of capitalism and competition in market ideology, for example, as their own operative norms.

In our group's final session in late October, Peyton talked through a theme that she had been thinking about: the lack of trust among colleagues at her school. While she didn't use Foucault's language, her ability to see, name, and critique hierarchical observation as a disciplinary instrument being utilized at her school is strongly evident:

> I was just writing about the idea of trust, and wondering why we don't have it anymore within our schools. I was thinking about my school. We're trying to move away from it this year, but last year it was really bad. Teachers started policing other teachers, to the extent of calling the papers and calling the superintendent because they basically didn't think the principal was policing enough. But what had created *that*, though, was that the principal and the superintendent had started policing us! They caused us to police one another!
>
> And I was thinking about the idea that we have to sign in for *every single meeting*. You know, policing is *only* about making sure that we're putting in the time. But if we put in extra time for curriculum night, or Fall Share, or all those other things that we're doing after hours every day, you don't ever hear them saying, 'Of course, go. I know you're doing your planning at home.' And just, why that trust went away. Because it didn't used to be that way. I mean, it's so interesting! That it's just policing, literally, *every, little, tiny thing.* It's crazy.

Administrators, too, are surveilled. They, too, are disciplined by means of the same instruments that they have the power to use on those "beneath" them. Hierarchical observation is about making individuals visible in the panopticon. While the intensity of this disciplinary instrument may decrease with each successively higher tier in the system, it is more than strong enough to be acutely felt at each administrative level. The system as a whole works because the instruments of discipline work effectively at every level. Awareness of this administrative reality was revealed when Sarah brought up an excerpt from my research proposal.

> You were talking about your interaction with the principal. And how, out of one side of her mouth she was very supportive and said, 'We value your voice. We value your creativity and your teaching style, blah, blah, blah. But just give the tests and comply. And do it our way,' meaning, 'because we think that's really more important.'

Rachel replied by saying, "Well, is it that it's more important, or is it that *they're* under tremendous pressure from *their* superiors? And they're frustrated. They're kind of sandwiched, too." I think again of the principal who comforted her "failing" teachers who had missed making Adequate Yearly Progress in only one of five areas by saying with a grin, "But another school in our district missed all five!" In light of such evidence of the effectiveness of hierarchical observation in getting the people within the public school panopticon to internalize and accept its priorities and values as their own, the introduction to panopticism in Chapter 6 may be more clearly understood: when the prisoners have accepted systemic values and expectations as their own, guards become superfluous. This modern technology of power is all about efficiency and the utilization of fear. A very large prison population can thus be effectively policed by a very small number of guards if the inmates can be manipulated into policing themselves. An entire workforce of teachers and an entire population of students and their parents can be domesticated if they can be taught to internalize the competitive, capitalistic values of the corporate-state, subordinating democratic concerns to market demands.

3. Normalizing Judgment

Hierarchical observation would be pointless in the absence of this instrument, about which Foucault writes: "the power of normalization imposes homogeneity; but it individualizes by making it possible to measure gaps, to determine levels, to fix specialties, and to render the differences useful."[5] The purpose of surveillance itself is to ensure that individuals at each level in the panopticon are behaving, measuring up to all of the values and expectations that are promoted by the system. The very idea that a condition called "normal" exists is what gives rise to seemingly commonsensical goals like "being on grade level." It is the power of normalizing judgment that makes being on grade level a "natural" and universally shared value in the public school panopticon. Another way to look at the phrase, "being on grade level," of course, is through critique of the foundational idea upon which it is based. Because twenty-five children are the same age, there is no sound reason for expecting that they should all be able to know and do the same things, in the same way, at the same time in their lives.

Because the overarching goal of discipline is to "increase the particular utility of each element of the multiplicity, but by means that are the most rapid and the least costly,"[6] normalizing judgment is exercised; and since the great majority of the individuals inside of the panopticon are invested in accepting and internalizing the expectations and values of the system, the "norm" becomes the basis for establishing policy. In this way, "being on grade level" becomes the obvious and natural goal for every child—instead of being revealed as a perverse slogan used to mask the fact that most schools are simply not arranged to suit the needs of individual children.

None of this is to say that normalizing judgment in itself is bad. General guidelines describing "typical" child development, for example, are useful to parents and teachers alike. The processes of normalization may even be considered essential in terms of parents' and teachers' responsibilities to socialize children—to prepare them for healthy interactions with others and for positive engagement in their communities. The problem is one of determining appropriate usage. If the goal of normalizing judgment is to gain compliance rather than to facilitate growth, then disciplinary success can be declared when the people have agreed to just "lay down and let 'em run all over you," which is how Sarah described her understanding of what compliance means.

When judgment is used as a normalizing instrument for the purposes that Foucault names of comparing, differentiating, hierarchizing, homogenizing, and excluding,[7] it serves panoptic ends rather than human ones. Several people in this study had experience with these various processes of normalization. Those who didn't always behave as submissively as they were supposed to, and even some who were only thinking about "misbehaving," talked about consequences in terms of negative labels being attached to them by those who are positioned a tier or two above them in the hierarchy. While negative labels or name-calling may not seem like an overly threatening consequence when viewed from this distance, these teachers' and parents' words make it clear that to be judged and found abnormal is not a trivial matter to them.

- I would love to do something like that, to invite you to come and speak to our PTA. But it's obvious, if I do that the principal would say, 'Oh, Boyoyo is now a rebel.' (Boyoyo)

- You feel that you have an entre into that school, and you don't want to blow that. You don't want to make anyone think that you're a troublemaker. (Sarah)

- We're not these menopausal women. They used to say that's what we were! That we don't have better things to do. You know, we're just out there causing havoc at the schools! (Elena)

- A lot of times when the school principal or teachers would see me coming, they're like, 'Oh, what is she going to do now?' I'm convinced that at the middle school I was the dragon lady. I swear the signal went off when I came in the building. You know, you think of what you hear in the ER, 'Code Red! Code Red!' (Selena)

- When you in any way rock the boat, or fragilize an administrator, yes. You risk letters of reprimand in your files. You risk being branded as a negative person, as somebody who's not a good team player. (Rachel)

- I'm considered the crazy person. I have those letters of reprimand in my children's files. You know, 'She's a crazy mother. The kid is really adorable but the mother's insane.' (Julia)

How are we to make sense of the fact that two middle-aged Latinas remember being called "menopausal women" in reaction to their activism on behalf of the children and families in their neighborhoods? ("They used to say that's what we were!") What should we think about the fact that several participants imagine charges of insanity as the system's response to their "misbehavior"? My view is that these examples are evidence of normalizing judgment at work, a disciplinary instrument being strategically deployed to contain and control disruptions in the system. "Menopausal" is a punishing term intended to put an assertive, middle-aged woman in her place. In pointing out a woman's deviation from her expected role of sexual viability and compliant submission, it is a normalizing term of discipline. (It's hard to imagine two middle-aged activist fathers dismissively referred to as "those impotent, balding men.") Beyond the targeting of voices by gender, "menopausal" as an epithet was an attempt in this case to neutralize the voices of two working class women of color. Would extremely affluent women who happened to be White be similarly demeaned? Possibly. The layers of normalizing judgment are complex.

Participants' consideration of being labeled "menopausal women" "rebel," "dragon lady," "troublemaker," "negative," and "crazy mother" as a perceived consequence for being noncompliant suggests their understanding of the processes of normalization at an experiential level. Indeed, each of these labels serves as a means for comparing, differentiating, hierarchizing, homogenizing, and excluding—in short, for creating a continuum for defining "good" and "bad" kinds of parent and teacher participation in schools.

4. The Examination

This disciplinary tool makes ingenious use of both hierarchical observation and normalizing judgment. The examination is itself "a normalizing gaze, a surveillance that makes it possible to qualify, to classify, and to punish."[8] It is through examination that individuals are made visible—whether that examination takes the form of a standardized test or an annual review; and the condition of compulsory visibility, according to Foucault, is exactly that which "maintains the disciplined individual in his subjection."[9] To be an object of power is to be seen; to be powerful is to control the gaze. Documentation is therefore an essential activity within the panopticon, as individuals are reduced to the cumulative contents of their performance files.

While the examination was framed in terms of standardized tests in our study group, it is important to note that this instrument of discipline applies to a broad spectrum of surveillance and documentation activities. In the state in which this study took place, for example, standardized tests have recently been replaced with a state-developed criterion-referenced test. While this move will theoretically make success at least feasible for all children (versus the norm-referenced style of test construction based on percentile rankings, guaranteeing test-score distribution along a bell curve), the underlying issue of elite-tier control of the public school panopticon and the exercise of disciplinary instruments like the examination remain. In the context of this discussion, it is also worth remembering some of the research findings on motivation that Alfie Kohn summarized: (1) People who participate in an activity where the stakes are raised (i.e., when extrinsic motivators are used), are less creative and do work of poorer quality than do those who participate in an activity for its own sake; and (2) our internal motivation suffers when we are threatened, watched, forced to work under a deadline, controlled, made to compete against other people, and expecting to be evaluated. "In fact," writes Kohn, "any time we are encouraged to focus on how well we are doing at something—as opposed to concentrating on the process of actually doing it—it is less likely that we will like the activity and keep doing it when given a choice."[10]

In illustrating the impact of this instrument of discipline upon the lives of the parents and teachers in our study group, at least three specific effects of the examination can be identified. First, a continual emphasis on examination in the schools is shaping understandings of what it means to teach and to parent. It usurps teachers' and parents' definitional authority to define their own roles and identities. While the teachers in this group spoke of their resistance to being defined by the examination (by refusing to do such things as to devote time to test preparation, to use "canned" curricula, and to "paper their walls" with standards, for example), they acknowledged the constant pressure that teachers are under to define their roles in terms of the examination's disciplinary perspective. Boyoyo described how hard it can be to resist defining "teacher" in this way.

> It is very hard. We just took those *Assess to Learn* tests. So I went to check the test and I say, 'Oh, we only have covered this little part. I haven't covered all this stuff!' And supposedly they have received it in elementary, but I don't know! So then I start feeling it. You start to feel again that pressure. And that makes me go, 'Okay. We're going to do this, and this, and this,' and I start putting on a lot of stuff. And I can see the kids, I can see their eyes, that they are not with me any more. I don't know where they are, but they are not with me. Because I was trying to, 'Oh, now I need to cover this and this and this, because they are going to ask them again and they are going to *fail* again.'
>
> And I was feeling that this weekend. I was getting all this tension. I was just putting a lot of questions about fractions, and what about this, and what about this? And kids were getting *lost* again. There were a few that were catching it. And I started going, 'Come *on*, you guys! Make the connection!' And I was getting all.... [Boyoyo makes a strangling noise; group laughter.]
>
> And that's when I go, ohhh. Just relax. Do a project. They are going to have fun, and they are going to learn this little part, and probably there will be a better chance that they are going to learn that *well*. Even if they don't learn the other stuff, because if you go the other way they are not going to learn for sure. So Monday we started with a project.

Peyton's perspective on how the examination is impacting the definition of what it means to teach also brings into question the issue of what it means to learn. She introduced the idea that an excessive emphasis on test performance runs contrary to the constructivist view of learning that is endorsed, according to Kohn, by "virtually all cognitive researchers today."[11]

> I had never made the connection before, but I think because of tests, because of the pressures, that we're now focusing on what kids don't know instead of what they do know. I remember being taught to find out what kids know so you can build on it. And now we just aggregate data to figure out what they didn't know

well on their test, so we can teach them what they didn't know. We don't even care what they do know. We don't even look at it.

The examination appears to be effective in claiming the authority—not only from individual teachers but from "virtually all cognitive researchers"—to define what it means to teach and to learn in "our" public schools.

Parents, too, spoke of the power that the examination has had in defining what they have thought their own role should be in their children's lives at school. For Selena, the examination in the form of standardized test scores encouraged her to define her own advocacy for her children in terms of the market. With standardized test scores in hand, she became a shopper in search of a good deal.

> I would use test scores to gauge, is this a good classroom for my daughter? And I used it as if I was coupon shopping! As I got more involved in the school, then I had access to which teachers' scores were really up there. You know, now I think if I could go back to that time, I *wouldn't* pay attention to that.

An emphasis on examination over collaborative discussion effectively disempowers parents as team players in the public schools. The twist in looking at this aspect of the examination is that sometimes it is the parents themselves who feel as if they are the subjects of the review. Elena explained the phenomenon in this way:

> But we get sucked *in* with the testing through parent-teacher conferences! When the test results come, the teacher will sit right there and say, "This is where your child fits at. Right here." And then you're like, *ohh,* my *god!* And my daughter, she freaks with testing. She never does good. So she was at the bottom of all those, and I felt like *I* was failing. I never really said the teacher was. I felt like *I* was doing something wrong.

Sarah agreed, saying, "And that's what the tests do to you as a parent. They make you think *you're* failing." Parents' perceptions of being examined and judged in schools are attached to a broader context than their children's performances on standardized tests. Two parent participants in the group, Elena and Selena, spoke of their participation in parent-teacher meetings at school as experiences in feeling examined themselves. "At the parent-teacher conferences there's six teachers against *one parent,*" said Elena. "And the whole time it's, 'Your student isn't doing *this,* this, this.' So it's, it's a big intimidation factor that a lot of us as parents feel." Selena described her experience from a decade ago as the mother of a child with special needs, attending Individualized Education Plan (IEP) meetings in which her *perception* of examination defined her behavior.

> Don't you have the social worker or somebody in those IEPs? My thing was, what if I said the wrong thing and they take my daughter away from me? Be-

cause the words 'social worker,' to me, means I'm not doing my job as a mom! And looking back at that, I would always think about that. One is a social worker. You know? And I took it negative. Only welfare people have social workers because they're on welfare and something's not right with their parenting skills. So *that's* what stayed on my mind! I've got to watch my P's and Q's. I can't show I'm mad, you know, because what if they take my daughter away from me? That's how stup. . . naive I was. [Laughs.] Or intimidated. Or not knowing. Not knowing.

Clearly, the examination as an instrument of discipline is powerful in its ability to define the words we live by. What it means to teach, to learn, and to be an effective advocate for one's own children are meanings that are significantly shaped by the surveilling and documenting processes of examination.

A second effect of an emphasis on examination is that school cultures are increasingly competitive and inhumane, particularly for those participants who are associated with schools in poorer neighborhoods. This more competitive, inhumane trend is evident in the words of several members of our study group:

- I've watched my school change. It used to be a place where the test came once a year and we just took it. We didn't prepare for it. We prepared kids to learn, every day of our lives. And so we weren't worried about the test. And now, I see that we are worrying more about the tests, and teaching kids how to take a test. How to fill in bubbles. That's what my school has turned into. Teachers teach to a test, now. (Peyton)

- I'm just hearing from different parents, what they're going through at this school. The parents aren't communicating with one another that their child was really sick and upset when they had to take these tests. And parents didn't want to share that with one another because they were embarrassed! And the one comment that one parent made, she goes, 'Elena, I never told anybody! My son is sick, always with a stomach ache.' It's just the weirdest thing. They focus so much on the testing, and the human element is missing. (Elena)

- We're going into corrective action next year because they've given us our chance. We were told this week that they're thinking of bringing in a whole new staff if they're not pleased with us by the end of the year. Of taking us and putting us somewhere else. (Julia)

- The state will take over, and nobody knows what that means. Does that then mean that they give us to Edison? (Rachel)

Some of these words give rise to the image of the public school panopticon as a giant board game with human tokens. Teachers who speak of being "put" somewhere else and "given" to Edison—based on their having been examined and found lacking—and parents who can see that "the human element is missing" provide evidence that for students and teachers alike, the schools in our nation's poorer neighborhoods can be dehumanizing places in which to live and work. The fact that a relationship can be detected, even in the context of this small study, between the existence of wealth and a humanizing approach to education in our schools is a public disgrace. It is a disgrace that has existed long before standardized testing became the panopticon's primary means of holding schools accountable to their publics; but somehow the disgrace seems deeper over a decade after Kozol's exposure of the savage inequalities that exist in the educational opportunities available to America's different "kinds" of children. Unfortunately, it does not appear to suit panoptic purposes to exercise the disciplinary instrument of examination for the purpose of assessing whether all children have access to a deeply humanizing experience with education.

A third effect of the examination as a disciplinary instrument in the public school panopticon is manifested in the way that it serves to sort and rank children, teachers, and schools. This sorting and ranking mechanism provides an "objective" means of defining variable worth—but perhaps more importantly, from a top-tier perspective, it provides the means by which to separate and neutralize people in the lower levels of the panopticon. Just as amoral familism is defined by its key features of individualism and isolation, the examination is defined by the key feature of competition. Therefore, this final effect of the examination is to exalt competition over cooperation, facilitating a culture of amoral familism in which students, teachers, schools, and districts are ranked and sorted. They are pitted one against the other in a race to claim the prize: a temporary stamp of success by an approving upper class.

An example of how examination as a tool of power affects the lives of the participants in this research group is illustrated in what I found to be one of the most powerful stories that emerged through the course of the study. It came up first in my initial interview with Ana, an activist and organizer in the Native American community. I had asked her what sense she was making of the word "accountability" in the public schools, and her response rocked me. Before I share this story, though, I need to set the stage by sharing my initial response to it.

This was the only time during the course of this study when I believe that my "whiteness" interfered with my ability to communicate well with a participant. As I listened to Ana's response to my question about accountability, I was unsure at first that she had understood what I was trying to get at. It took me awhile to realize, as I listened, that Ana understood exactly what I was asking, and that while I was quietly wondering whether or not she had understood me she was going about the process of answering my question in her own way. The following exchange with Ana represents my personal epitome of experience in confronting the unconscious arrogance that can come with being born and bred into the dominant language and culture. Intellectual knowledge of "direct" and "circular" communication patterns grew into real understanding for me when I was able to consciously experience my own assumptions about how conversation is supposed to work. When I finally saw where Ana was taking my question, I realized that she was indeed addressing it in a profoundly personal, powerful, and historic way. As I look at her words now through the lens I am using here, I see that she was at the same time showing me another effect of examination in a disciplinary system: to rank and sort, to separate and neutralize, and to "objectively" assign variable values to the children, teachers, schools, and entire communities that exist within the public school panopticon.

I asked Ana, "How is accountability in schools being defined? And how should it be defined?" I include the length of this exchange in order to allow the reader to share my own experience of discovery, from the uncertainty of wondering whether my question had been heard to the profundity of the analogy to which Ana was leading me.

Ana: Well, see, that's the situation with the Native peoples here. They conquered us, but without a fight. And they realized that we wouldn't go down, that we would fight for what we had. So they were, like, okay, we'll oppress them by putting them on reservations, and we'll control them by not allowing them to hunt buffalo. We'll kill off all the buffalo, their way of living. We'll acculturate them to our way, we'll acclimate them to make them like us. We'll force our religion on them. Our religion, so then they will become more civilized.

We had our own culture. We had our own religion. Actually, I don't want to say religion. Our spirituality. And that's how they were changing us, to control us. To divide and conquer. And then they went through the phase that they conquered us, they took our food away, they took our land away, made us live on reservations. They made us dependent on them, the government did, by taking our food away. They were rationing food to us. And then they took away food and said we're not going to feed you any more because Indians are uprising. You know, practicing your cultural beliefs, your spirituality. And then, when even that didn't succeed they tried to kill us off, to exterminate us through different diseases. Which, we survived that. And then they thought, well, we'll take the kids away from their parents and put them in boarding schools. And that's when the students were beaten. They were sexually abused, physically abused, psychologically abused. So they tried to take that culture and language away. And then *that* didn't work. We still survived *that*.

So, now, they taught us the way of government. The way the government works, which is not the way our tribal government works. I mean, our grassroots way of, I don't want to say governing the people, but our natural way of keeping people together. Our culture together. But our governmental tribes are now using the U.S. Congress's methods of governing the people, which is not really working. We want to go back to our traditional ways. To a grassroots way of teaching, of thinking.

A long time ago, before the colonizers came, we were all equal. We all had a say. And all this, I don't know, internalized oppression and everything, it has to intertwine. To intertwine with how the government wanted us to be. And they wanted us to be dependent on them in regards to money, funding, food. But we're coming, the Native American people, the Indian people are coming to a way where we want to be more self determined, like we're supposed to be. So we try to pull away from all the government funding. And this is where the federal government is saying, well, you're self determined. We can't help you. They divide and conquer. That is their thinking.

That's what I see in this situation, what you're talking about. The government wants us to think, or whoever wants us to think in a standardized way. I can relate to that, because of what has happened to the Native American people, all the time. You know, but we still survived. I call us the survivors. Of *all* that.

Kaia: What a perspective! That the standardized tests of today are just a modern expression of what happened 500 years ago. You know, the people that I'm interviewing, again and again I ask them about the standardized tests and about standardizing everything. And again and again, the theme that I'm hearing from people is that it's working. That the system works perfectly. The system works exactly as it was intended to work. To make sure that there are workers, and that there are leaders. And that the savage inequalities exist for a good reason. That the system is working as it was designed to. Oh, jeez. The idea that this is on a par with, you know, small pox ridden blankets[12] and . . .

Ana: Boarding school.

Kaia: The boarding schools. The taking, literally taking the children away from their families and away from their cultures and away from who they are. That this is just another . . . That this is the same thing.

Ana: So, you know, that's how I can relate to it. And that's where I think that it's really [sighs], how do you say, true to feel that that's what we're doing. You know, in regards to the Patriot Act and how the wealthy are the ones controlling the country. Globalization.

Ana's perspective on the accountability movement in education illustrates the final effect of examination that I could find as I looked at participants' words with the idea of disciplinary review in mind. This effect is in the "objective" ordering that the examination provides. Individuals are not only ranked and sorted by this means, but also separated and neutralized in the process as they are helped to internalize the labels of proficient, adequate, and failing that are "earned" as a result of their very public performances.

Ana's story suggests that the accountability movement in schools is merely another strategy, part of an historic pattern to oppress her people. I was eager for other members of our group to hear and discuss this perspective, so I asked Ana if she would share it with them. The following conversation took place after she did so, during our group's third session together. I include the length of this exchange to encourage the reader's imaginative experience of participants' questions, connections, and discoveries.

Kaia: In terms of the accountability movement, I think Ana's analogy is that a teacher handing out that test is the soldier handing out the blankets with small pox. Does that analogy work or not? Where does it break down, and where does it work? Is that a good analogy to use?

Julia: For me it is.

Kaia: Why?

Julia: I've always disliked testing. But when I came to hate it was three years ago when... This still makes me cry. I just sat there and bawled for an hour and a half, literally wiping the tears from my face, watching these kids take this test. One of my students had just been in the country two weeks, and he was forced to take a test in English! And I *had* to give it to him. And the only reason I did it is because I wanted to stay and help him, and the only way I could do that was if I stuck around.

Kaia: Let's keep poking at the analogy. Where does it work? Where does it fail?

Mariela: Well, who are *we* then? What is *our* role? Are we the soldiers who give these blankets out, knowing that they're poisonous? Are we knowing, and we are doing it anyway? [There is a pause. Mariela's questions hang in the air, briefly, in silence.]

Julia: [Quietly.] Yeah. I feel like that, sometimes.

Peyton: Or are we soldiers watching other soldiers do it? [There is a loud reaction from the group. Several people talk at once.] As a primary teacher I don't pass them out, but I'm watching other people do it.

Mariela: Mm hmm. Standing silently . . .

Julia: And it's that balance. Where do I *weigh* that balance? Do I quit my job? Or do I say, okay. I'll give them the small pox, but then I'll *treat* them? Or do I say, no, I won't give them the small pox, but somebody else will and then they'll *die*! You know?

Sarah: Yeah. The responsibility. Who's responsible?

Mariela: *Do* all the blankets *have* small pox? Am I creating problems for your son, Sarah, when I give *him* the test? Or is he going to be fine? You know?

Julia: He's immune to small pox.

Mariela: Yeah! Does he have an immunity?

Kaia: Some kids got a vaccination!

Mariela: Right! You know, the white kids that have already been exposed to small pox, they're not going to get it! You know? They'll be fine. [Laughs.] Because I think your son is going to be fine. In giving him the test, he didn't vomit from it or anything, did he? Did he feel stressed, or . . .

Sarah: He just loved getting free breakfast.

Mariela: Yeah! They served them free breakfast all month. [Laughs.] All month!

Foucault wrote that the examination is "a normalizing gaze, a surveillance that makes it possible to qualify, to classify, and to punish. It establishes over individuals a visibility through which one differentiates them and judges them."[13] Ana's take on the disciplinary role of examination helped the teachers in our group to personalize our own roles in this process of qualifying, classifying, and punishing children in the name of accountability. I don't know what went on inside of each group member during the heartbeats of silence that followed Mariela's questions of, "Well, who are *we* then? What is *our* role? Are we the soldiers who give these blankets out, knowing that they're poisonous? Are we knowing, and we are doing it anyway?" The question that followed that three-count of heartbeats recognizes and challenges the very foundation of amoral familism upon which the panopticon is built. Peyton asked, "Or are we soldiers watching other soldiers do it?"

The examination as an instrument of discipline in the public school panopticon serves at least three purposes, which I have described and illustrated through the words of the parents and teachers in this study group. In summary, the examination: (1) usurps teachers' and parents' definitional authority to define their own roles and identities; (2) creates an increasingly competitive and inhumane culture in the schools, serving the panoptic goal of separating the people and neutralizing their potential political force; and (3) further separates and neutralizes people by providing an "objective" means by which to sort, rank, and define variable worth for all who live and work within the public school panopticon.

I have thus far named, described, and illustrated what I believe are the four most powerful instruments of discipline identified by Foucault: (1) the timetable, (2) hierarchical observation, (3) normalizing judgment, and (4) the examination. He also named "collective training" and "exercises" as two other panoptic tools that are used in order to "extract from bodies the maximum time and force . . . by means that are the most rapid and the least costly."[14]

5. Collective Training

One place to begin understanding the idea of collective training as an efficient means of getting the most out of public school workers for the least amount of effort and expense is to look at how students are grouped. I have already written about the phenomenon of the almost universally internalized goal of making sure that all students are performing "on grade level." Clearly, this organizational structure is designed for systemic efficiency, not to accommodate children's variable levels of readiness to learn. This reality was revealed when Alex spoke of her experience as a middle school teacher where she "saw, time and time again, how students are thrown into these classes with thirty, thirty-five other kids, where most days they don't ever hear the sound of their own name." Grouping children by age and then demanding that they all progress at the same rate and in the same ways is lunacy from a child development perspective. From a business perspective, however, efficiency and cost-effectiveness are the pre-eminent values, not healthy child development. From this perspective, collective training makes all kinds of sense.

Students aren't the only workers in the system who are collectively trained, as every teacher knows. Alex spoke of her own experience with this particular instrument of "efficiency," a word that begs a new definition in the context of her description.

> [The book *High Stakes*] made me think about my own experiences in staff meetings, where someone comes in and gives us our new reading, or our new math, or our new whatever that's going to save the day. And I know the reality is that we all sit there and we're grading our papers, or we're drinking our coffee, and we're doing our own thing and nodding every once in awhile to make them think that we're listening to them.

The shortcomings of collective training were further illustrated in a brief exchange between Sarah and Mariela.

> Sarah: It's very hard to have compulsory meetings for an entire staff, because at any given time the staff's needs are different.

> Mariela: But we do it for an entire district of six-year-olds, and expect them all to meet the same thing at the same time.

> Sarah: I know. I know. And that's the crime! Everybody has different needs at different times. And that's the crime.

Teachers' familiarity with the process of being "professionally developed"—somewhat like photographic film—where they attend meetings and in-service sessions with agendas they have had no voice in defining is testament to the success of instituting collective training as a natural and inevitable method of management. In this arrangement teachers themselves are the objects of faithless management, with no more definitional authority to manage their own growth and development than "an entire district of six-year-olds."

6. Exercises

Foucault does not elaborate on what he takes "exercises" to mean as a disciplinary tool. In examining these parents' and teachers' words through the lens of discipline, however, I identified four additional instruments—one of which I initially named "superficiality/lip service." On reflection, I think the group discussion excerpts that I initially identified in this way may actually address what Foucault intended with the name of "exercises" for this instrument.

One example of an exercise in superficiality that the teacher participants in our group discussed was the relatively new phenomenon in school accountability called the site visit. While "visits" from district office or the state department of education have the ring of neighborly exchange, it is clear to all who participate in them that there is no semblance of reciprocity in the experience. Rather, the site visit is merely one of many mechanisms utilized in the public school panopticon for the purpose of ensuring the visibility of its workers. As an embodiment of panoptic discipline, the site visit belongs in the category of the exercise. In the experience of the teacher participants in this group, anyway, it is a hollow ritual without depth or substance.

In our tenth meeting together, the teachers in our group described for parents the site visits that had been instituted in their school districts, ostensibly as a means of holding teachers and students accountable for teaching and learning their prescribed content standards. Rachel described her recent experience of receiving "visitors" in her classroom and being audited by them in this way.

> We were given beforehand a sheet of paper. Extraordinary! We're in the fourth week of school, our class lists have just been defined, and one of the categories was, "Children know class procedures." We were examined by elementary school teachers. I had an elementary school librarian and somebody else come in, I think for about forty-five seconds. Walked in, sat down, and left.

> And then *after* the visit, the farce continues. Because we know as teachers that *nothing* has changed in our school. That we are, in fact, doing *less* well than we were last year in terms of best practices, for what we decided should be practices in our school. And yet we had a *cake* party the day after the visit! Congratulating us on how well we were doing. They came in on Thursday, and on Friday we had the cake party. And everybody patted themselves on the back, how wonderful we are. But we all know that we've gone three steps back. But because that rubric was met in a very artificial way, oh, everything's fine.

Shallow exercises tend to consume time and focus attention in ways that become more beneficial with every step one takes up the hierarchical ladder. This is evident in the fact that definitional authority and visibility exist in inverse proportions in the public school panopticon: the further one gets from the classroom, the less strongly does the principle of compulsory visibility apply and the more definitional authority is available for people in the upper tiers of the hierarchy to define the terms and conditions of their work.

To illustrate, I return to Rachel's opening comment in her description of the site visit. She said, "We're in the fourth week of school, our class lists have just been defined, and one of the categories was, 'Children know class procedures.'" The accountability spotlight of this site visit is trained, full beam, on Rachel. It shines less brightly on her administrators who had allowed a third of the first quarter to pass before finalizing class lists. It shines less brightly still on state policymakers who assumed the right to dictate classroom realities without hav-ing benefit of professional experience or expertise in schools. The accountability spotlight shines weakly, if at all, on federal policymakers who have mandated that school success be measured with norm-referenced instruments that, by de-sign, privilege some children over others and that measure relative performance rather than actual achievement. It shines not at all on the corporate and political elite who attend the education summits, who have presumed the authority to define both the standard of "excellence in education" and the means of measur-ing it—at the same time that they have themselves abandoned responsibility for the public welfare. Instead, the spotlight shines inexorably downward.

Alex, too, spoke of the superficiality of the site visit. I can still hear the laughter in her voice as she described for us her experience with it. I can hear, too, the ongoing jokes about whether I'd be holding a cake party for the group at the close of our sessions together. (I did, of course.) That laughter is important. It represents a simple refusal to accept the role of the disciplined individual that we in the lower tiers of the panoptic hierarchy are relentlessly pressured to play. It signifies, too, an ability not only to see power at work, but to challenge "the direction that is coming from the top," as Boyoyo would say. Alex is a teacher who can see absurdity in the panopticon; her laughter was contagious as she described her experience of the site visit as an exercise in superficiality.

> The day that they came to my school I wasn't even there. I wanted to go to a workshop and asked my principal if I could go, and he said of course, that's fine. I mean, that's how seriously he was taking any of this. Not seriously at all. But people in my school, still, it's like they couldn't relax about it! I was get-ting my sub plans ready for the next day, in the copy room making copies, and there were people in there copying the standards! And putting them on colored paper to put on their wall! [Group laughter.] I'm like, 'What are you doing?' 'Well, you know, we're getting our visit tomorrow.' And I'm like, 'And who are you getting your visit from? You're getting your visit from other elemen-tary school teachers!' They still had to create such drama about it!

> And so the teachers came for our site visit, and they did their same procedure, even though I had a sub. Where they interviewed the *sub* about the standards! [Laughs hard, group laughs.] I know the woman who was my sub, and she just thought it was a scream! I mean, they're interviewing her about my classroom and about whether or not I'm meeting the standards in my classroom! [Group laughter.] I mean, that's again where it's just so absurd! It's like, how can you take *any* of this *seriously*?

> And so I get my report back for how I'm doing in my classroom. [Sarah: And it's fine! (Group laughter.)] Right! And they also, they interview the students. They had questions to ask the students about the standards. Well [laughs], my second and third graders, they have thinking standards that we talk about a lot. Clarity, logic, fairness, and, um, what's the fourth? We talk about them all the time. So that when they're asking questions, it's, 'Can you be more clear? Are you being relevant?' Things like that. So the interviewer writes down, 'The

kids knew about thinking standards, question mark, question mark, question mark.' [Group laughter.] But my kids have no concept of, well, we're on standard II-B-1-little-a, or whatever. But they have thinking standards, and isn't that something? [Laughs.] In my opinion that's a lot more meaningful. But they didn't know what that was all about.

In addition to site visits as one example of exercises or hollow rituals that serve to focus the beam of accountability downward, participants named other superficial reforms and hollow rituals that they saw being implemented in the public schools.

- All parents are supposed to get these brochures. 'This is what your kid should do in first grade, second grade.' You should see the lingo that they've got on there. As a parent, this is crap. You're still keeping us, as parents, in the dark. (Elena)

- How do you assess a habit of mind? If you can't say, "You have 98 percent on the habits of mind..." The way that the standards have been created is so that they can easily be assessed. (Alex)

- Somebody asked earlier why teachers just didn't keep teaching the way they want to. Why do they do all this? And so I thought about what's happening in my school, and I started listing why. And it was because the principal was calling for our quarterly foci. And because we needed to have our scope and sequence turned in. And that we had to go to meetings on testing. And our staff meetings are geared around student segments. And principal visits are all around the business aspect now, versus the child-centered aspect. (Peyton)

- Sometimes I'm forced to do things with students that take up so much time, and I have to do them to be accountable to somebody. And it's hard for me to give up the time that I would rather be using to give *myself* information. (Mariela)

Whether we call them hollow rituals and performances or superficial exercises, what site visits, quantitatively defined standards, incomprehensible brochures, and shallow data-mania in the schools (vs. focused, rigorous, student-centered observation and assessment) accomplish is to flood the panopticon with activity. What gets lost in the paper storm are qualitative questions about the purposes that members of the public might want their public schools to serve. What gets lost is time. Imagine if every staff meeting and every inservice day for a year were devoted to seriously engaging parents, students, educators, legislators, business people, and other members of a community in three basic questions: what do we agree about when it comes to our hopes for the education of children in our neighborhood? Where do we disagree? What might be some of the ways in which we can enact our agreements and respectfully explore our differences? Unfortunately, the discipline of superficial exercises and hollow rituals is well enough entrenched to prohibit the use of time in such a large and public way. It seems to me that finding smaller ways to create exactly this kind of horizontal and vertical conjunction is our challenge.

The instruments of discipline that I have examined thus far are examples that Foucault suggested that did, indeed, bear out as a presence in these teachers' and parents' lives at school. Three additional instruments emerged through analysis of group discussion transcripts using Foucault's lens as my guide: the expert, the memo, and control of mainstream media.

7. The Expert

This instrument of discipline refers to the pervasive systemic reliance on external authority for providing guidance, support, and expertise in the schools. The expert can come in many forms. It could be a $5,000-a-day speaker brought in to "motivate" a school staff; it could be a teacher-proofed curriculum that dictates what should be taught in such detail that "a monkey could teach it"; it could come in the form of a publication written by anyone but public school teachers and parents about the dismal state of education in America and what should be done about it; it could come in the form of a test that has the power to override every judgment that a teacher has made about the quality and quantity of student achievement over the course of a year. The parents and teachers in our group described the forms that "the expert" takes as a disciplinary agent in their schools.

- I guess the District spent five million dollars to get an instructional coach in every school. And we're all looking at each other, like, 'Did anyone ask us if we wanted an instructional coach?' (Alex)

- I think that the whole idea of having standards, the implications of that are that we don't have faith in the abilities of our teachers, and our school systems in general, to be able to do good for our students. So we have to bring in standards from outside, to tell them what is good. (Sarah)

- I just wonder why teachers bother when ultimately the kids fail the test. Nobody cares what the kids' DRA [Diagnostic Reading Assessment] score is, and nobody cares what the report card says, and nobody cares what their progress was! Because I could say, they're doing fine, doing fine, doing fine, failed. Oh, I guess they weren't doing fine. (Peyton)

- They're taking out of my hands the assessment of a child. And I'm the one, I sat in this classroom 180 days with that child. I sat with the parents. I met with them. I know this child's background, and McGraw-Hill does not. (Julia)

- I don't want to teach in a school where I have to do Four Block, and they tell me 'It's 9:06, read page...' I don't want to do that! (Mariela)

8. The Memo

I have already described the use of one memo that simultaneously served the disciplinary functions of controlling teachers' time and making them visible. This memo was in the form of an addendum to a letter written by a school principal and mailed to her staff prior to the start of the school year. When I asked participants if they thought their colleagues would be offended by that addendum had it been written to them, Peyton responded in a way that clarified the role of the memo as an instrument of discipline.

> Percentage-wise, I'd say it would offend probably only, like, 5 percent. Because I do think it is about information. But because we were asked to look at it through a different eye just now we saw different things. But because there's so many of these coming all of the time, you get to the point of, 'What do I need to know?' And you pull out the information and go to the next flier that's in your box.

I add the memo to this list of disciplinary instruments because it is unusually and usefully flexible as a form of disciplinary power. It doesn't require the physical presence of an actual person who will take responsibility for its contents; it can shield local authority figures from discontent or unpopularity by placing responsibility on some distant authority that has mandated its contents (e.g., the district office, state legislators, federal law); it can be endlessly used to fill teachers' inboxes with information, replacing the need for human interaction between managers and workers; it can embody punishment as a physical presence in a personnel file.

Rachel's story illustrates the power of the memo as an instrument of discipline. "Last year I tried to go up to the administrators and talk about the ludicrousness of certain things, and I got a letter of reprimand in my file! So now, I'm quiet! I don't open my *mouth*!"

9. Control of Mainstream Media

This is the final instrument of discipline that I could identify through participants' words. In the hands of the powerful, the corporate media work to keep the beam of the accountability spotlight sharply and exclusively focused on the lower tiers of the panopticon. Mariela described her perception of the media's role in the accountability movement in this way:

> I think it's the media that is making us think that things are falling apart. It's not from personal experience! People rate their own schools, their own teachers very highly. It's the system that they don't rate highly. And so I think people's faith seems to be based on what people are *hearing* rather than what they're experiencing.

Corporate ownership of mainstream media and the extraordinarily narrow range of perspectives that is available to people in the United States on issues of public concern are well-documented phenomena. When corporate interests rule both the public school panopticon and the popular means of informing the people who fund them of its status, the loss of local definitional authority in the schools is a thoroughly unsurprising result.

In Conclusion... So What?

All told, I have named, described, and illustrated through participants' words nine instruments of discipline that are in use every day, in every level of the public school panopticon, to achieve the overarching purpose of discipline: to decrease the people's political power while maximizing their productivity and utility in efficient, cost-effective ways. Toward this end, these nine instruments serve the four basic functions of discipline: (1) defining, organizing, and regulating "reality;" (2) separating and neutralizing people; (3) finding efficient ways to utilize people and maximize their productivity; and (4) infiltrating, studying, and documenting everything and everyone that is subject to its power. (See Appendix B for a summary of disciplinary functions and instruments.)

The purpose of this analysis, in which I used the lenses of disciplinary functions and instruments to frame my perspective, was to make the following point: so far, the accountability movement in education has been successfully directed from the elite tier of the public school panopticon because that tier has been able to maintain exclusive control over the crucial element of visibility. My argument has been that if those of us who have been made visible by the accountability spotlight can identify the ways, both large and small, in which that control has been accomplished, then we will be empowered to resist being wholly objectified in this way. If we can learn to spot the instruments of discipline when they are being used to define reality for us, to neutralize our individual and collective power, to make efficient use of us, and to position only those in the lower tiers as the appropriate objects of scrutiny and visibility, then we will be empowered to undertake the work of reclaiming our own definitional authority in our own schools.

Right now, though, I admit that this grand idea seems impossibly out of reach. Even though I have found a great deal of hope through the process of researching my questions, I won't deny that dismay and defeat had seats at the table during many of our group discussions. The following exchange between three parents in the group, for example, took place during our fourth meeting.

> Sarah: How do we get over this barrier [of race] so that we can focus on the prize? So that we can say, 'Hey! These tests are a bunch of crap! Let's focus on getting rid of them.' Or, 'Let's focus on making the schools better for everybody's kids! Because everybody's kids have to live with everybody!'

Elena: But that's not the real world. You know, we've got to be honest here.

Sarah: Except what if those parents [of privilege] read the same literature that we're reading?

Elena: I don't think so.

Kate: I don't see that. I think there's a lot of ignorance there. It's this, 'There is not a problem at *our* school. There is not an issue at our school, because everyone is doing okay.'

Sarah: If you personally, at your little microcosm level, aren't struggling with this . . .

Kate: Why bother?

The problem is so big. Making the problem manageable will be my focus in the next chapter.

Notes

1. Michel Foucault, *The Foucault Reader* (New York: Pantheon Books, 1984), 209.

2. Foucault, *Foucault Reader*, 209.

3. "Teachers are the guard dogs of the ideology of the ruling classes." Arturo Ornelas, personal communication, April 1, 1999.

4. Foucault, *Foucault Reader*, 209.

5. Foucault, *Foucault Reader*, 196

6. Foucault, *Foucault Reader*, 209.

7. Foucault, *Foucault Reader*, 197.

8. Foucault, *Foucault Reader*, 197.

9. Foucault, *Foucault Reader*, 199.

10. Alfie Kohn, *Punished by Rewards* (New York: Houghton Mifflin Company, 1993), 80.

11. Alfie Kohn, *The Schools Our Children Deserve: Moving Beyond Traditional Classrooms and 'Tougher Standards'* (New York: Houghton Mifflin Company, 1999), 133.

12. A reference to Lord Jeffrey Amherst's alleged experimentation with germ warfare against the Indians at Fort Pitt in 1763. "Could it not be contrived to send the *Small Pox* among those disaffected tribes of Indians?" he asked Colonel Henry Bouquet. "We must on this occasion use every stratagem in our power to reduce them" <http://www.nativeweb.org/pages/legal/amherst/lord_jeff.html>.

13. Foucault, *Foucault Reader*, 197.

14. Foucault, *Foucault Reader*, 209.

CHAPTER 8

Reframing the Panopticon

With so much weight being exerted to encourage every player in the public school panopticon to internalize its culture of amoral familism, it's easy to feel overwhelmed and impotent. The scope of the problem is enormous, and the grip of amoral familism is strong—peculiarly so in more affluent contexts, as the participants in this study demonstrated. Noam Chomsky addressed this very issue in a recent interview with David Barsamian. At the end of the interview, Barsamian asked, "Someone reading this interview may say, 'Chomsky has all this command of facts and history. But what do I do as an individual?' How would you respond to that?" Chomsky's reply was to say:

> The first thing you ought to do is verify what I present. Just because I say it doesn't make it true. So check it out, see what looks correct, what looks wrong, look at other material which wasn't discussed, figure out what the truth really is. That's what you've got a brain for.
>
> If you think that the general thrust of it is correct, there should be no problem in doing something about it. We're not going to be thrown into prison and face torture. We're not going to get assassinated. We have enormous privilege. We have tremendous freedom. That means endless opportunities.
>
> I should tell you that every night I get many letters, and after every talk I get many questions from people who say, 'I want to change things. What can I do?' I never hear these questions from peasants in southern Colombia or Kurds in southeastern Turkey under miserable repression or anybody who is suffering. They don't ask what they can do; they tell you what they're doing.
>
> Somehow the fact of enormous privilege and freedom carries with it a sense of impotence, which is a strange, but striking phenomenon. The fact is, we can do just about anything. There is no difficulty, wherever you are, in finding groups that are working hard on things that concern you.
>
> But that's not the kind of answer that people want. The answer that they want, I think, in the back of their minds is, what can I do that will be quick and easy

and bring about an end to these problems? . . . That's not the way things work. If you want to make changes in the world, you're going to have to be there day after day doing the boring, straightforward work of getting a couple of people interested and building a slightly bigger organization and carrying out the next move and suffering frustration and finally getting somewhere. That's how the world changes.[1]

As I go about the process of refining my questions about education now, in light of what I learned with these teachers and parents, Sarah's voice has been a critical one for me to keep hearing. As a "white woman of privilege" who works in her home doing the best she can to take care of her family, Sarah represents to me the deeply concerned, intensely impotent citizen that lives inside many of us who are living lives of enormous privilege, tremendous freedom, and endless opportunities. Her words could have been spoken by almost every person I know who is living a life of personal comfort:

> What you're essentially asking, to me, is how do we all become active rebels? And I don't know whether I want to be an active rebel for anybody except my two kids! And I know that's morally bankrupt. But I don't know whether I have the energy to be anybody but morally bankrupt. And I think that that's probably true of a lot of other parents. I don't know the answer. How, if at all, do we make a difference. Except for our own kids! I don't know how we change it for the kids who really need it the most, who need us to be their voices in a power system.

The sheer enormity of the problem is beyond daunting; but I think there is a way to frame the problem of the accountability movement in a way that is potentially empowering, even for those of us who may have become impotent with privilege. Ironically, the panopticon itself offers an answer.

Another Look at the Public School Panopticon

Imagine the structure of the public school panopticon as it currently exists: it is a pyramid divided into a series of hierarchical rows, or tiers, and each tier is divided horizontally into a number of individual cells. The higher the tier, the fewer the cells there are. As it currently exists, the functions of discipline are defined in service to the interests of those who occupy the uppermost cells in the system. The orientation of energy and accountability in the system is "upward," aimed toward meeting the needs of those who occupy the top tiers. In other words, the corporate and political elite are effectively using the instruments of discipline for the purposes of (1) defining, organizing, and regulating "reality;" (2) separating and neutralizing people; (3) finding efficient ways to utilize people and maximize their productivity; and (4) infiltrating, studying, and documenting everything and everyone that is subject to the power of the public school panopticon.

In continuing to imagine that pyramidal structure, visualize Foucault's "solid separations" that have been created between all of the cells in the system. Visualize cell walls that are strong and thick, impermeable enough to thwart the people's casual attempts at horizontal or vertical conjunctions. These cell walls have been constructed over time, not with two-by-fours, sheetrock, hammers, and nails—but with the instruments of discipline: timetables, hierarchical observation, normalizing judgment, examinations, collective training, superficial exercises, experts, memos, and corporate control of the mass media. The thickness of the walls varies from cell to cell, depending on how thoroughly the people inside have internalized the system's values and expectations, and depending also on the force that is applied when the disciplinary tools are used. Imagine, for example, that a principal has found ways to allow the people in her school (including her students) to be creative, to collaborate in powerful ways, and to participate in deciding what accountability means and how to measure success. Then imagine a principal in another school who admonishes her teachers not to take risks but to "follow the rules of the game." In the first school where the exercise of strong voices is facilitated, the cell walls would be more permeable, not as thick, as in the second.

My own experience of twenty-five years in education leads me to believe that the second school defines today's norm, particularly in our "failing" schools, and the first represents a systemic anomaly. I believe that there was more variability in cell wall thickness ten years ago, even five, than there is today. The strength of the beam in the accountability spotlight has increased in recent years, causing the instruments of discipline to be used more frequently and more forcefully in many schools. The walls that exist between students, parents, teachers, principals, and on up the hierarchy today are, consequently, more uniformly thick. My mental picture of the public school panopticon as it currently exists, then, is drawn with dark and solid lines between each tier in the hierarchy and between almost all of the cells in all but the uppermost rows. As Boyoyo put it, in today's system "there is no osmosis."

This is a powerful image, because for me, the image itself holds an answer to the problem of crushing enormity. With this picture of the public school panopticon in mind, I am learning to shift my focus from changing the system to changing the construction of my own cell walls. The essential questions for me then become: how do I use my knowledge of the instruments of discipline to help make my walls—and my floor and my ceiling—more permeable? How do I encourage osmosis in my microscopic corner of the panopticon so that essential nutrients can get through to the cells in my area? And finally, if healthy osmotic functioning can be achieved in my little corner, how can I help people in other areas to do the same thing?

Osmosis: Choosing Health, Choosing Life

While speaking recently with a group of graduate students in a methods class, I introduced the idea of Bentham's panopticon in describing Foucault's theory about how power operates in the modern world. I shared Boyoyo's thought, that in today's school system there is no osmosis. When I asked students what sense they could make of the model I had drawn on the board, there was lively conversation—but the "Aha!" moment arrived for me a week later. Stacy Schauerhamer, a student in that class, gave me permission to quote a part of the dialogue journal that she submitted the week after that class discussion had taken place. She titled her reflection "Balance and the Triangle," in reference to the picture of the "continuous, individualizing pyramid" that I had drawn on the board.

April 22nd
Balance and the Triangle

Osmosis is the movement of a liquid from a solution with a low solute concentration to a solution with a high solute concentration until there is an equal concentration on both sides. Also it can be a gradual process of learning.

Osmosis in the panopticon is the movement of information from an area or person who has lots to a person who needs more. It's all about balancing the information received and the information given. If this is true then the people on the bottom of the panopticon should be receiving equal amounts of information as the top. Where it breaks down is when the person above or below decides that their membrane is impermeable. No information is getting in or out. So how do we overcome this block in the flow? We use the second part of the definition of osmosis. Gradually the information will start to leak through. Sometimes we who want the information will need to chip away at the wall until a little information is getting in and out. The osmosis process will happen but it may not be quickly. Those who do not want things to be equal will try to stop this gradual change. The overriding factor is the need to have balance. We all strive for it in our individual lives.

My last thought is if the panopticon becomes balanced will it be in the shape of a pyramid anymore?

What effect will such thoughts have on Stacy in the first years of her career as a new teacher? My hope is that the idea of having some control over the construction of her own walls and floors and ceilings (as well as for the shape of the system's structure overall) will be empowering for her, and that she will be more able to resist panoptic efforts to prevent her from finding a balance of information and power with her students, parents, colleagues, and employers. My fear for her, and for all teachers, frankly, is that if they are not able to find ways to make their professional "walls" permeable and to achieve "osmotic balance," that they will die as teachers. Whether that metaphoric death means that they leave the profession within the first few years (as we know many do), or that they remain in the classroom but not in the profession (as we know many do), the stakes are high for them. They are equally high for everyone else in the system. I know scores of parents, teachers, students, and administrators who are starving for a sense of balance, connection, and meaning in their professional lives. I could even make the argument that even those in the upper tiers who are seemingly well served by the current structure are also "dying" slowly in the absence of panoptic osmosis.

Panoptic osmosis is exactly what I am proposing as the goal. It is not to do away with the structure itself; I am pragmatic enough to believe that a strong hierarchical organization is needed to provide order in a system involving nearly fifty million students and three and a half million educators. But in a panopticon that breathes, in which cell walls are permeable and the people can get the nutrients that they need, two changes to the continuous, individualizing pyramid would result. One, the orientation of energy would flow "downward," toward students who occupy the foundational tiers in the hierarchy. After all, a structure is only as stable as its foundation is strong. With this downward flow of energy, accountability efforts would be designed with children's needs rather than "national interests" in mind. They would be devoted to ensuring that schools are places where all students can feel safe, valuable, capable, and powerful enough to be able to risk investing their best efforts and their most vulnerable selves in challenging, relevant, and active learning. When the orientation of energy flows "upward" to satisfy the requirements of those in the uppermost tiers, as it currently does, it is our foundation that we risk: our children, our society, and the ideals of democracy.

The second change that osmosis would facilitate is that dotted lines would replace the dark, thick ones that currently define the boundaries between most of the cells in the panopticon. Access to others, horizontally and vertically, would promote visibility and accountability throughout the system. The one-way spotlight of the current accountability movement would be transformed into the broad and far-reaching beam of lamplight, and this would illuminate every hierarchical tier with equal intensity. Visibility in this more egalitarian context would not be about top-down surveillance, but about having enough confidence, courage, and humility to make our work public at every hierarchical level, embracing our accountability to foundational tiers. For this second change to happen, we in the lower and middle tiers must be able to not only recognize but also resist the instruments of discipline when they are autocratically applied.

These two changes, successfully implemented in local spaces, would transform the continuous, individualizing pyramid into a collective, child-centered pyramid (see Appendix C: *Osmosis and the Evolution of the Public School Panopticon*). I am not so naïve as to imagine this utopian vision is within reach of the public school system as a whole at this time; but I know from experience that it is possible to take small steps in local spaces toward achieving osmosis in the panopticon. It is possible to cultivate small, healthy spaces for genuine engagement with our students, families, and colleagues.

The panopticon needs to evolve because those dark, thick lines in the current structure represent the presence of disease. Cells are dehydrated and withering for lack of healthy exchange. It is as if the system itself is diabetic. A person with diabetes faces the possibility of death because of a fundamental problem with osmosis. Abundant nutrients in a diabetic person's bloodstream cannot get through the cell membrane without insulin; in the absence of insulin each cell is literally starving in the midst of plenty. Without it, a diabetic person would eventually become comatose and die. With an injection of insulin, glucose molecules are given the vehicle they need to get into the cells. They can hitch a ride, so to speak, and the cells can receive the nutrients they need. This is the image I have in mind for teachers, parents, students, administrators and others who may be "starving" in the public school panopticon in the absence of a common vision and a sense of shared hope for the future. Vision and hope require conversation to make those cell walls permeable, just as nutrients require insulin to gain access.

During her final interview when I asked Rachel if she wanted to keep meeting and continue our discussions as a group, she said, "Yes! I have to! This is *food* to me." I am convinced that Rachel represents a small but incredibly important group of people who are currently "dying" in our public schools. I believe that in every school there is a handful of such people withering away in the midst of plenty. The books, the ideas, the people are out there—they just can't get in. Timetables, hierarchical observation and the other instruments of discipline discourage that kind of permeability. For Rachel, our discussion group was the shot of insulin she needed. "This is *food* to me," she said.

I think this particular population that Rachel represents is especially important because these teachers, students, parents, and administrators can already see the questions that need asking. They may not know the terminology associated with the "functions and instruments of discipline," but they understand intimately what they mean at the level of experience. These people are important because they represent a place to begin a conversation that is broader than the one that I started with twelve parents and teachers. This initial conversation was essential for me, though. I learned something from it. The energy that is generated when people gather purposefully to talk with each other—to find and to create connections through focused discussion of important texts and ideas—is transformative. This power of focused conversation, that is, of volatile knowing, is potentially revolutionary.

If the project of re-inverting visibility served to empower many of the teachers and parents in the context of this small group, it is a project worth pursuing on a larger scale.

Where to from Here?

The "so what?" sub-question that I set out to answer through this research project with teachers and parents was: what, if anything, would participants want to do once they became better informed about the history and ramifications of the accountability movement in education? In short, would any individual or collective action result?

The differences that I can point to in terms of the effects of participation in this study are mostly attitudinal. Many pages of transcript excerpts, for example, contain participants' comments categorized under the following headings: *I feel empowered to make a difference; I can better articulate my beliefs and influence others; I have been sharing my books with other people; It made me want to be an activist and do something; I'm starting to think of me as one person who can change it; I feel more secure about myself now/I'm more confident; I am not wanting to take it any more.*

Beyond attitudinal changes, however, participants also brainstormed ideas over the course of several meetings about what they thought needed to happen next. This list of ideas fills a gap in my own thinking and writing about how to go about accomplishing the kind of inter-cell permeability that I am advocating. The question of how the "solid separations" between cells in the panopticon is accomplished is more easily answered than the question of how to make those cell walls permeable. Those solid separations are accomplished by using the instruments of discipline to atomize and fragment the people—thus explaining the themes of disconnection/competition and the crisis of faith discussed in Chapter 5. That accomplishment is also ensured by maintaining definitional authority over the words by which people live and work within the public school panopticon. These two over-arching strategies explain how *im*permeability is facilitated. Once that is understood, though, the crucial question remains. How are we to promote osmosis in the panopticon?

My own list of ideas for facilitating permeability is short: (1) engage in focused readings and discussions with others who occupy positions that are located horizontally and vertically to your own; and (2) become familiar with how the instruments of discipline are applied in your life at school, and in that familiarity, learn how to resist and co-opt those strategies in the exercise of power. Thanks to participants' brainstormed ideas about what needs to happen next, that short list can be significantly extended. Several more pages of transcript excerpts are categorized under the heading of "ideas for actions to take/what needs to happen." I add these categories to the list of possible ways to facilitate osmosis in the panopticon, prompting its evolution toward a more permeable, healthy, and child-centered structure: (3) identify visionary leaders; (4) educate and influence current political leaders; (5) educate other parents and teachers; (6) encourage other teachers to trust themselves and teach, and support those who refuse to give in to the testing pressure; (7) build bridges and join forces between and among parents, educators, and schools; (8) create a public space in our own lives for dialogue with others about what we *do* want in and from our schools; (9) open pilot schools; (10) use the media to reach a broader audience.

Facilitating osmosis in the public school panopticon through these and other means yet to be imagined provides a wealth of ideas for future research. The new research scenario that is forming in my mind at this point is this: if that "starving" handful of teachers and parents and administrators (and potentially students) that I imagine exists in every school could be brought together in such a way as to create representation from every school in one district, and if the texts and the findings from this study could be used as the basis for generating regular, focused conversation with such a group, what identifiable impact might such activity have in the schools and neighborhood communities within that district? With the goal of promoting osmosis in the panopticon by forming horizontal and vertical conjunctions within it, I would offer such a group the following questions for their ongoing discussions:

1. What do the instruments of discipline actually look like in your school? in your district? in your classroom? Who/what is and is not *visible* because of how these instruments are used in these contexts? What is and is not accomplished because of that?

2. What specific examples of healthy osmosis can you identify in your school, district, and classroom? What examples would indicate a lack of osmotic functioning?

3. Where do you see *faith* in action in your school, district, and classroom? Where do you see its absence? What are the observable consequences of faith/lack of faith in students, families, teachers, and administrators?

4. How is "parent involvement" defined in your school, district, and classroom? What is and is not accomplished because of how it is defined?

5. How can you use your knowledge of the instruments of discipline? Who or what would you want to illuminate or make visible with them?

6. Who enjoys definitional authority in your school, district, and classroom for words like education, teaching, learning, achievement, and success? What do these words currently mean in each of those contexts? What do you want them to mean?

7. How do you differentiate between a "good" teacher and a "lousy" teacher? How can you tell what "good" is in a school and in a classroom?

8. If you had access to the mainstream media, what would you want to say?

9. Does amoral familism exist in your school, district, or classroom? How can you tell whether Chomsky's "responsible men" have been successful or not in eroding "the natural and deep-seated values of sympathy and solidarity" in your state, school, district, and classroom?

10. What would be on your top-ten list of changes you would like to see in your school, district, and classroom? How would you prioritize them? Working from the assumption that one meaning of democracy has to do with the individual's right to effect change at a local level, what steps would you need to take in order to make the first thing on that list happen?

Conclusion

I have written that my discovery through the process of conducting this research project is simply this, that the energy that is generated when people gather purposefully to talk with each other—to find and to create connections through focused discussion of important texts and ideas—is transformative. I have claimed that this power of focused conversation is potentially revolutionary. Selena and Peyton, a parent and a teacher, provide the evidence of that finding with which I will close this work.

Selena: In reality, this whole thing, it's challenging the way I think. And I think if you were to ask me those first questions you asked me before we started this project I'd be lost. What is education? What is democracy? What does this mean? And I'm just wondering, what are my words going to be after I've left here? Because everything's changed now.

Peyton: I'm the same way. I just feel like, well, I thought I knew! But now, where do I go and what sense do I make of what I'm reading? It's challenging my pedagogy! It's challenging my philosophy of what education is.

People discovering their questions are already on the road to definitional authority. And people discovering their questions together are already building the kind of democratic faith in each other that will make the trip worthwhile.

Notes

1. David Barsamian, "Noam Chomsky: *The Progressive Interview*" *The Progressive* (May 2004), 39.

APPENDIX A

METHODOLOGY

Research Question

How do teachers and parents make sense of the accountability movement?

Guiding Questions

1. How do participants' identities as parents and teachers influence group discussions and participants' experiences of those discussions?

2. Will individual or collective action result?

The purpose of the first guiding question was to serve as a mechanism for making teacher-parent relationships an explicit subtext of the study. The historic imbalance of power that exists between these two groups[1] is something that I recognized in the context of this project, which was specifically designed to engage parents and teachers in discussion together. Neglecting to take this reality into consideration, I believed, would constrain the group's ability to genuinely explore aspects of the accountability discourse together. In making parent-teacher relationships an explicit element of the study, I worked to open this topic with participants and to make it safe for discussion, thereby enhancing the depth and authenticity of the group's experience. I was convinced that this was an important goal in a time when the common-sense understanding of "parent involvement" has been politically constructed around the ultimate value of individual student achievement, thus encouraging a culture of amoral familism—rather than to reflect value, for example, for all parents' sympathy and solidarity on behalf of all children's potential achievements, promoting a culture of child-centered egalitarianism. The purpose for the second guiding question was rooted in my assumption that some kind of change would occur as a result of participation in this study.

These guiding frameworks helped me to get at layers of my research question that were not obviously apparent elements of inquiry. The first guiding question mined the phrase "teachers and parents"; the second explored the phrase "make sense of" in terms of participants' personal responses to "becom[ing] more informed and sophisticated" constructors of meaning[2] relative to the accountability movement.

Project Overview

Over the course of six months, participants and I worked together as a group, reading and discussing a variety of texts that provided a critical perspective on different aspects of the accountability movement (e.g., privatization, an inequitable opportunity structure, the de-professionalization of teachers, and the instrumental construction of "parent involvement"). I had initially intended to provide a tentative list of readings to the group and a tentative schedule outlining suggested readings and meeting dates, with the idea that we would revise and finalize that schedule together. I abandoned this plan after our initial group meetings, however, for two reasons. One, the variety of academic backgrounds in the group necessitated a re-evaluation of the texts I had originally envisioned using and prompted a search on my part for more accessible readings. Secondly, participants indicated early in our process that they wanted me to choose the readings for the group, trusting that my familiarity with the literature would serve them and the purposes of my study well. I shared my bias against market ideology as the basis for governing public schools with the group, and I presented each of the texts that I chose (listed below) as representative of the kind of critical information about education that does not enjoy mainstream visibility.

In our group meetings, I facilitated text-based discussions on these texts in the tradition of Socratic dialogue and Critical Friends Group protocol. (A Critical Friends Group is a specific kind of learning community in schools. In these groups educators serve as critical advocates for each other as members examine their own professional practices and their students' performance and progress, using a variety of structured protocols to guide their work together. One of these is the text-based discussion protocol I used to facilitate group discussions; it is a more structured version of Socratic discussion.) In keeping with the discussion protocol that we followed, my role was that of a participant as well as a facilitator; I positioned myself in the group as a constructivist participant-observer, a role I will describe in further detail below.

Over the course of twelve meetings in six months, the texts that we read and discussed together were, in order, *High Stakes* by Dale Johnson and Bonnie Johnson (2002), *What Happened to Recess and Why Are Our Children Struggling in Kindergarten* by Susan Ohanian (2002), *Will Standards Save Public Education?* by Deborah Meier (2000), *The Manufactured Crisis* by David Berliner and Bruce Biddle (1995), and *The Schools Our Children Deserve* by Alfie Kohn (1999). We also read *A Nation at Risk* by the National Commission on Excellence in Education (1983), an excerpt from C. Douglas Lummis's *Radical*

Democracy (1996), and an excerpt from Michael Engel's *The Struggle for Control of Public Education: Market Ideology vs. Democratic Values* (2000).

In addition to participant-observation, I used a number of other methods for gathering information. These methods and my purpose for using them are described in detail below, with the aim of holding myself publicly accountable to the ideal described by Anfara, Brown, and Mangione: "Good naturalistic inquiry shows the hand and opens the mind of the investigator to his or her reader."[3] The accountability discourse these authors engage in is in refreshing contrast to the one that this study was designed to explore.

Philosophical Orientation

My orientation is to critical research. Sharan Merriam describes critical theory as a perspective that posits education as "a social institution designed for social and cultural reproduction and transformation," and which concerns itself with the "ideological critique of power, privilege, and oppression in areas of educational practice."[4] My disciplinary perspective on this project is sociological, rooted as it is in the issues of equity, access, class, race, and gender.

What I am presenting here is a qualitative case study, approached through the paradigmatic lens of constructivism. The ontological relativism of this research paradigm makes it one that is well suited to the purpose and design of my study. This relativism, according to Guba and Lincoln, "assumes multiple, apprehendable, and sometimes conflicting social realities that are the products of human intellects, but that may change as their constructors become more informed and sophisticated."[5] My inquiry into how familiarity with critical literature affected participants' constructions of a variety of issues in education presumed the existence of a multiplicity of constructions; it is ideologically aligned with constructivism's relativistic view of the nature of reality.

The epistemological perspective of a constructivist paradigm is equally well suited to my project. It is described by Guba and Lincoln as "transactional and subjectivist." From this perspective, "the investigator and the object of investigation are assumed to be interactively linked so that the 'findings' are *literally created* as the investigation proceeds."[6] A transactional and subjectivist epistemology attempts to address power imbalances between the knower and the known, or the investigator and her participants. This reflects an *emic* perspective in the research, in which participants' "original (emic) constructions deserve equal consideration with those of other, more powerful audiences and of the inquirer (etic)."[7] Equal consideration for the voices of all contributors is a theme that resonates not only with my perspective as a researcher, but with my identity as a teacher and citizen. Indeed, a qualitative research project dedicated to the ideal of popular democracy *requires* an epistemological commitment to an emic perspective in order for the findings—and the investigator—to have credibility. In this context, the challenge to "walk the talk" is particularly appropriate.

Finally, a qualitative approach was warranted, even essential, as Guba and Lincoln describe constructivism's methodology as "hermeneutic/dialectic"[8] and naturally qualitative. Patton defines qualitative research as

> an effort to understand situations in their uniqueness as part of a particular context and the interactions there. This understanding is an end in itself, so that it is not attempting to predict what may happen in the future necessarily, but to understand the nature of that setting—what it means for participants to be in that setting, what their lives are like, what's going on for them, what their meanings are, what the world looks like in that particular setting—and in the analysis to be able to communicate that faithfully to others who are interested in that setting. . . . The analysis strives for depth of understanding.[9]

Given the nature of my research question (i.e., its ambitious breadth and depth), I chose case study methodology as the best means for investigating it. This method provided for the deep and focused examination that the question required. Merriam defines this type of qualitative research as "an intensive, holistic description and analysis of a single instance, phenomenon, or social unit."[10] She cites Smith's[11] conception of a case as a "bounded system" to name what she calls "the single most defining characteristic of case study research"[12]—a clearly delimited object of study. My group of participants was the "case" that I studied. My overall intent was interpretive, as the data I collected helped me to "develop conceptual categories or to illustrate, support, or challenge theoretical assumptions held prior to the data gathering."[13]

Assumptions

I chose this case with some assumptions in mind. One is that details do, indeed, undermine ideology, and that when one dominating ideology is undermined there is room for others to expand. In other words, I assumed that if market ideology would be undermined in my participants' and my constructions and potential reconstructions of the purpose of education and the role of schools in society, we would be open to exploring other frameworks for defining such critical issues in education. This assumption is based in personal experience. Having been raised in an ultra-conservative, working class, and wholly white environment, I spent the first decade of my career accepting the bootstrap rhetoric of equal opportunity for all in America. I became a leader in my school district and I participated in championing the outcome-based education movement and the rising focus on standardization and accountability. I attribute the radical reconstruction of my ideological perspective to my own continuing education—to having had access to the works of critical theorists like Donaldo Macedo, whose experiences support his conclusion that "the U.S. educational system is not a failure. The failure it generates represents its ultimate victory to the extent that large groups of people, including the so-called minorities, were never intended to be educated."[14] In the context of the world, Macedo's social criticism is a miniscule detail, as is that of Maxine Greene, Paulo Freire, Howard Zinn and countless others. But the questions that those details provoke have expanded my world. My assumption was that information would expand others' views, too.

Another assumption followed from the first. I assumed that informational details [about such things as the 29 percent of students who vomited while taking the Texas Assessment of Academic Skills[15] and the millions of dollars that are going into investors' pockets instead of into social and educational supports for impoverished children and families] would help our group's "social imagination"[16] to flourish. Maxine Greene describes this kind of imagination as "the capacity to invent visions of what should be and what might be in our deficient society, on the streets where we live, in our schools."[17]

Finally, I assumed that if social imagination did, indeed, flourish, some kind of change would occur. Whether the change would be internal and personal or external and public, I did not know. My findings relative to these assumptions are presented in the final chapters of this work.

Participant Selection

My twelve participants were six teachers and six parents associated with a variety of public schools in an urban area of the Southwest. In identifying these twelve people, my goal was to maximize the diversity of the public schools represented in terms of their socioeconomic perspective and demographic composition, while maintaining a workable discussion-group size. I did not limit myself to elementary-, middle school-, or high school-oriented participants. Rather, I sought teachers and parents who were: (1) identified (by themselves or others) as being people who thrive on "big picture" discussions about every level of education and/or society; (2) open-minded and interested in the perspectives of others; and (3) recognized for their talent (as parents and/or teachers). In my experience I have found that there are usually a small number of such people at most schools, potential visionaries and activists who often feel isolated and powerless, hungering for community and dialogue. These were the participants I was looking for. I did not exclude a participant who was both a parent and teacher, but I did work to ensure that the group was evenly represented in both categories.

I built this participant group by means of criterion-based selection and network sampling.[18] Potential participants who fit established criteria were recommended to me by various contacts within the university and public school systems. In order to facilitate the creation of a safe environment for genuine dialogue, free from the politics and history of any given site, my goal was to ensure that all participants came from different schools unless participants themselves urged otherwise. In the end, this school-affiliation diversity was broad but not perfect. The twelve participants in the group represented eight schools. Par-

ticipants' school affiliations are listed below, along with each school's state rat-
ings for the 2003–2004 and 2004–2005 school years.[19] (Each participant's primary identity for the purpose of the study is noted: T=Teacher, P=Parent. Several teachers in the group were also parents; one parent had been a teacher.)

Participants	School Level	2004-2005 Rating	2003-2004 Rating
Alex (T)	Elementary School	Met AYP*	Exemplary
Sarah (P)/Mariela (T)	Elementary School	Met AYP	Meets Standards
Kate (P)/Peyton (T)	Elementary School	Met AYP	Meets Standards
Julia (T)/Boyoyo (T)	Middle School	Did Not Meet AYP	Probationary
Tessa (P)	Middle School	Did Not Meet AYP	Meets Standards
Ana (P)	Middle School	Did Not Meet AYP	Meets Standards
Rachel (T)	High School	Did Not Meet AYP	Meets Standards
Selena (P)/Elena (P)	High School	Did Not Meet AYP	Meets Standards

* Adequate Yearly Progress is a designation of success/failure that originates in federal legislation, the 2002 reauthorization of the Elementary and Secondary Education Act called *No Child Left Behind* (NCLB).

Boyoyo was the lone male in our group. While I was able to achieve my
goal of creating a diverse group in many ways, I was unable to balance the
group's gender profile. Of the fifty-three people referred to me by colleagues
and friends in the early stages of group formation, only twelve were male (23
percent), even though I specifically asked for male referrals. Of the twenty-four
of these fifty-three who matched my participant selection criteria and who were
invited to participate, seven were male (29 percent) and seventeen were female
(71 percent). The fact that I tried to create at least a semblance of gender balance
is evident in that I invited seven of twelve male referrals (58 percent) and seventeen of forty-one of the female referrals (42 percent). In the end, thirteen of the
seventeen women I invited said yes (77 percent), although two of these had to
drop out because of incompatible schedules with the rest of the group. Only one
of the seven men invited agreed to participate (14 percent). This data is interesting in that it points to the status of education as "women's work," arguably an
explanatory factor for the lack of local definitional authority in the schools.

Data Collection

In keeping with the constructivist view of ontology, epistemology, and
methodology, I used a variety of methods for gathering data. Ontological relativism posits the existence of multiple realities, necessitating a variety of ap-
proaches for apprehending them. A transactional and subjectivist understanding
of the knower-known relationship (i.e., epistemology) suggests that different
kinds of interactional opportunities would potentially facilitate the achievement
of breadth and depth in terms of the findings that participants and I would create
together. Finally, a hermeneutic and dialectic methodology requires multiple

opportunities for the construction and reconstruction of ideas from both emic and etic perspectives. By using a number of different methods for collecting data, I increased the number of opportunities for me and for participants to reform and refine our understandings, increasing the likelihood that those understandings would be "more informed and sophisticated than any of the predecessor constructions."[20]

In addition to addressing the particular concerns of a constructivist research paradigm, the use of a number of different data-collection techniques served the more general purpose of enhancing the trustworthiness of my study. The triangulation of data coming from a variety of sources helped to ensure that my findings are both credible and dependable. Qualitative researchers name a variety of methods for gathering data, the most common three being interviews, observation, and document inspection.[21] I used each of these strategies, in addition to keeping a researcher's journal for the duration of the study. The four techniques and their purposes relative to this project are described in more detail below.

Participant Observation

I facilitated eleven text-based discussions with participants on critical literature in education. I conducted two of these discussions per month, after an initial orientation meeting with the participant group. Each session was approximately two and a half hours long, expanded at participants' request from the two-hour time frame I had originally planned. Each text-based discussion was audio-taped and transcribed by me.

Merriam names several concerns about which a researcher in the role of participant-observer must be aware. For one, the ambiguity of the position from the researcher's perspective can be frustrating, as participant observation has been characterized as "a schizophrenic activity" in which "the researcher usually participates but not to the extent of becoming totally absorbed in the activity."[22] Maintaining balance is an obvious challenge for the participant-observer. Other concerns associated with this dual stance include the researcher's ability to monitor the flow of research activities, to organize and manage the mountains of data in which s/he is immersed, and to avoid over-identifying with participants.[23] A final problem inherent in participant observation is one with which I was most concerned, particularly in view of my plan to serve as facilitator for my group's text-based discussions. This concern has to do with "the extent to which the observer investigator affects what is being observed."[24] (See the Credibility section below for information about steps I took to address this threat to the trustworthiness of my study.)

Despite the difficulties associated with this strategy for gathering data, the benefits of the participant-observer approach warranted its use in the context of this study. The purpose of text-based discussions was to give all participants, including myself, a broader perspective of the accountability movement, based on deep and focused exposure to critical literature and to the variety of perspectives that the teachers and parents in our group would contribute. Exploration of my research question (How do teachers and parents make sense of the accountability movement?) required the discursive intimacy that the participant-observer stance allows; the same need existed for the exploration of my guiding questions (How do participants' identities as parents and teachers influence group discussions and participants' experiences of those discussions; Will individual or collective action result?). The data that I gathered by means of participant observation was a rich body of data for my dissertation. In actuality, it was the primary source.

Document Inspection

At the conclusion of each group discussion, each participant (including myself) wrote a brief reflection on their experience in that discussion. Additionally, I invited each member to keep a participant journal or to e-mail me with thoughts, questions, ideas, and concerns that occurred to them during the weeks between our group sessions. I provided each participant with a notebook for journaling purposes during our first group meeting, believing that my access to this kind of information would enable me to better understand each member's perspective of the process as it was happening, and of the project as it progressed.

From a constructivist perspective, I believed that these personal journals would be extremely important sources of information. Transactional (mutually created) and subjective understandings are the very definition of epistemology in this paradigm. Inspection of these documents would serve at least two purposes: to confirm or challenge patterns in data that emerged from other sources (serving the purpose of establishing trustworthiness through the triangulation of data); and to provide personal insights relative to my guiding questions. Unfortunately, since only two participants followed up on the journaling aspect of participation in the study, my plan for providing this third-level perspective on my data (in addition to participant observation and interviews) was compromised. I did use the written reflection on group discussions to guide my facilitation of subsequent meetings, and I did read the journals that were submitted to me. I did not, however, incorporate the two journals I received into my analysis of data because I did not want to introduce an imbalanced perspective on my participants into that analysis.

Interviews

I conducted two individual interviews with all participants—one at the beginning of the six-month period of data collection, and one at the end. Purposes for the first round of interviews were to gather background information, to understand why each person was interested in participating, to get a feel for the concerns and questions about education and society that participants brought to the group, to learn about participants' initial constructions of words like democracy and citizen, and to hear how these teachers and parents would talk about their personal sense of power and/or powerlessness relative to their educational/social concerns (related to Chomsky's notion of sympathy and solidarity). The second round of interviews, conducted at the conclusion of our group meetings, was necessary for understanding whether/how participants had reconstructed their ideas and for learning what participation in the project meant to them. An additional topic for the second round was for me to learn how parents and teachers thought about their identity in the group. I wanted to know whether participants thought that the categories of "parent" and "teacher" were meaningful in terms of how the group functioned.

Interviews in both rounds ranged in length from ninety minutes to two and a half hours. I audio-taped and transcribed all interviews. In doing so, I recognized the dangers that accompany what Norman Denzin calls "embalmed transcribed speech."[25] While I do not identify strongly with a post-structural approach to knowing, I value Denzin's caution against the risk of "a doubling of agency" that transcription invites:

> When the text becomes the agency that represents the voices of the other, the other becomes an object spoken for. A doubling of agency occurs behind the text because the agent is the author of the text doing the interpreting. The other becomes an extension of the author's voice.[26]

The pertinent observation by Kathy Charmaz, that "postmodernism can *inform* realist study of experience rather than simply serve as justification for abandoning it,"[27] resonates with me; it explains my appreciation for Denzin's warning even as I reject its implications. My goal, after all, was to understand participants' constructions and potential reconstructions of ideas related to the accountability movement, not to learn The Truth. Therefore, I interviewed participants and transcribed those interviews because I believe there is value in the process of trying to pin down what we think we believe in any given moment— of talking our way through the reconstruction of ideas. I accepted the risk of "embalming" others' speech because I believe that, while Truth will never be established, perceptions of truth emerge through talking. I know that I sometimes discover what I believe to be true only when I hear myself saying it. For this reason, I believe that the interview and follow-up review of its transcription offers significant benefit to the research and learning processes.

I took steps to guard against any overt or covert "doubling of agency" on my part and against inaccurate representations of others' meanings. I conducted member checks every other week, starting with our eighth meeting, by presenting the code-mapping schema I was in the process of developing. My purpose in this was to learn whether participants' views of emerging themes cohered with my own. I took advantage of two additional opportunities for member checking after the conclusion of my six-month period of data collection. Half of the research participants decided to continue meeting on a monthly basis; during two of these meetings, I presented for critique the findings that were emerging through my analysis. From at least a part of the initial research group, I was able to confirm in this way that my findings were consistent with these participants' experience of the study.

Researcher's Journal

I kept a researcher's journal throughout the course of the study. Merriam calls this a fieldwork journal, "an introspective record . . . [that] includes his or her ideas, fears, mistakes, confusion, and reactions to the experience and can include thoughts about the research methodology itself."[28] This was the means I used for recording my observations about the project as it unfolded. Here is where I recorded such things as my personal reflections following each text-based discussion; areas of inquiry that needed follow-up with participants or that required further review of related literature; ideas about patterns that seemed to be emerging from the data I was collecting; and questions about methodological or ethical concerns that required the guidance of outside consultants.

These four data-collection methods (participant observation, document inspection, interviews, and a researcher's journal) are well aligned with the perspective of constructivism. With the exception of the participants' journals, they yielded the data I needed in order to address my research question, and taken together, they represent a strength of design that justifies confidence in my findings.

Data Analysis

I used the constant comparative method of analysis initially described in 1967 by its originators, Barney G. Glaser and Anselm L. Strauss, in *The Discovery of Grounded Theory*. Merriam offers a concise summary of this method:

> The basic strategy . . . is to do just what its name implies—constantly compare. The researcher begins with a particular incident from an interview, field notes, or document and compares it with another incident in the same set of data or in another set. These comparisons lead to tentative categories that are then compared to each other and to other instances. Comparisons are constantly made within and between levels of conceptualization until a theory can be formulated.[29]

While my approach to data analysis has its roots in this model, my analytic intent was other than what early proponents of grounded theory originally (and subsequently) described.[30] The purpose of analysis in the context of this study was not to generate theory in order to explain objective experience, but to generate a trustworthy interpretation of the findings that my participants would lead me to; not to provide a "window on reality," as Charmaz put it, but simply "a rendering, one interpretation among multiple interpretations, of a shared or individual reality."[31] This interpretive epistemological and ontological orientation, as well as the fact that I make no pretense of positioning my research in a theo-retical vacuum, indicates a departure from the positivistic roots of grounded theory in favor of a revised version that Charmaz calls "constructivist grounded theory." Her conception of a grounded theory continuum, encompassing both objectivist and constructivist perspectives, describes the analytical niche that I found in this method:

> The power of grounded theory lies in its tools for understanding empirical worlds. We can reclaim these tools from their positivist underpinnings to form a revised, more open-ended practice of grounded theory that stresses its emer-gent, constructivist elements. We can use grounded theory methods as flexible, heuristic strategies rather than as formulaic procedures.[32]

In this spirit, I used three specific strategies deriving from grounded theory to analyze my data: coding (line-by-line and focused), memo writing, and theo-retical sampling. A brief description of each, based on Charmaz's work in de-lineating a constructivist grounded theory, follows.

Coding Data

Charmaz uses three terms to describe the process of identifying themes in the data: line-by-line coding, focused coding, and action codes. My analysis began with the application of the first two of these. While my intent was to be-gin coding as soon as I had transcribed data available to me (from individual interviews and group meetings) and then to continue this process throughout the data collection phase, the reality of my experience fell short of this ideal. Just keeping up with transcription of group discussions, two and a half hour sessions involving anywhere from five to thirteen participants, was challenging. I there-fore only began coding two-thirds of the way into my data collection period, after our seventh group session. Once I began, I used a line-by-line strategy through the duration of my coding process. This strategy allowed me to focus on coding minute bits of information, helping to ensure that the data itself guided my analysis rather than my own beliefs and theories. Line-by-line coding also served to keep potentially relevant themes from getting lost in the larger data chunks of sentences and paragraphs. By this means I eventually established an initial set of eighty-five codes that subsequently guided my analysis.

I used these tentative lenses, this initial set of eighty-five codes, in the sub-sequent focused coding of data. This strategy allowed me to conceptually orga-nize the mass of information that I collected. Focused coding (interspersed by occasional line-by-line coding as a check against the dangers of me "leading" my data and of losing significant follow-up questions) yielded the categories I eventually used to synthesize and explain my findings. These, in turn, "shape[d] [my] developing analytic framework. . . . Categories turn[ed] description into conceptual analysis by specifying properties analytically."[33]

Memo Writing

Ryan and Bernard describe memo-ing as "one of the principal techniques for recording relationships among themes."[34] Charmaz positions it as "the intermediate step between coding and the first draft of the completed analysis. . . . Through memo writing," she explains, "we elaborate processes, assumptions, and actions that are subsumed under our codes."[35]

I used this analysis strategy for a number of reasons, not least of which is the fact that it provides a formal account of how I made sense of the categories that emerged from my coded data. Since the integrity of my analytic framework is dependent upon my ability to find meaningful and genuine relationships among categories, it was important that I built into my design a means to track that meaning-making process. As Charmaz puts it, "Memo writing aids us in linking analytic interpretation with empirical reality."[36] The formal articulation of what could otherwise be an internal and un-inspected process helped me not only to be rigorous in my analysis, ensuring that findings are consistent with the data; these memos also provide a trail that an external reader can follow in order to corroborate or refute the dependability of my final product.

Charmaz offers a number of other reasons that make memo writing an important strategy. Among other benefits, the process "helps to spark our thinking and encourages us to look at our data and codes in new ways," it helps us to "define leads for collecting data," and it "keeps us focused on our analyses and involved in our research."[37]

I took advantage of both computer-aided and paper-and-pencil formats in creating this audit trail. Notes in my researcher's journal point to connections in the making. I also found the memo-ing capabilities in HyperResearch, the computer program I used for coding, to be an extremely useful feature for this purpose.

Theoretical Sampling

Memo writing served an additional purpose in that it helped me to identify conceptual gaps as my explanation and interpretation of the data developed. When this happens, Charmaz explains, "we grounded theorists . . . go back to the field and collect delimited data to fill those conceptual gaps and holes—we conduct theoretical sampling. At this point, we choose to sample specific issues only; we look for precise information to shed light on the emerging theory."[38]

Ryan and Bernard describe the impetus for grounded theorists as wanting "to understand people's experiences in as rigorous and detailed a manner as possible. They want to identify categories and concepts that emerge from text and link these concepts into substantive and formal theories."[39] Kathy Charmaz's argument for a constructivist grounded theory allowed me to situate my approach to data analysis within a framework that accommodates the ontological, epistemological, and methodological paradigm in which my project was grounded.

My use of theoretical sampling was limited to conversations with the half of my participants who had elected to continue meeting on a monthly basis after their formal participation in the study concluded. In presenting my findings as they evolved in this informal context, I was able to refine and deepen the theoretical connections I was making through the processes of coding and categorizing my data.

Trustworthiness

A fertile obsession, validity is the researcher's mask of authority (Lather, 1993, p. 674) that allows a particular regime of truth within a particular text (and community of scholars) to work its way on the reader.[40]

I appreciate Denzin's objection to what he sees as a ploy for gaining legitimacy for qualitative research by riding the coattails of quantitative positivism's privileged position. I reject, however, the idea that if I value the need for validity and reliability in my research that I am simply hiding behind a mask of authority as I work to advance my own regime of truth upon unsuspecting readers. Having found nothing yet to adequately replace the constructs of validity and reliability in my mind, I would be negligent to dismiss them. Therefore, though Guba and Lincoln acknowledge that "the issue of quality criteria in constructivism is . . . not well resolved, and [that] further critique is needed,"[41] I am more philosophically aligned with their notions of credibility (internal validity), transferability (external validity), and dependability (reliability) than with Denzin's call for "poststructural validity,"[42] or with other constructions of quality control measures that have been proposed in recent years.[43]

Credibility (Internal Validity)

The credibility or internal validity of a study has to do with what Merriam describes as "the question of how research findings match reality. . . . Do the findings capture what is really there? Are investigators observing and measuring what they think they are measuring? Internal validity in all research thus hinges on the meaning of reality."[44]

Constructivism's ontological perspective, as noted earlier, is that of "relativism, which assumes multiple, apprehendable, and sometimes conflicting social realities that are the products of human intellects, but that may change as their constructors become more informed and sophisticated."[45] It is with this perspective on knowing in mind that I introduce the strategies[46] that I used to ensure the credibility of my findings:

Triangulation

The credibility of my findings is enhanced because of the many data collection techniques and sources of data that were available to me. (As noted previously, the fact that only two of my twelve participants kept a journal as an aspect of their participation in the study caused me to rely on three instead of four sources of data: group discussion transcripts, interview transcripts, and participant observations recorded in my own journal.)

Member checks

By offering participants a copy of their interview transcript and a copy of this dissertation manuscript, and by consulting with them during the process of data analysis (during and after the data collection period), the danger of "the other becom[ing] an extension of the author's voice"[47] was addressed and hopefully, eliminated.

Long-term observation

I did not base my findings on observations of merely one or two sessions of group discussion and interaction, but rather on six months of observation in twelve group discussions and on two rounds of participant interviews. The duration of my study was aimed at providing sufficient time for in-depth reading and discussion without over-taxing participants' commitment to the project.

Collaborative mode of research

The constructivist paradigm described by Guba and Lincoln and reported here clearly addresses the fact that participants and I were "interactively linked so that the 'findings' were *literally created* as the investigation proceeds."[48] In this context, manipulation or distortion of findings on my part would be difficult to achieve. The three themes that emerged through my analysis of group discussion transcripts were created meeting by meeting, month by month, with all of the participants in the group.

Researcher's biases

I made a point of making my own position clear to participants regarding my philosophical and theoretical position, my assumptions that I brought to the project, and my relationship to others in the study as a participant-observer. One concrete strategy that I employed toward this end was to invite participants to read my research proposal and to use it as the basis of one of our text-based discussions. This was an effective approach in making sure that participants were aware of my background, my biases, and my research agenda.

These measures, taken together, ensure that my findings are congruent with my participants' realities, and that the study is credible from an internal perspective.

Two final notes about the internal credibility of this study have to do with issues that I named earlier. One is the concern that I had at the start of the project as I envisioned myself in the dual role of participant-observer. As facilitator and participant in group discussions, I recognized the potential danger of my inadvertent leading of group discussions down paths that I might deem correct. One protection against this danger was the depth of experience that I have in the facilitation of text-based discussions. However, knowing that I couldn't presume to say that I am always able to control the temptation to "teach" people the "right" knowledge, I built a second protection into my design in making this very concern known to all participants. In introducing them to the discussion protocol, I specifically invited them to watch for and call attention to leading questions, facial expressions, and body language. As a final protection, I ensured through my participant selection process that at least one participant was also well versed in facilitating text-based discussions. I asked that participant to take on the responsibility of monitoring my facilitation and to publicly call me on moments when my facilitation appeared directive or leading. While the fact that she never did this over the course of our twelve meetings together does not guarantee that my facilitation was never directive or leading, my public precautions minimized the threat.

I debated with myself at length over the role I should play in the group's text-based discussions. In the end, I decided that the role of facilitator was appropriate mostly because the role options left to me were I *not* to facilitate discussions would have been even more potentially dangerous to the integrity of my study. If I were a full-fledged participant rather than a facilitator, I would have had less responsibility for ensuring that all voices were heard and less responsibility for monitoring the group's adherence to the ground rules for text-based discussions. On the other hand, if I were to refrain from participating and either videotape discussions or sit in as an observer, instead, I feared that the experience of being watched would negatively impact the quality and spontaneity of discussion. Finally, while it was permissible for me to actively participate in the group discussions (according to the text-based discussion protocol that I used), that participation was naturally more curtailed with me in the facilitator's chair than if I had not had to assume the responsibilities of facilitation.

A second concern was my worry that my imposition of pre-selected texts on the group would violate the very notion of popular democracy that I advocate. As participants themselves helped me to realize, this concern was unfounded. It was at their request, since my familiarity with critical literature on the accountability movement in education was greater than theirs, that I selected the texts for our discussions.

Dependability (Reliability)

In a qualitative paradigm, my goal is not to isolate and control variables, ensuring that my results will be replicable in other settings. It is, rather, as Merriam explains: to make sure that outside readers would "concur that, given the data collected, the results make sense—they are consistent and dependable. The question then is not whether findings will be found again but *whether the results are consistent with the data collected.*"[49] Strategies I used to ensure dependability were:

The investigator's position

In order to ascertain whether my results make sense given the data that I present, readers will require detailed contextual information about such things as "my position vis-a-vis the group being studied, the basis for selecting informants and a description of them, and the social context from which data were collected."[50] In the writing of this work, I have taken pains to ensure that my position is clear to readers in the same degree that I made it known to participants.

Triangulation (as previously described)

Audit trail

The likelihood that my findings are dependable, that is, that they make sense in view of the data that I collected, is strengthened by my adherence to the analytical process of memo writing. These analytical memos served as a tracking mechanism for my thinking processes as I moved through the work of coding, categorizing, and interpreting data—effectively meeting the obligation for a dependability check that Merriam describes: "In order for an audit to take place, the investigator must describe in detail how data were collected, how categories were derived, and how decisions were made throughout the inquiry."[51] My writing partner, Carol Brandt, was an invaluable help to me in reviewing my audit trail and helping me to think through this process.

Transferability (External Validity)

In conducting this study, I obviously had hope that the work would benefit not only my participants and me, but also people in other settings who are concerned with similar issues. Rather than worry about the generalizability of my findings as quantitative researchers must—who take care to ensure such things as "equivalency between the sample and population from which it was drawn, control of sample size, random sampling, and so on"[52]—my standard is what Firestone[53] called "case-to-case" transfer. Also called "reader or user generalizability," my obligation relative to transferability is to describe the context of my study in enough detail so that outside readers can determine for themselves whether my findings are of any use in their context. Rich, thick description is the strategy that I used to meet this obligation.

Confirmability (Objectivity)

A final set of terms that are used to contrast qualitative and quantitative methods is confirmability versus objectivity. I bring no pretense of objectivity to this project. Rather, I have done everything in my power—through the use of the strategies named above for ensuring credibility, dependability, and transferability—to ensure that my study is confirmable. No one explains the rationale behind this kind of orientation to knowing better than Howard Zinn:

> Why should we cherish 'objectivity,' as if ideas were innocent, as if they don't serve one interest or another? Surely, we want to be objective if that means telling the truth as we see it, not concealing information that may be embarrassing to our point of view. But we don't want to be objective if it means pretending that ideas don't play a part in the social struggles of our time, that we don't take sides in those struggles.

> Indeed, it is impossible to be neutral. In a world already moving in certain directions, where wealth and power are already distributed in certain ways, neutrality means accepting the way things are now. It is a world of clashing interests—war against peace, nationalism against internationalism, equality against greed, and democracy against elitism—and it seems to me both impossible and undesirable to be neutral in those conflicts.[54]

Significance and Limitations of the Study

The main limitation of this study has to do with the participant group. Although I have built a case arguing for popular democracy in the governance of public schools, it is clear that my participant group was a privileged one in terms of the social, financial, and cultural capital they brought to the project. Clearly, people who have the time to read, think, and meet for discussion about philosophical and political ideas were viewing the issues I have outlined here from a position of relative advantage. They were people, like me, who do not work multiple jobs and who have the advantages of food, shelter, and safety that at least a degree of financial privilege in our society brings. They were also, for the most part, a socially and culturally privileged group of participants, having the confidence to read and discuss these kinds of texts—confidence that education and experience in discussing ideas can bring.

While I recognize this potentially narrow perspective as a limitation of the study, I will argue that the same perspective also represents an important strength of my research. In a time when the voices of the poor are not powerful enough to be heard[55] and the voices of the super-affluent will not likely be used to diminish their own financial, political, and cultural advantages, it is the "middle class" voice of relative privilege that I was interested in hearing. In this regard I think often of my oldest sister—a therapist, teacher, wife, and mother of two—who agonizes over the social and educational injustices that she observes. Like me and millions of other moderately affluent Americans, she is part of what Amy Goodman calls "the silenced majority"[56]—silenced, Goodman says, by a corporate media that is dedicated to serving private rather than public interests. Isolated, my sister has felt powerless, as have I—a pair of unwilling amoral familists tucked away in the privilege of our middle class homes. Silenced, unless we choose to break out of our isolation and speak with others about our varied conceptions of the public good. The significance of this research project is that it offered such an opportunity for the parents and teachers who lived it.

The ultimate significance of this study lies in the contribution it may make to empowering other teachers and parents to break the silence that typically exists between them, to disrupt the status of market values in our schools, and in doing so, to realize the democratic potential of parents' and teachers' partnership in volatile knowing.

"There comes a time when silence is betrayal," warned Dr. Martin Luther King, Jr.[57] If the ideals of public education are to survive on our watch, that time is now.

Notes

1. Michelle Fine, "[Ap]parent Involvement: Reflections on Parents, Power, and Urban Public Schools," *Teachers College Record* 94, no. 4 (Summer 1993); Kimberly Waggoner and Alison Griffith. "Parent Involvement in Education." *Journal for a Just & Caring Education* 4, no. 1 (January 1998); Kathryn Nakagawa, "Unthreading the Ties that Bind: Questioning the Discourse of Parent Involvement," *Educational Policy* 14, no. 4 (September 2000).

2. Evon G. Guba and Yvonne S. Lincoln, "Competing Paradigms in Qualitative Research" in *Handbook of Qualitative Research*, edited by Norman K. Denzin and Yvonne S. Lincoln (Thousand Oaks, Calif.: Sage, 1994), 111.

3. Vincent A. Anfara, Kathleen M. Brown, and Terri L. Mangione. "Qualitative Analysis on Stage: Making the Research Process More Public." *Educational Researcher* 31, no. 7 (2002): 29.

4. Sharan Merriam, *Qualitative Research and Case Study Applications in Education* (San Francisco: Jossey-Bass Publishers, 1998), 4.

5. Guba and Lincoln, "Competing Paradigms in Qualitative Research," 111.

6. Guba and Lincoln, "Competing Paradigms in Qualitative Research," 111, emphasis in original.

7. Guba and Lincoln, "Competing Paradigms in Qualitative Research," 114.

8. Guba and Lincoln, "Competing Paradigms in Qualitative Research," 112. Note: Hermeneutic means "interpretive; explanatory" and dialectic, "the art or practice of logical discussion as employed in investigating the truth of a theory or opinion." Jess Stein,

ed., *The Random House Dictionary of the English Language: The Unabridged Edition*, (New York: Random House, 1967), 397, 665.

9. Patton in Merriam, *Qualitative Research and Case Study Applications in Education*, 6.

10. Merriam, *Qualitative Research and Case Study Applications in Education*, 27.

11. Smith in Merriam, *Qualitative Research and Case Study Applications in Education*.

12. Merriam, *Qualitative Research and Case Study Applications in Education*, 27.

13. Merriam, *Qualitative Research and Case Study Applications in Education*, 38.

14. Donaldo P. Macedo, "Literacy for Stupidification: The Pedagogy of Big Lies" in *Breaking Free: The Transformative Power of Critical Pedagogy*, edited by Donaldo P. Macedo (Cambridge, Mass: Harvard Educational Review, 1996), 55.

15. Dale Johnson and Bonnie Johnson, *High Stakes: Children, Testing, and Failure in American Schools* (Lanham, Md.: Rowman & Littlefield Publishers, 2002).

16. Maxine Greene, *Releasing the Imagination: Essays on Education, the Arts, and Social Change* (San Francisco: Jossey-Bass Publishers, 1995), 5.

17. Greene, *Releasing the Imagination*, 5.

18. Merriam, *Qualitative Research and Case Study Applications in Education*.

19. <http://www.ped.state.nm.us/div/acc.assess/accountability/index.html>.

20. Guba and Lincoln, "Competing Paradigms in Qualitative Research," 111.

21. Merriam, *Qualitative Research and Case Study Applications in Education*; Margaret LeCompte and Judith Preissle. *Ethnography and Qualitative Design in Educational Research* (2nd ed.) (San Diego: Academic Press, 1993); Valerie. J. Janesick, "The Dance of Qualitative Research Design: Metaphor, Methodolatry, and Meaning" in *Handbook of Qualitative Research*, edited by Norman K. Denzin and Yvonne S. Lincoln, 209–219 (Thousand Oaks, Calif.: Sage, 1994); Irving Seidman, *Interviewing as Qualitative Research* (2nd ed.) (New York: Teachers College Press, 1998); Andrea Fontana and James. H. Frey, "The Interview: From Structured Questions to Negotiated Text" in *Handbook of Qualitative Research* (2nd ed.), edited by Norman K. Denzin and Yvonne S. Lincoln, 645–672 (Thousand Oaks, Calif.: Sage, 2000); Michael V. Angrosino and Kimberly A. Mays de Pérez, "Rethinking Observation: From Method to Context" in *Handbook of Qualitative Research* (2nd ed.), edited by Norman K. Denzin and Yvonne S. Lincoln, 673–702 (Thousand Oaks, Calif.: Sage, 2000); Ian Hodder, "The Interpretation of Documents and Material Culture" in *Handbook of Qualitative Research* (2nd ed.), edited by Norman K. Denzin and Yvonne S. Lincoln, 703–715 (Thousand Oaks, Calif.: Sage, 2000).

22. Merriam, *Qualitative Research and Case Study Applications in Education*, 103.

23. Gans in Merriam, *Qualitative Research and Case Study Applications in Education*.

24. Merriam, *Qualitative Research and Case Study Applications in Education*, 103.

25. Norman Denzin, *Interpretive Ethnography: Ethnographic Practices for the 21st Century* (Thousand Oaks, Calif.: Sage, 1997), 41.

26. Denzin, *Interpretive Ethnographic Practices for the 21st Century*, 44.

27. Kathy Charmaz, "Grounded Theory: Objectivist and Constructivist Methods" in *Handbook of Qualitative Research* (2nd ed.), edited by Norman K. Denzin and Yvonne S. Lincoln (Thousand Oaks, Calif.: Sage, 2000), 528, emphasis in original.

28. Merriam, *Qualitative Research and Case Study Applications in Education*, 110.

29. Merriam, *Qualitative Research and Case Study Applications in Education*, 159.

30. See Charmaz, "Grounded Theory," for a brief history on the development of grounded theory.

31. Charmaz, "Grounded Theory," 523.

32. Charmaz, "Grounded Theory," 510.

33. Charmaz, "Grounded Theory," 516.

34. Gery W. Ryan and H. Russell Bernard, "Data Management and Analysis Methods" in *Handbook of Qualitative Research* (2nd ed.), edited by Norman K. Denzin and Yvonne S. Lincoln (Thousand Oaks, Calif.: Sage, 2000), 783.

35. Charmaz, "Grounded Theory," 517.

36. Charmaz, "Grounded Theory," 517.

37. Charmaz, "Grounded Theory," 517.

38. Charmaz, "Grounded Theory," 519.

39. Ryan and Bernard, "Data Management and Analysis Methods," 782.

40. Denzin, *Interpretive Ethnography*, 7.

41. Guba and Lincoln, "Competing Paradigms in Qualitative Research," 114.

42. Denzin, *Interpretive Ethnography*, 20.

43. See Anfara, et al., "Qualitative Analysis on Stage."

44. Merriam, *Qualitative Research and Case Study Applications in Education*, 201.

45. Guba and Lincoln, "Competing Paradigms in Qualitative Research," 111.

46. From Merriam, *Qualitative Research and Case Study Applications in Education*.

47. Denzin, *Interpretive Ethnography*, 44.

48. Guba and Lincoln, "Competing Paradigms in Qualitative Research," 111, emphasis in original.

49. Merriam, *Qualitative Research and Case Study Applications in Education*, 206, emphasis in original.

50. Merriam, *Qualitative Research and Case Study Applications in Education*, 206–207.

51. Merriam, *Qualitative Research and Case Study Applications in Education*, 207.

52. Merriam, *Qualitative Research and Case Study Applications in Education*, 207.

53. Firestone in Merriam, *Qualitative Research and Case Study Applications in Education*.

54. Howard Zinn, *Declarations of Independence: Cross-examining American Ideology* (New York: Harper Perennial, 1990), 6–7.

55. Michael Apple, *Education the "Right" Way* (New York: RoutledgeFalmer, 2001).

56. Amy Goodman, "Democracy Now: The Independent Media in Times of War," *The University of New Mexico 21st Century Speakers Series*, Albuquerque, New Mexico, January 18, 2003.

57. Martin Luther King, Jr., cited by Goodman, "Democracy Now."

APPENDIX B	Foucault's Functions of Discipline in the Public School Panopticon			
Foucault's Instruments of Discipline	Disciplinary Function A *Define, organize, and regulate reality*	Disciplinary Function B *Separate and neutralize people*	Disciplinary Function C *Utilize people fully and efficiently*	Disciplinary Function D *Infiltrate, study, and document*
Disciplinary Instrument #1 *The timetable*	definitional authority is exercised by the upper tiers over how people in lower tiers spend their time; the lower the tier, the more controlled is their time	schedules are created in a way that makes it hard for people to connect; time is tightly controlled, limiting opportunities for horizontal and vertical collaboration	"on task" behavior and productivity are emphasized; schedules are created so that people are always "on"; when workers are always "on" during their workday, time for planning comes from evenings/weekends	
Disciplinary Instrument #2 *Hierarchical observation*		the uneven distribution of power creates a hierarchy which keeps people vertically separated; vertical and horizontal surveillance separates by creating a "policed" environment	with systemic values internalized at every level, control is efficient; the people are their own "guards" or enforcers of those values and expectations	observation occurs within the system, at every hierarchical level; every individual is made visible through detailed documentation of performances
Disciplinary Instrument #3 *Normalizing judgment*	"good" and "bad" are defined according to systemic values; ways of being that serve the elite panoptic tier are established as normal; reality is operatively defined by these norms	people at each level are rewarded or punished depending on whether or not they have been found "normal" according to operational definitions and measurements; ranking systems formalize the value of "normalcy"	normalizing judgment makes practices like age-grouping "natural"; people learn to internalize the idea that the essential goal is efficient achievement of the norm (vs. pursuit of "the good" according to personal/public values)	

Foucault's Instruments of Discipline	Foucault's Functions of Discipline in the Public School Panopticon			
	Disciplinary Function A *Define, organize, and regulate reality*	Disciplinary Function B *Separate and neutralize people*	Disciplinary Function C *Utilize people fully and efficiently*	Disciplinary Function D *Infiltrate, study, and document*
Disciplinary Instrument #4 *The examination*	the examination is where hierarchical observation and normalizing judgment come together; it is the instrument that embodies systemic values and measures each individual's position relative to them; it is the most visible expression of what those in power (at every level) have decided is most important	examination is the means by which people are ranked and sorted according to their performances; horizontal and vertical connections between people are made difficult because of the culture of competition that results		performances are constantly measured against this expression of what is real and important; periodic documentation of each individual's achievement relative to those norms makes that person visible and fixes him/her at a specific point on the system's good-bad continuum
Disciplinary Instrument #5 *Collective training*	people are grouped and trained in service to systemic needs and goals, not their own; collective training provides an efficient organizational structure for operationalizing the instrument of normalizing judgment	individuals in the system are separated by means of how their "training" is organized (administrators and students, for example, never study anything together; parents and teachers rarely do); collective training of individuals at each tier prevents people from identifying common goals and interests	collective training (whether one-size-fits-all professional development model for teachers or the grouping of twenty-five twelve-year-olds in a seventh grade class) demonstrates the fact that schools are not designed to serve human needs; efficient arrangement of children and teachers reveals the reality that the reverse is actually the case	

APPENDIX B (p. 3 of 4)	Foucault's Functions of Discipline in the Public School Panopticon			
Foucault's Instruments of Discipline	Disciplinary Function A *Define, organize, and regulate reality*	Disciplinary Function B *Separate and neutralize people*	Disciplinary Function C *Utilize people fully and efficiently*	Disciplinary Function D *Infiltrate, study, and document*
Disciplinary Instrument #6 *Superficial Exercises*	substantive questions, discussions, and activities are avoided; reality is instead defined by a kind of mind-numbing adherence to activity for its own sake; the question of what all of the activity has to do with a collective understanding of "the big picture" of reality just doesn't come up	superficial exercises keep people too busy to think, much less to be able to connect with anyone else; when everyone is busily doing without pausing to reflect on their activity together, they may not question whether their activity is contributing to a vision of reality that is not their own		
Disciplinary Instrument #7 *The expert*	the elite tier of the panopticon reserves for itself the right to define what knowledge is; official knowledge is real and valuable, while the students', parents', and educators' personal experiences and expertise are not	people in schools do not have authority to identify, define, and solve their problems; they are divorced from their own experience and expertise as outside experts are brought in to identify, define, and direct the solutions to problems for them; expertise within a school is devalued, dismissed as unofficial knowledge	when "the expert" is in the form of canned curricula or legislation mandating a phonics-only approach to reading, for example, efficiency can be maximized by ensuring that all instruction takes place at the same time, in the same way; creativity and passion are abandoned in favor of efficiency and predictability	formal documents like *A Nation at Risk* and *No Child Left Behind* are the embodiment of panoptic authority in the public schools; they provide the necessary authorization for the continuous and detailed surveillance that takes place at every level of the system; they are the mechanisms by which visibility is controlled

APPENDIX B (p. 4 of 4)	Foucault's Functions of Discipline in the Public School Panopticon			
Foucault's Instruments of Discipline	Disciplinary Function A *Define, organize, and regulate reality*	Disciplinary Function B *Separate and neutralize people*	Disciplinary Function C *Utilize people fully and efficiently*	Disciplinary Function D *Infiltrate, study, and document*
Disciplinary Instrument #8 *The memo*		the memo allows managers to avoid face-to-face interaction in the form of discussion, debate, and negotiation with workers; it dispenses with human interaction	the memo "saves" time, and in the process it takes away from workers the chance to argue, to make sense of what they are doing and why; saving time and denying chances for workers to have input are two efficient strategies, from a manager's perspective	
Disciplinary Instrument #9 *Media control*	the elite panoptic tier owns the ultimate means of defining, organizing, and regulating reality in its ownership of the mass media; teachers and parents are unaware of some of the questions that urgently need to be asked about the state of education because it is not the media's job to shed light on the issues they represent	citizens are isolated and neutralized by a media system invested in promoting consumerism over citizenship; media portrayals of complex issues ("achievement" in schools) are baldly presented as truth; in the absence of complicating details, people are encouraged to accept sound bytes as reality	to control the people's perception of reality is to pre-empt the likelihood of horizontal conjunctions forming amongst the workers; it is efficient to keep the people focused on their function within the panopticon, in service to the elite tier of that structure, rather than allow them to see the questions that need asking in service to those who occupy the foundational tiers	

APPENDIX C

OSMOSIS & THE EVOLUTION OF THE PUBLIC SCHOOL PANOPTICON

A Representation of Foucault's
Continuous Individualizing Pyramid (1984)
Lack of Systemic Cell-Wall Permeability Leads to Starvation

Volatility/Changeability in the Schools via
the *Collective, Child-Centered Pyramid* (Tollefson)
Healthy Osmotic Functioning Allows Nourishment & Growth

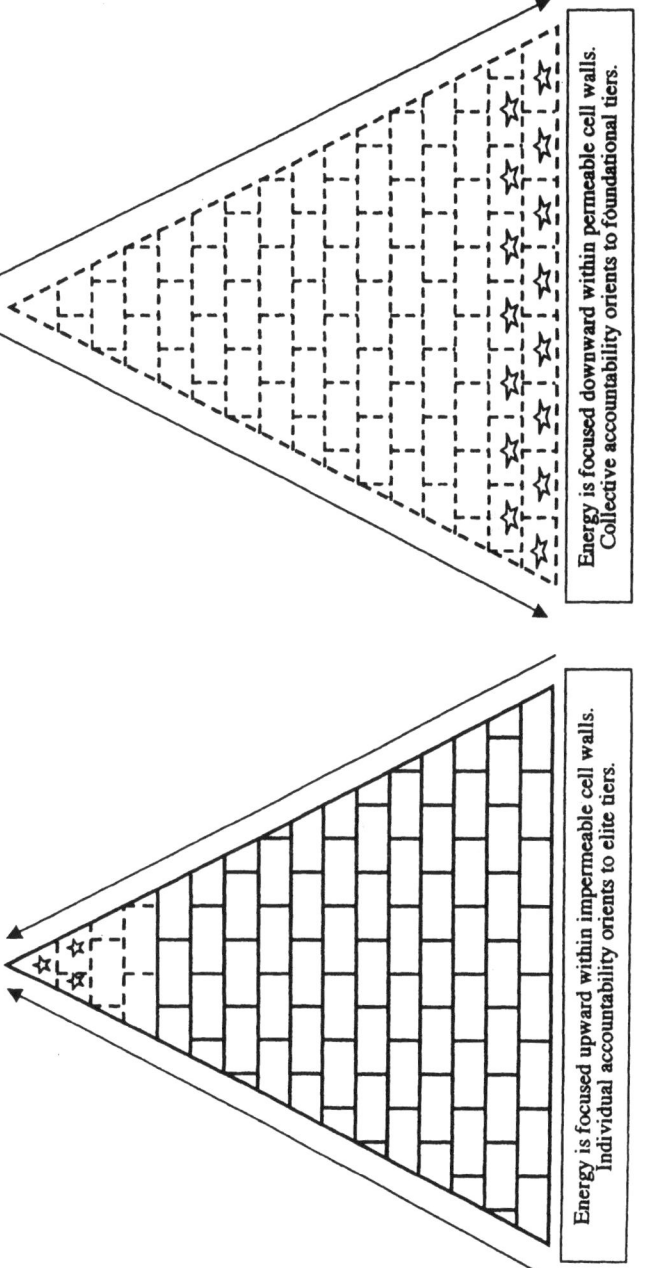

Energy is focused upward within impermeable cell walls.
Individual accountability orients to elite tiers.

Energy is focused downward within permeable cell walls.
Collective accountability orients to foundational tiers.

Bibliography

Albrecht, James E. "A Nation at Risk: Another View." *Phi Delta Kappan* 76, no. 10 (June 1984): 684–685.

Anfara, Vincent A., Kathleen M. Brown, and Terri L. Mangione. "Qualitative Analysis on Stage: Making the Research Process More Public." *Educational Researcher* 31, no. 7 (2002): 28–38.

Angrosino, Michael V., and Kimberly A. Mays de Pérez. "Rethinking Observation: From Method to Context" in *Handbook of Qualitative Research* (2nd ed.), edited by Norman K. Denzin and Yvonne S. Lincoln, 673–702. Thousand Oaks, Calif.: Sage, 2000.

Apple, Michael. *Education the "Right" Way.* New York: RoutledgeFalmer, 2001.

"Back to School, Thinking Globally." *New York Times*, September 6, 2005, Editorial Section. Retrieved from http://www.nytimes.com/pages/pageone/ on September 6, 2005.

Ball, Stephen J. "Education Markets, Choice, and Social Class: The Market as a Class Strategy in the UK and the USA." *British Journal of Sociology of Education* 14, no. 1 (March 1993). Retrieved from the University of New Mexico General Libraries Online Database, EBSCO Academic Elite, Accession Number 9707182762. Accessed November 14, 2002.

Barsamian, David. "Noam Chomsky: *The Progressive Interview.*" *The Progressive* (May 2004): 35–39.

Berliner, David C., and Bruce J. Biddle. *The Manufactured Crisis: Myths, Fraud, and the Attack on America's Public Schools.* Cambridge, Mass.: Perseus Books, 1995.

Beyer, Landon E. "Educational Reform: The Political Roots of *A Nation at Risk.*" *Curriculum Inquiry* 15, no. 1 (1985): 37–56.

Birenbaum-Carmeli, Daphna. "Parents Who Get What They Want: On the Empowerment of the Powerful." *Sociological Review* 47, no. 1 (February1999). Retrieved from the University of New Mexico General Libraries Online Database, EBSCO Academic Elite, Accession Number 1847216. Accessed November 13, 2002.

Bracey, Gerald. "The 14th Bracey Report on the Condition of Public Education." *Phi Delta Kappan* (October 2004): 149–167.

———. "The 15th Bracey Report on the Condition of Public Education." *Phi Delta Kappan* (October 2005): 138–153.

———. "The 16th Bracey Report on the Condition of Public Education." *Phi Delta Kappan* (October 2006): 151–166.

Charmaz, Kathy. "Grounded Theory: Objectivist and Constructivist Methods" in *Handbook of Qualitative Research* (2nd ed.), edited by Norman K. Denzin and Yvonne S. Lincoln, 509–535. Thousand Oaks, Calif.: Sage, 2000.

Children's Defense Fund. "The State of Children in America's Union: A 2002 Action Guide to *Leave No Child Behind.*" http://www.childrensdefense.org/. http://www.civilrights.org/issues/census/details.cfm?id=8367. Accessed November 13, 2002.

Chomsky, Noam. "Renewing Tom Paine's Challenge" in *Our Media Not Theirs*, by Robert McChesney and John Nichols, 15–23. New York: Seven Stories Press, 2002.

Christensen, Doran. "The Politics of Educational Reform: What Vested Interests Are at Stake?" Paper presented at the American Educational Studies Association, Chicago, 1987. ERIC #ED290735.

Considine, David M. and Gail E. Haley. *Visual Messages: Integrating Imagery into Instruction.* Englewood, Colo.: Teacher Ideas Press, 1999.

deMause, Neil, and Steve Rendall. "The Poor Will Always Be With Us—Just Not on the TV News." *Fairness & Accuracy in Reporting.* Retrieved from http://www.fair.org/index.php?page=3172. Accessed September 22, 2007.

Denzin, Norman. *Interpretive Ethnography: Ethnographic Practices for the 21st Century.* Thousand Oaks, Calif.: Sage, 1997.

Denzin, Norman, and Yvonne Lincoln, eds. *Handbook of Qualitative Research.* Thousand Oaks, Calif.: Sage, 1994.

Dewey, John. "The Democratic Conception in Education" (1916), in *Educating the Democratic Mind*, by Walter C. Parker. Albany: State University of New York Press, 1996.

Donlevy, Jim. "The Dilemma of High-Stakes Testing: What Are Schools For?" *International Journal of Instructional Media* 27, no. 4 (2000): 331–338.

Ednalino, Percy. "Teacher Won't Administer CSAP Tests." *Denver Post,* January 27, 2001.

Elshtain, Jean Bethke. *Democracy on Trial.* New York: Basic Books, 1995.

Engel, Michael. *The Struggle for Control of Public Education: Market Ideology vs. Democratic Values.* Philadelphia: Temple University Press, 2000.

"Facts on Uninsured Children." *American Medical Student Association* (September 2007). Retrieved from http://www.amsa.org/cph/CHIPfact.cfm on September 22, 2007.

"FAIR: Media Giants Cast Aside Regulatory 'Chains'." *Fairness and Accuracy in Reporting* (March 2002). Retrieved from http://www.fair.org/index.php?page=1659. Accessed August 15, 2002.

"FAIR Presents: The Underreported Impact of Welfare Reform." *Fairness and Accuracy in Reporting* citing "Local TV News Project," Journalism.org, 2002. Report found at http://www.journalism.org/resources/research/reports/localTV/2002/postsept11.asp.

"FairTest, the National Center for Fair and Open Testing." http://www.fairtest.org.

Fine, Michelle. "[Ap]parent Involvement: Reflections on Parents, Power, and Urban Public Schools." *Teachers College Record* 94, no. 4 (Summer 1993). Retrieved from the University of New Mexico General Libraries Online Database, EBSCO Academic Elite, Accession Number 9401240207. Accessed November 13, 2002.

Fiske, Edward B. "Problem for Education: Commission Looks to Rise in Federal Role, While Reagan Looks to a Diminished Role." *The New York Times*, 1983, B15.

Fontana, Andrea, and James. H. Frey. "The Interview: From Structured Questions to Negotiated Text" in *Handbook of Qualitative Research* (2nd ed.), edited by Norman K. Denzin and Yvonne S. Lincoln, 645–672. Thousand Oaks, Calif.: Sage, 2000.

Foucault, Michel. *Discipline and Punish*. New York: Vintage Books, 1977.

———. *The Foucault Reader*. New York: Pantheon Books, 1984.

Gardner, William E. "A Nation at Risk: Some Critical Comments." *Journal of Teacher Education* 35, no. 1 (1984): 13–15.

Gilligan, Carol. *In a Different Voice*. Cambridge, Mass.: Harvard Univ. Press, 1983.

Giroux, Henry. "Pedagogy of the Depressed: Beyond the New Politics of Cynicism." *College Literature* 28, no. 3 (Fall 2001). Retrieved from the University of New Mexico General Libraries Online Database, EBSCO Academic Search Elite, Accession Number 5176897. Accessed October 22, 2002.

Goodman, Amy. "Democracy Now: The Independent Media in Times of War." *The University of New Mexico 21st Century Speakers Series,* Albuquerque, New Mexico, January 18, 2003.

Greene, Maxine. *The Dialectic of Freedom*. New York: Teachers College Press, 1988.

———. "Diversity and Inclusion: Toward a Curriculum for Human Beings." *Teachers College Record* 95, no. 2 (1993): 210–221.

———. *Releasing the Imagination: Essays on Education, the Arts, and Social Change*. San Francisco: Jossey-Bass Publishers, 1995.

Guba, Evon G. and Yvonne S. Lincoln. "Competing Paradigms in Qualitative Research" in *Handbook of Qualitative Research*, edited by Norman K. Denzin and Yvonne S. Lincoln, 105–117. Thousand Oaks, Calif.: Sage, 1994.

Hazen, Don, and Julie Winokur. *We the Media: A Citizen's Guide to Fighting for Media Democracy*. New York: The New Press, 1997.

Hickey, Neil. "Behind the Mergers: Q & A." *Columbia Journalism Review* (May/June 2002). Retrieved August 15, 2002 from http://www.cjr.org/year/02/3/hickey.asp.

Hlebowitsch, Peter S. "Playing Power Politics: How *A Nation at Risk* Achieved Its National Stature." *Journal of Research and Development in Education* 23, no. 2 (1990): 82–88.

Hodder, Ian. "The Interpretation of Documents and Material Culture" in *Handbook of Qualitative Research* (2nd ed.), edited by Norman K. Denzin and Yvonne S. Lincoln, 703–715. Thousand Oaks, Calif.: Sage, 2000.

Hoffman, James. V. "The De-Democratization of Schools and Literacy in America." *Reading Teacher* 53, no. 8 (2000): 616–624.

Janesick, Valerie. J. "The Dance of Qualitative Research Design: Metaphor, Methodolatry, and Meaning" in *Handbook of Qualitative Research*, edited by Norman K. Denzin and Yvonne S. Lincoln, 209–219. Thousand Oaks, Calif.: Sage, 1994.

Johnson, Dale and Bonnie Johnson. *High Stakes: Children, Testing, and Failure in American Schools*. Lanham, Md.: Rowman & Littlefield Publishers, 2002.

Karp, Stan. "Let Them Eat Tests." *Rethinking Schools* 16, no. 4 (2002): 3–4.

Kauffman, Liz, ed. *Webster's Dictionary*. Quillmaker, New Jersey: Watermill Press, 1997.

Keefe, Elizabeth and Kaia Tollefson, review of *High Stakes: Children, Testing, and Failure in American Schools*. *Journal of Anthropological Research* 59, no. 1 (2003): 136–137.

Kohn, Alfie. *Punished by Rewards*. New York: Houghton Mifflin Company, 1993.

————. *What to Look for in a Classroom... and Other Essays.* San Francisco: Jossey-Bass Publishers, 1998.

————. *The Schools Our Children Deserve: Moving Beyond Traditional Classrooms and 'Tougher Standards'.* New York: Houghton Mifflin Company, 1999.

————. "Standardized Testing and Its Victims." *Education Week* 20, no. 4 (2000): 60, 46–47 .

————. "The Case Against 'Tougher Standards,'" http://www.alfiekohn.org, 2001.

Kozol, Jonathan. *Savage Inequalities: Children in America's Schools.* New York: Harper Perennial, 1991.

————. *Shame of the Nation.* New York: Crown Publishers, 2005.

Krugman, Paul. "The Waiting Game." *The New York Times,* July 16, 2007.

LeCompte, Margaret, and Judith Preissle. *Ethnography and Qualitative Design in Educational Research* (2nd ed.). San Diego: Academic Press, 1993.

Lummis, C. Douglas. *Radical Democracy.* Ithaca, New York: Cornell Univ. Press, 1996.

Lunenberg, Fred C. "The Current Educational Reform Movement: History, Progress to Date, and the Future." *Education & Urban Society* 25, no. 1 (1992): 3–18.

Macedo, Donaldo P. "Literacy for Stupidification: The Pedagogy of Big Lies" in *Breaking Free: The Transformative Power of Critical Pedagogy,* edited by Donaldo P. Macedo. Cambridge, Mass.: Harvard Educational Review, 1996.

Marx, Karl. *Early Writings.* New York: Penguin Books, 1844/1992.

McChesney, Robert. "The Global Media Giants: The Nine Firms that Dominate the World." *Fairness & Accuracy in Reporting* (November/December 1997) http://www.fair.org/index.php?page=1406.

McChesney, Robert and John Nichols. *Our Media Not Theirs.* New York: Seven Stories Press, 2002.

McGrew, Jannell. "Rosa Parks: A Woman Who Changed a Nation." *Montgomery Advertiser,* 1998. www.montgomeryadvertiser.com/1news/specialreports/rosa/. Accessed November 9, 2002.

McNeil, Linda, and Angela Valenzuela. "The Harmful Impact of the TAAS System of Testing in Texas: Beneath the Accountability Rhetoric." Harvard University: The Civil Rights Project, 2000. Retrieved from *The Civil Rights Project, Harvard University,* http://www.law.harvard.edu/groups/civilrights/conferences/testing98/drafts/mcneil_valenzuela.html on February 15, 2001.

Meier, Deborah. *Will Standards Save Public Education?* Boston: Beacon Press, 2000.

Meier, Deborah, and George Wood, eds. *Many Children Left Behind: How the No Child Left Behind Act Is Damaging Our Children and Our Schools.* Boston: Beacon Press, 2004.

Merriam, Sharan. *Qualitative Research and Case Study Applications in Education.* San Francisco: Jossey-Bass Publishers, 1998.

Metcalf, Stephen. "Reading Between the Lines." Retrieved from *The Nation,* http://www.thenation.com/doc.mhtml?i=20020128&s=metcalf (2002) on January 16, 2003.

Miller, Mark. C. "The Big Ten Media Giants" in *Project Censored 2003,* Peter Phillips and Project Censored, 231–240. New York: Seven Stories Press, 2002.

Miller-Kahn, Linda, and Mary L. Smith. "School Choice Policies in the Political Spectacle." *Education Policy Analysis Archives* 9, no. 50 (2001). Retrieved from http://epaa.asu.edu/epaa/v9n50.html, accessed November 11, 2002.

Nakagawa, Kathryn. "Unthreading the Ties that Bind: Questioning the Discourse of Parent Involvement." *Educational Policy* 14, no. 4 (September 2000). Retrieved from the University of New Mexico General Libraries Online Database, EBSCO Academic Search Elite, Accession Number 3474991. Accessed November 13, 2002.

National Commission on Excellence in Education (NCEE). "A Nation at Risk: The Imperative for Educational Reform." U.S. Department of Education, 1983. Retrieved from http://www.ed.gov/pubs/NatAtRisk/ on February 16, 2001.

Naureckas, Jim. "Media Monopoly: Long History, Short Memories." *Fairness & Accuracy in Reporting,* 2002. Retrieved from www.fair.org/extra/9511/monop.html on August 15, 2002.

New Mexico Media Literacy Project (NMMLP). Retrieved from http://www.nmmlp.org on January 15, 2003.

"No Child Left Behind." *United States Department of Education.* Retrieved from http://www.nclb.gov/ on January 18, 2003.

Ohanian, Susan. *What Happened to Recess and Why Are Our Children Struggling in Kindergarten?* New York: McGraw-Hill, 2002.

Parker, Walter C., ed. *Educating the Democratic Mind.* Albany, New York: State University of New York Press, 1996.

Passow, A. Harry. "Tackling the Reform Reports of the 1980s." *Phi Delta Kappan* 65, no. 10 (June 1984): 674–683.

Phillips, Peter, and Project Censored. *Censored 2003: The Top 25 Censored Stories.* New York: Seven Stories Press, 2002.

Rethinking Schools. "The History and Philosophy of Rethinking Schools." Retrieved from http://www.rethinkingschools.org on January 15, 2003.

Rogers, Spence. "Increasing Student Motivation to Learn." Presentation at the National Schools Conference Institute's *Effective Schools Conference,* Phoenix, 1998.

Ryan, Gery W., and H. Russell Bernard. "Data Management and Analysis Methods" in *Handbook of Qualitative Research* (2nd ed.), edited by Norman K. Denzin and Yvonne S. Lincoln, 769–802. Thousand Oaks, Calif.: Sage, 2000.

Sacks, Peter. *Standardized Minds: The High Price of America's Testing Culture and What We Can Do to Change It.* Cambridge, Mass.: Perseus Publishing, 1999.

Saunders, Doug. "For-Profit U.S. Schools Sell Off Their Textbooks." *Toronto Globe,* October 30, 2002. Retrieved from www.commondreams.org/headlines02/1030-02.htm on November 4, 2002.

Seidman, Irving. *Interviewing as Qualitative Research* (2nd ed.). New York: Teachers College Press, 1998.

Sheldon, Kennon M., and Bruce J. Biddle. "Standards, Accountability, and School Reform: Perils and Pitfalls." *Teachers College Record* 100, no. 1 (1998): 164–181.

Smrekar, Claire E., and Lora Cohen-Vogel. "The Voices of Parents: Rethinking the Intersection of Family and School." *Peabody Journal of Education* 76, no. 2 (2001): 75–100. Retrieved from the University of New Mexico General Libraries Online Database, EBSCO Academic Search Elite, Accession Number 6463089 on November 13, 2002.

Stedman, Lawrence. "Respecting the Evidence: The Achievement Crisis Is Real." *Education Policy Analysis Archives* 4, no. 7 (April 4, 1996). Retrieved from http://epaa.asu.edu/epaa/v4n7.html on November 11, 2002.

————. "The Achievement Crisis Is Real: A Review of *The Manufactured Crisis*." *Education Policy Analysis Archives* 4, no. 1 (January 23, 1996). Retrieved from http://olam.ed.asu.edu/epaa/v4n1.html on November 11, 2002.

Stein, Jess (ed.). *The Random House Dictionary of the English Language: The Unabridged Edition*. New York: Random House, 1967.

University of Maine. "The United States Health Care System: Best in the World, or Just the Most Expensive?" (2001) Retrieved from dll.umaine.edu/ble/U.S.%20HCweb.pdf at the University of Maine website on September 6, 2005.

University of Virginia Library. "Electronic Text Center for the Thomas Jefferson Digital Archive." Retrieved from http://etext.virginia.edu/jefferson/ on September 6, 2005.

Vincent, Carol. "Parent Empowerment? Collective Action and Inaction in Education." *Oxford Review of Education* 22, no. 4 (December 1996). Retrieved from the University of New Mexico General Libraries Online Database, EBSCO Academic Search Elite, Accession Number 9701220990. Accessed November 13, 2002.

Waggoner, Kimberly, and Alison Griffith. "Parent Involvement in Education." *Journal for a Just & Caring Education* 4, no. 1 (January 1998). Retrieved from the University of New Mexico General Libraries Online Database, EBSCO Academic Search Elite, Accession Number 219120. Accessed November 13, 2002.

Walden, Everett L. "Public Education: Sin Eater for *A Nation at Risk*." *Clearing House* 65, no. 4 (Mar/Apr 1992): 215–216. Retrieved from the University of New Mexico General Libraries Online Database, EBSCO Academic Search Elite, Accession Number 9705075555. Accessed February 22, 2001.

Wellstone, Paul. "High Stakes Tests: A Harsh Agenda for America's Children." Address at Teachers College, Columbia University. Retrieved from http://wellstone.senate.gov/columbia.htm on February 22, 2001.

Zinn, Howard. *Terrorism and War*. New York: Seven Stories Press, 2002.

————. *A People's History of the United States: 1492–Present*. New York: Harper Collins, 1995.

————. *Declarations of Independence: Cross-examining American Ideology*. New York: Harper Perennial, 1990.

Index

About the Author

Kaia Tollefson's career in education began in Kodiak, Alaska, in 1983. She was a middle school teacher there for nine years and worked in administration for the next five—first as a curriculum and staff development coordinator and then as an elementary school principal. She discovered a passion for teacher education while pursuing her doctoral degree in language, literacy, and sociocultural studies, awarded by the University of New Mexico in 2004. Her most recent experience in teaching children was in 2002, when she returned to the classroom to teach fifth grade. One of her professional goals is to find ways to refresh and reground her roots in the public schools, never getting too far away from understanding what it means to be a classroom teacher. She is currently an assistant professor of education at California State University Channel Islands, working in teacher education, coaching a Critical Friends Group, and exploring the relationship between the concept of voice and the processes of teaching and learning.

18811836R00131

Printed in Great Britain
by Amazon